英語徹底耳練！

てっていみみれん

Learn to have an ear for English

CD 2枚付

青山学院大学教授
外池滋生 編著
Joseph T. McKim
外池一子

実務教育出版

はじめに

■スイッチの切り替え

　最近の言語理論では、人間は言語を処理する共通の装置を持っていて、それをそれぞれの母語にあわせて調整して使っていると考えます。

　その装置にはいくつかのスイッチが付いており、そのスイッチを特定の言語にあわせて設定するとその言語を処理できるようになると考えるのです。日本語と英語とでは、語順がよい例です。[**read** a book]：[本を**読む**]、[**from** Tokyo]：[**東京から**]、[**picture** of John]：[ジョンの**写真**]の対に見られるように、英語では中心をなす語（太字）は先頭にあるのに対して、日本語では末尾にあります。日本語話者が英語を学ぶときに「中心となる語の位置」を決定するこのスイッチを切り替えなければなりません。

　音声に関しても同様の切り替えが必要です（日本語話者は言葉に詰まったときに「エー」と言い、英語話者は er と言いますが、これらも、これから話をしようというときに調音器官を中立的な体勢にもって行くための準備といえます）。

　本書『英語徹底耳練！』は、この言語処理スイッチを、切り替えることができる力を身に付けるための CD ブックです。言葉は、もとより思想、感情、情報を伝える道具ですから、その英文から何かを学ぶものがなければ聴き取る甲斐もないので、本書では、内容を吟味したオリジナル英文 50 本を収録しました。それを、**英語圏の発音の多様化を意識して、米国を中心に英国、カナダ、オーストラリアのネイティブ音声で構成**しています。これは TOEIC テストのリスニングセクション Part3（会話問題）、4（説明文問題）の対策にも役立ちます。本書を、あなたの脳の中の「英語言語処理装置」の性能を高めることにお役立てください。

外池　滋生

目次

- はじめに ─── 1
- 耳練(リスニング・トレーニング)の課題 ─── 4
- 本書の構成 ─── 6
- CDの内容 ─── 8

耳練 1-20 Short Conversation （TOEIC Part3 対応）

① A Man in a Hurry（急いでいる男）─── 10
② Absenteeism（欠勤問題）─── 14
③ Ankle Injury（足首の捻挫）─── 18
④ Contract（契約）─── 22
⑤ A Commercial Property（商業物件）─── 26
⑥ Agenda（議題）─── 30
⑦ Managers' Conference（管理職会議）─── 34
⑧ A Telephone Sale Call（売込み電話）─── 38
⑨ An Ambitious Young Man（野心的な若者）─── 42
⑩ Faulty Product（欠陥品）─── 46
⑪ Crowded Airplane（混み合う機内）─── 50
⑫ Headhunting（ヘッドハンティング）─── 54
⑬ A Million Messages（たくさんの伝言）─── 58
⑭ Weekend Plans（週末の予定）─── 62
⑮ Shake-up（人事の大刷新）─── 66
⑯ Franchise Seminar（フランチャイズ・セミナー）─── 70
⑰ Baseball Tickets（野球のチケット）─── 74
⑱ Employee Orientation（新入社員オリエンテーション）─── 78
⑲ Office Renovation（オフィスの改装）─── 82
⑳ Looking for a job（職探し）─── 86

耳練 21-40 Short Talk （TOEIC Part4 対応）

① A Mountain Bike Prototype（マウンテンバイクの試作品）─── 90
② Radio Flea Market（ラジオ・フリーマーケット）─── 94
③ Business News（ビジネスニュース）─── 98
④ New Annex（新しい別館）─── 102
⑤ Banquet Hall Reservation（宴会場の予約）─── 106
⑥ Book Commercial（本の宣伝）─── 110
⑦ Condominium Association Meeting（マンション管理組合の総会）─── 114
⑧ Spanish Test（スペイン語検定試験）─── 118
⑨ Association of Small Publishers（小規模出版社協会）─── 122
⑩ Factory Tour（工場ツアー）─── 126

Contents

⑪ Pet Lovers Incorporated (ペットラバーズ社) — 130
⑫ Outsourcing (アウトソーシング) — 134
⑬ Ellis Island (エリス島) — 138
⑭ Sunburst Coffee (サンバースト・コーヒー) — 142
⑮ Paper Reduction (紙の費用削減) — 146
⑯ Job Fair (就職説明会) — 150
⑰ Election Report (開票速報) — 154
⑱ Enterprise Zone Program
　 (企業誘致地域プログラム) — 158
⑲ Conflict Resolution (対立解消) — 162
⑳ Clean Electricity (クリーンな電気) — 166

目練 41-50 Long Passage

❶ Workplace Burnout (仕事で燃え尽き症候群) — 172
❷ Compulsive Hoarding (物を捨てられない人たち) — 175
❸ Left-handedness (左利き) — 178
❹ Why Not Go to the Movies? (映画に行こう) — 181
❺ Is Curry Addictive? (カレーは中毒性があるか?) — 184
❻ Ecotourism (エコツーリズム) — 187
❼ Intrusive Marketers (しつこい売込み) — 190
❽ Fighting Plagiarism (剽窃との闘い) — 193
❾ Abraham Lincoln (エイブラハム・リンカーン) — 197
❿ Martin Luther King, Jr. (キング牧師) — 201

■ さらに、本書を徹底活用するために!

- Useful Expressions 一覧 ———————————————— 206
- Listening Challenge 120 (練習問題) ————————— 214
- Listening Challenge 120　正解記号一覧 —————— 234
- index ———————————————————————————— 235

耳練（リスニング・トレーニング）の課題

■ 5つの「知る」べきこと

本書の各ユニットに進む前に、英語を聴き取るためのトレーニングに重要な5つのポイントについて簡単に解説します。

1. 聴き分けるべき「単語」を知る

聴き取り（Listening Comprehension）は、語彙力、構文解析力は言うに及ばず、一般常識などあらゆる能力を総動員しなければならない高度な知的作業ですが、その前にまず連続する音の中から個々の単語を聴き分けなければなりません。色とりどりでさまざまな模様のある絨毯の上に落ちた何かを探すときに、その形と色を知らなければ見つけることは容易ではありません。それと同じように、**連続する音の中から単語を聴き分けるためには、その単語がどのように聴こえるかを知らなければなりません。**

2. 前後関係で単語の「発音は変わる」を知る

個々の単語は、それが現れる場所によって違って聴こえます。例えば good は、That's good のような文末では d が開放されるか、されないか、Good evening のように母音に続くか、Good morning のように子音が続くかによって、異なって発音されます。これらすべての中に good を聴き分けるためには、**さまざまな組合せで使われる多くの英文に触れる必要があります。**同様のことは他のすべての単語について言えますが、聴き分けることが難しい単語をその都度つぶしていく（理解する）しか方法はないのです。しかし、この方法を続けることである段階から飛躍的に、聴き取りの精度がアップします。

> ● 聴き分けるためには自分で発音できることが大事
> 聴こえたように発音することができなければ、本当に聴き分けることはできませんから（ここは、とても大事な点）、発音練習を採り入れ、自分で繰り返し声に出して練習してみる（口練）ことが必要です。

3. 英語の「リズム」を知る

英語は、強く発音される（強勢を持った）母音が、ほぼ等間隔に並ぶようなリズムを持った言語です。たとえば強勢を持つ音節を「〇」で、強勢を持たない音節を「。」で表すと、
Plus, I'm taking some strong medication for the pain は、
〇／。〇。。　〇。。〇。。。〇のように強勢に挟まれた部分は、弱い音節が少なければ短い区切りを入れ、多い場合は早く発音して強勢が等間隔になるよう発音されます。**このリズムを意識することが**、英語を聴き取るうえでも、話すうえでもたいへん大事です。

4. 日本語と英語の「音節構造の違い」を知る

日本語には「今日（kyoo）」「今晩（komban）」「明後日（asatte）」のような場合以外では子音の連続や子音で終わる語はありませんが、英語では strength のように音節の初めにも終わりにも子音の連続を持つ語がたくさんあります。したがって、語と語の間ではさらに複雑な子音連続が生じたり、また語末の子音が次の語頭の母音と連続して一つの音節として発音されることが頻繁に生じます。日本語話者にとってこの点で重要なことは、発音上は「**母音のないところに母音を入れない**」、その逆に「**子音と母音が連続するところでは連続させる**」の2つです。聴き取りのうえでは「**母音のないところに母音を聴こうと期待しない**」ことが大事です。

5. 英語圏の「発音の多様性」を知る

　本書の CD 音声の大部分は北米英語ですが、イギリス英語やオーストラリア英語も何割か収録されています。これらの英語の間の違い、特に**発音やイントネーションの違い**は、実際に聴いてみることが一番ですが、いくつか目立つ相違を簡単に説明します。

　① 綴り字「o」の発音：lot の場合
　　・アメリカ英語　→　[lɑt]（「ア」のように発音）
　　・イギリス、オーストラリア英語　→　[lɔt]（「オ」のように発音）
　② can't の場合
　　・アメリカ英語　→　[kænt]
　　・イギリス、オーストラリア英語　→　[kɑːnt]
　③ better、matter などの語中「t」の場合
　　・アメリカ英語　→　日本語の「ラ行」の音に近い発音
　　・イギリス、オーストラリア英語　→　摩擦の多い「t」として発音
＊ オーストラリア英語のみの特徴としては、アメリカ、イギリス英語で［エイ］と発音されるところが、［アイ］に近い音で発音される。（ただし、本 CD の吹き込み者は標準化された英語のナレーターで、［アイ］も一般のオーストラリア英語話者ほど際立ってはいない）

■ 効果絶大な「耳練」のすすめ方

　以上のことに留意しながら、本書の耳練1の Short Conversation から順番に Short Talk、Long Passage までを何度も解説と照らし合わせながら聴くことによって、一字一句もらさず聴き取り、かつ同時にその意味が理解できるところまで練習をしていけば、聴き取り能力は驚異的な進歩をとげ、それまで聴き取ることのできなかったテレビのニュースなども格段に理解できるようになります。スクリプトや解説をすぐに参照するのではなく、どうしてもわからないところだけを、それも全部見るのではなく最初の単語だけ見るようにして、なるべく自分の努力で聴き分けることができる喜びを実感しながら進めてください。

　基本的な耳練のすすめ方は図のとおりです。各ユニットに掲載の「耳練チェックマトリックス」表に、1st try から 3rd try まで、3段階のチェック欄を設けてありますが、これは「3回」ということではなく、あくまで「3段階」です。1段階ごとに繰り返し聴くことで、「聴き取る」力は鍛えられていきます。**時間はかかりますが、本書の効果は絶大です。**

●耳練のすすめ方

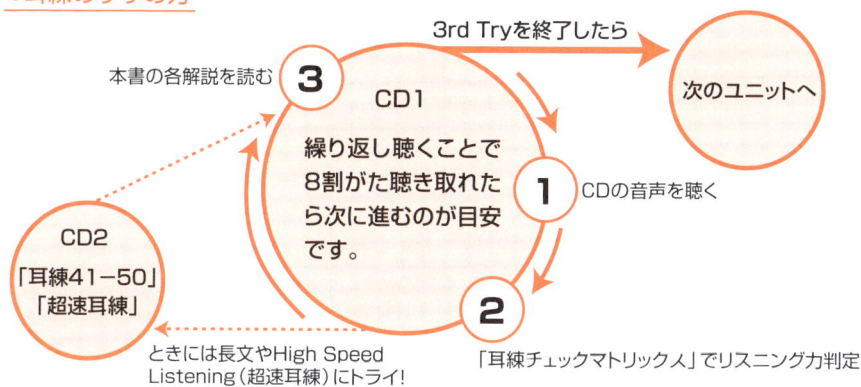

3rd Try を終了したら → 次のユニットへ

3 CD1　繰り返し聴くことで8割がた聴き取れたら次に進むのが目安です。
本書の各解説を読む

1 CD の音声を聴く

2 「耳練チェックマトリックス」でリスニング力判定

CD2 「耳練41-50」「超速耳練」
ときには長文や High Speed Listening（超速耳練）にトライ！

本書の構成

■ TOEICリスニング対策編

多彩な場面設定のShort Conversation&Short Talk 40本を収録！

- **CDトラックNo**
- **使用した英語の種類**
  アメリカ、イギリス、カナダ、オーストラリアの英語のどれを採用したかを表示しています。

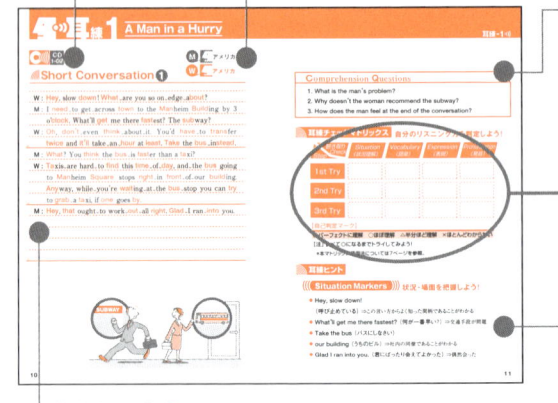

- **Comprehension Questions**
  理解度の基準になります。巻末に「Listening Challenge」として選択肢と併せて掲載しています。

- **耳練ヒント—Situation Markers**
  英文の状況や場面を把握するためのヒントです。

- **音声収録内容**
  ネイティブの発音による約1分間の英文の内容です。初めは英文を見ずに音声のみで聴き取ることを心がけましょう。（文字の色が黄色の部分は強勢ポイントです – Short Conversationのみ）

- **Pronunciation**
  英文を聴き取るためのポイントを表示しています。

- **Vocabulary**
  重要な単語や熟語などの意味等の解説です。

- **Key Expressions**
  本文中の重要表現を取り上げ、文法等の解説をしています。先頭の数字は、英文の該当行数を示しています。

- **日本語訳**
  英文の日本語訳です。

- **Useful Expressions**
  Key Expressionsでガイドされた表現をさらに言い換えて英文表記しています。音声はCDで聴くことができ、リピート練習もできます。

●「耳練チェックマトリックス」が学習方法をガイド

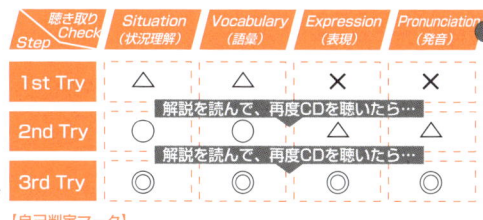

Step 聴き取りCheck	Situation (状況理解)	Vocabulary (語彙)	Expression (表現)	Pronunciation (発音)
1st Try	○	△	×	×
2nd Try	解説を読んで、再度CDを聴いたら…		△	△
3rd Try	解説を読んで、再度CDを聴いたら…			
	◎	◎	◎	◎

[自己判定マーク]
◎ パーフェクトに理解　○ ほぼ理解　△ 半分ほど理解　× ほとんどわからない
[注] すべて◎になるまでトライしてみよう!

● **聴き取りCheck項目**

英文の聴き取りに必須の4項目を表示しています。「◎」以外の判定をした項目については、次ページからの解説を読み、再チャレンジしてください。1段階ごとに繰り返し聴くことで、「聴き取る」力が鍛えられます。(各項目名は、次ページからの解説の見出しと同一です。)

■ 一般長文編

聴き応え、読み応えあるオリジナル英文エッセイ10本を収録!

- **4か国のネイティブによる約3〜4分間の英文朗読**
- **興味深い話題、さまざまな表現、使える英文満載**

耳練の仕上げとして長文にチャレンジすることが基本ですが、耳練1−40の途中でも効果あり。短い英文がより聴き取りやすくなります。

■ 巻末構成

Useful Expressions一覧
・本文中に解説された重要表現を一覧にしています。CD音声で発音を聴くこともできますし、リピート練習も可能です。

Listening Challenge120(練習問題)
・本文中のComprehension Questionsと選択肢(4択)を掲載。CDトラックNoを指定し、その英文に関する練習問題ができます。(*質問、選択肢の音声は収録されていません)

index
・本文中に収録された重要な約1,200語を索引に収録しています。

■ 本書CDはリスニング・トレーニングの最強ツール!

本書のCDには次の特長があります。

特長①　4か国、総勢6名のネイティブによる音声収録!
・英語の多様性、TOEICリスニング対策のために、米国、英国、カナダ、オーストラリアの発音を収録しています。

特長②　3パターンの音声スピードを採用!

Slow Speed	耳練 1−5 (Short Conversation)・耳練21−25(Short Talk)
Natural Speed	耳練 6−20 (Short Conversation)・耳練26−40(Short Talk)
	耳練41−50(Long Passage)
High Speed Listening (超速耳練)	耳練1−50の中から14本(P8参照)

＊ High Speed Listening (超速耳練) は、通常の音声を機械処理し、25%スピードアップしています。

CDの内容

🔊 **CD1**　Track 1　解説：外池滋生

耳練1−20 Short Conversation

Track 2	A Man in a Hurry (M:アメリカ W:アメリカ)	Track 12	Crowded Airplane (M:アメリカ W:イギリス)
Track 3	Absenteeism (M:アメリカ W:アメリカ)	Track 13	Headhunting (M:アメリカ W:イギリス)
Track 4	Ankle Injury (M:アメリカ W:アメリカ)	Track 14	A Million Messages (M:アメリカ W:アメリカ)
Track 5	Contract (M:アメリカ W:イギリス)	Track 15	Weekend Plans (M:アメリカ W:アメリカ)
Track 6	A Commercial Property (M:アメリカ W:アメリカ)	Track 16	Shake-up (M:イギリス W:アメリカ)
Track 7	Agenda (M:アメリカ W:アメリカ)	Track 17	Franchise Seminar (M:アメリカ W:カナダ)
Track 8	Managers' Conference (M:アメリカ W:アメリカ)	Track 18	Baseball Tickets (M:アメリカ W:カナダ)
Track 9	A Telephone Sale Call (M:アメリカ W:アメリカ)	Track 19	Employee Orientation (M:アメリカ W:カナダ)
Track 10	An Ambitious Young Man (M:アメリカ W:アメリカ)	Track 20	Office Renovation (M:アメリカ W:オーストラリア)
Track 11	Faulty Product (M:アメリカ W:イギリス)	Track 21	Looking for a job (M:アメリカ W:オーストラリア)

耳練21−40 Short Talk

Track 22	A Mountain Bike Prototype (アメリカ)	Track 32	Pet Lovers Incorporated (イギリス)
Track 23	Radio Flea Market (アメリカ)	Track 33	Outsourcing (イギリス)
Track 24	Business News (アメリカ)	Track 34	Ellis Island (アメリカ)
Track 25	New Annex (アメリカ)	Track 35	Sunburst Coffee (イギリス)
Track 26	Banquet Hall Reservation (アメリカ)	Track 36	Paper Reduction (イギリス)
Track 27	Book Commercial (アメリカ)	Track 37	Job Fair (カナダ)
Track 28	Condominium Association Meeting (アメリカ)	Track 38	Election Report (カナダ)
Track 29	Spanish Test (イギリス)	Track 39	Enterprise Zone Program (アメリカ)
Track 30	Association of Small Publishers (アメリカ)	Track 40	Conflict Resolution (オーストラリア)
Track 31	Factory Tour (アメリカ)	Track 41	Clean Electricity (オーストラリア)

Useful Expressions

Track 42−61	Short Conversation (アメリカ)	Track 62−81	Short Talk (アメリカ)

🔊 **CD2**　Track 1　解説：Joseph T. McKim

耳練41−50 Long Passage

Track 2	Workplace Burnout (アメリカ)	Track 7	Ecotourism (アメリカ)
Track 3	Compulsive Hoarding (アメリカ)	Track 8	Intrusive Marketers (アメリカ)
Track 4	Left-handedness (カナダ)	Track 9	Fighting Plagiarism (オーストラリア)
Track 5	Why Not Go to the Movies? (アメリカ)	Track 10	Abraham Lincoln (アメリカ)
Track 6	Is Curry Addictive? (イギリス)	Track 11	Martin Luther King, Jr. (アメリカ)

特別付録　**超速耳練 (High Speed Listening)**
ナチュラルスピードを機械的に25%スピードアップ！

Track 13	Agenda (P30)	Track 18	Book Commercial (P110)	Track 23	Left-handedness (P178)
Track 14	A telephone Sale Call (P38)	Track 19	Spanish Test (P118)	Track 24	Is Curry Addictive? (P184)
Track 15	Faulty Product (P46)	Track 20	Outsourcing (P134)	Track 25	Fighting Plagiarism (P193)
Track 16	Franchise Seminar (P70)	Track 21	Job Fair (P150)	Track 26	Abraram Lincoln (P197)
Track 17	Looking for a job (P86)	Track 22	Conflict Resolution (P162)		

※（ ）内の数字はスクリプトの掲載ページです。

英語
徹底耳練　**耳**練**1-40**［TOEICリスニング対策編］

1 A Man in a Hurry

Short Conversation ❶

W: Hey, slow down! What are you so on edge about?
M: I need to get across town to the Manheim Building by 3 o'clock. What'll get me there fastest? The subway?
W: Oh, don't even think about it. You'd have to transfer twice and it'll take an hour at least. Take the bus instead.
M: What? You think the bus is faster than a taxi?
W: Taxis are hard to find this time of day, and the bus going to Manheim Square stops right in front of our building. Anyway, while you're waiting at the bus stop you can try to grab a taxi, if one goes by.
M: Hey, that ought to work out all right. Glad I ran into you.

Comprehension Questions

1. What is the man's problem?
2. Why doesn't the woman recommend the subway?
3. How does the man feel at the end of the conversation?

耳練チェックマトリックス　自分のリスニング力を判定しよう！

聴き取りCheck / Step	Situation（状況理解）	Vocabulary（語彙）	Expression（表現）	Pronunciation（発音）
1st Try				
2nd Try				
3rd Try				

【自己判定マーク】
◎パーフェクトに理解　○ほぼ理解　△半分ほど理解　×ほとんどわからない

［注］すべて◎になるまでトライしてみよう！

＊本マトリックス活用法については7ページを参照。

耳練ヒント

Situation Markers　状況・場面を把握しよう！

- Hey, slow down!
  （呼び止めている）⇒この言い方からよく知った間柄であることがわかる
- What'll get me there fastest?（何が一番早い？）⇒交通手段が問題
- Take the bus（バスにしなさい）
- our building（うちのビル）⇒社内の同僚であることがわかる
- Glad I ran into you.（君にばったり会えてよかった）⇒偶然会った

耳練-1 A Man in a Hurry

耳練ポイント

Vocabulary －単語の意味を確認しよう！

- □ slow down／速度を落とす（ここでは「ちょっと待って」と急いでいる人を呼び止める働き）
- □ on edge／慌てている、興奮している
- □ by (3 o'clock)／(3時)までに
- □ subway／地下鉄
- □ transfer／乗り換える
- □ instead／代わりに
- □ right in front of ～／～の（真）正面に、前に
- □ grab／つかまえる

Key Expressions －重要フレーズを聴き取ろう！

02 **get across town**「街を横切る、反対側に行く」無冠詞の town は現在いる都市をさす

03 **What'll get me there fastest?**「何で行けば一番早く行けるかな？」what は交通手段をさしている

04 **don't even think about it**「とんでもない」「そんなことは考えもしてはならない」強調的な命令の定型表現として覚えておきたい。

04 **You'd have to ～**「～しなければならない」You'd となっているのは、地下鉄に乗ればという仮定が含まれているから ⇒Useful Expressions

05 **an hour at least** = at least an hour「少なくとも1時間」

06 **What?**「何だって？」「えっ？」驚きを表す

06 **the bus is faster than a taxi** バスは決まったバス会社の決まった路線であるから the がつき、タクシーの場合はどれでも来たものに乗るから a がついている

07 **Taxis are hard to find**「タクシーは見つけづらい、つかまりにくい」

07 **this time of day**「（一日の）この時間では」at が省略されている。day が無冠詞であるのは、どの日でもという意味で、特定の日ではないから

07 **the bus going to Manheim Square**「マンハイム・スクエア行きのバス」実際にはこの路線を走っているバスは何台もあるが、この場合 the bus は路線を表している

10 **grab a taxi**「タクシーをつかまえる」catch a taxi とも言う

10 **if one goes by**「通りかかったら」one は a taxi のこと

11 **that ought to work out all right** 文字どおりには「それがうまくいくはずだ」that は女性の提案内容。work out all right は「結局うまくいく」の意
⇒Useful Expressions

11 **Glad I ran into you.** = I am glad I ran into you. 類似の省略の例としては Sorry I'm late.（遅れてごめん）。run into は「ばったり出会う」⇒Useful Expressions

Pronunciation　－聴き取りポイントに注意しよう！

01　What‿are you so on‿edge‿about? の連音
04　Oh, don't‿even think‿about‿it. の連音
06　What? の語末の弱いtに注意
08　stops‿right in‿front‿of‿our building の連音
09　while‿you're waiting‿at‿the bus‿stop の連音
11　that ought‿to work‿out‿all right の連音とthatのtが聞こえないこと

日本語訳　－英文の内容を確認しよう！

急いでいる男

女：ねえ、ちょっと待って。何をそんなに慌てているの？
男：3時までに町の反対側にあるマンハイム・ビルに行かなければならないんだけれど、何で行けば一番早く行けるかな？　地下鉄？
女：とんでもない。2度乗り換えなきゃならないから、少なくとも1時間はかかるわよ。バスにしたほうがいいわ。
男：えっ？　タクシーよりもバスのほうが早いって言うの？
女：この時間はタクシーをつかまえるのは難しいし、マンハイム広場行きのバスならうちのビルの目の前で止まるのよ。それに、バスを待っている間にもしタクシーが来たらつかまえることもできるわ。
男：うん、そりゃいいね。君にばったり会ってよかったよ。

Useful Expressions ❶　－このままそっくり暗記しよう！

1. You'd have to wait in line to register.（登録するなら、列に並ばなければなりません）
2. Your plan ought to work out all right.（君の計画はうまくいくはずだ）
3. I ran into an old friend of mine yesterday.（昨日ばったり古い友人に会った）

CDで発音の確認とリピート練習ができます。 CD 1-42

Absenteeism

Short Conversation ❷

W: I don't understand why we keep having a problem with absenteeism.
M: It's because management only pays lip service to the problem. If we want workers to stop taking so many days off, we have to provide a day care center in the building so that mothers can leave their kids there.
W: Oh, management will never go for a day care center after spending so much of the budget on a new cafeteria.
M: That's exactly why absenteeism is a problem. Management cares more about all these less important things.
W: I see. But isn't there anything that we can do about the problem, Bob?
M: We could draft a report about absenteeism to let management know that it's affecting our productivity.

耳練-2

Comprehension Questions

1. What are the speakers mainly discussing?
2. What criticism does the man make about management?
3. What does the man propose doing about the problem?

耳練チェックマトリックス 自分のリスニング力を判定しよう！

聴き取りCheck Step	Situation（状況理解）	Vocabulary（語彙）	Expression（表現）	Pronunciation（発音）
1st Try				
2nd Try				
3rd Try				

【自己判定マーク】
◎パーフェクトに理解　○ほぼ理解　△半分ほど理解　×ほとんどわからない

［注］すべて◎になるまでトライしてみよう！

＊本マトリックス活用法については7ページを参照。

耳練ヒント

Situation Markers 状況・場面を把握しよう！

- we keep having a problem with absenteeism
  （欠勤の問題が絶えない）⇒職場の同僚
- management only pays lip service
  （経営側が口先だけの対応をする）⇒経営側に問題がある
- day care center in the building so that mothers can leave their kids there
  （社内の保育所に母親が子供を預けられるようにする）⇒子育て中の母親の欠勤が問題
- draft a report（報告書を作成する）⇒経営側に訴える

耳練-2 Absenteeism

耳練ポイント

Vocabulary －単語の意味を確認しよう！

- absenteeism／欠勤、欠席
- management／経営側、経営陣
- lip service／実行を伴わない口先だけの対応
- provide／提供する、作る
- day care center／保育所、託児所
- kids／子供たち
- go for／賛成する、支持する
- budget／予算
- cafeteria／社員食堂
- draft／作成する
- affect／影響する
- productivity／生産性

Key Expressions －重要フレーズを聴き取ろう！

01 **we keep having a problem with absenteeism**
「欠勤の問題がなくならない」have a problem with ～「～という問題がある」

03 **It's because ～**「～だからさ」

03 **only pays lip service to the problem**「その問題に対して口先だけの対応しかしない」

04 **taking days off**「休む、欠勤する」一日の欠勤であれば take a day off
Cf. a day off 休みの日　⇒Useful Expressions

06 **so that mothers can leave their kids there**「母親たちが子供を預けられるように」

07 **management will never go for a day care center**
「経営側は託児所に賛成なんかするはずがない」go for～で「～を求めてその方向に動く」の意から「～に賛成する、～を実行する」の意味になる。したがって Let's go for it.（では[それを]やろう）という用法もある　⇒Useful Expressions

09 **That's exactly why absenteeism is a problem.**「だからこそ欠勤が問題なんだ」
that はその前に女性が言った内容。why～は～である理由。したがって文字どおりには「それが～の理由だ」転じて「だからこそ～だ」となる。単にThat's why.（だからだよ）という使い方もできる　⇒Useful Expressions

14 **it's affecting our productivity**
「それがわれわれの生産性に影響を与えている」

Pronunciation　−聴き取りポイントに注意しよう!

01　I don't understand の連音
05　days off［デイゾf］となっている。have to では v が f になっている
08　much of［マッチョv］となっている
09　That's exactly［ツイg］となっている
10　less important things つながりに注意
11　But isn't there の But の t が開放されず、聞こえなくなっている
13　draft a report about の連音

日本語訳　−英文の内容を確認しよう!

欠勤問題

女：どうしてうちの会社で欠勤の問題がなくならないのか理解できないわ。

男：それは、経営側がその問題に口先だけの対応をしているからさ。従業員に休みをあまりとって欲しくないなら、建物(社)内に保育所を作って、母親が子供を預けられるようにしないとだめさ。

女：新しいカフェテリアに予算のかなりの部分を使ったんだから、経営側は保育所なんて作るはずないわ。

男：まさにそれが欠勤問題の元凶さ。経営側にとってはそういう些細なことのほうが大事なのさ。

女：なるほど。でも私たちで問題を解決するために何かできることがないかしら?

男：報告書を書いて、欠勤が生産性に影響が出ていることを経営側に知らせることはできるね。

Useful Expressions ❷　−このままそっくり暗記しよう!

1. He took a day off today.（彼は今日はお休みです）
2. Jack will never go for such an idea.（ジャックはそんな考えには賛成するはずがない）
3. That's exactly why I am here.（だからこそ私が来たのです）

CDで発音の確認とリピート練習ができます。

3 Ankle Injury

Short Conversation ③

M: アメリカ
W: アメリカ

M: Hello, Jane? Listen, about the reception for the Minister of Trade from Nigeria... I twisted my ankle playing basketball yesterday, and I don't think I can make it.

W: Are you sure? We don't often get a chance to rub elbows with our Board of Directors.

M: Yes, but I don't think I'd make a very good impression on them. My foot's all bandaged up, and I'm walking with crutches. Plus, I'm taking some strong medication for the pain.

W: Well, that's a shame, but I guess you'd better stay home. I'll explain what happened, so don't worry about it.

M: Thanks. Hope you enjoy the reception. And let me know if you learn anything important there.

W: Sure. I'll talk to you later. Take care.

耳練-3

Comprehension Questions

1. Why can't the man attend the reception?
2. Who will be at the reception?
3. What does the man want the woman to do later?

耳練チェックマトリックス 自分のリスニング力を判定しよう！

聴き取りCheck Step	Situation （状況理解）	Vocabulary （語彙）	Expression （表現）	Pronunciation （発音）
1st Try				
2nd Try				
3rd Try				

【自己判定マーク】
◎パーフェクトに理解　○ほぼ理解　△半分ほど理解　×ほとんどわからない
［注］すべて◎になるまでトライしてみよう！
＊本マトリックス活用法については7ページを参照。

耳練ヒント

Situation Markers 状況・場面を把握しよう！

- Hello, Jane?（電話の会話）⇒Janeと呼んでいることから親しい間柄
- about the reception ⇒おそらくレセプションに出ることになっている
- I don't think I can make it（出られそうにない）
- so don't worry about it（心配しないで）⇒出られなくてもよい
- Take care.（お大事に）

耳練-3 Ankle Injury

耳練ポイント

Vocabulary －単語の意味を確認しよう！

- reception／レセプション、歓迎会
- the Minister of Trade from Nigeria／ナイジェリアの貿易相
- twist one's ankle／足首をひねる、捻挫する（sprain one's ankle とも言う）
- make it／（会への出席、目的地への到着など）問題となっていることをやり遂げること（疑問文、否定文で使われることが多い）
- get a chance／機会を得る
- our Board of Directors／わが社の役員たち
- impression／印象
- bandaged up／包帯でぐるぐる巻きになっている
- crutches／松葉杖
- medication／（処方してもらった）薬

Key Expressions －重要フレーズを聴き取ろう！

01 **Listen,**「ねえ」親しい間柄で相手の注意を喚起する表現

04 **Are you sure?**「本当？」Are you sure you can't make it? の意味

04 **rub elbows with ～**「～と親しく接する」
肘がさわるほどの近距離で話をするの意から。日本語の「膝を交える」や「袖すりあう」と似ている。elbows が複数であるのは shake hands with ～（握手をする）、become friends with ～（友達になる）と同様 ⇒Useful Expressions

06 **I don't think I'd make a very good impression on them.**
「彼ら＝役員たちにいい印象を与えるとは思わない」前置詞 on を用いることが重要。I'd となっているのは「たとえ出席しても」という仮定法が含まれているから ⇒Useful Expressions

08 **Plus**「それに」Besides や In addition などと同様、追加的な理由などを導入する

08 **I'm taking some strong medication for the pain.**
「痛み止めのために強い薬を飲んでいる」動詞 take に注意

10 **that's a shame**「残念、もったいない」shame は「恥」であるが、このような用法では「せっかくの機会が活用できなくて残念」という意味 ⇒Useful Expressions

10 **I guess ～**「～なんでしょうね」I think ～は自分の意見を述べるのに対して、I guess ～は自分以外の人の意見への同意を表す。I suppose も同様

11 **what happened**「起こったこと」というのは、バスケットボールで足首を捻挫したこと

12 **Hope you enjoy the reception.** = I hope you enjoy the reception.

14 **I'll talk to you later. Take care.**
「じゃあまた」「健康などに気をつけて」いずれもよく使うので覚えておきたい

Pronunciation －聴き取りポイントに注意しよう！

01 about⌣the , Minister⌣of の連音
03 I don't⌣think⌣I can make⌣it の連音
04 get⌣a chance［ゲラチャンス］と聞こえる
04 rub⌣elbows with⌣our Board⌣of Directors の連音
07 my foot's⌣all bandaged⌣up の連音
10 Well, that's⌣a shame の連音
11 about⌣it の連音と語末のtのため［アバウリ］と聞こえる
13 if⌣you の連音
14 Take⌣care の連音

日本語訳 －英文の内容を確認しよう！

足首の捻挫

男：もしもし、ジェーン？　ねえ、ナイジェリアの貿易大臣のレセプションの件なんだけれど…実は昨日バスケットをしていて足首を捻挫しちゃってさ、それで出席できそうにないんだ。

女：本当に？　重役会の人たちと同席する数少ない機会なのに。

男：そうなんだけれど、でも重役たちにいい印象を与えられそうもないんだ。足は包帯でぐるぐる巻きだし、松葉杖をついている。それに、痛み止めの強い薬も飲んでいるんだ。

女：わかったわ、残念だけれど、家にいたほうがいいようね。事情は説明しておくから、心配しないで。

男：ありがとう。レセプションを楽しめるといいね。それからそこで何か大事な情報をつかんだら、教えてくれるかい。

女：いいわよ。じゃあ後でね。お大事に。

Useful Expressions ❸ －このままそっくり暗記しよう！

1. Did you get to rub elbows with your new colleagues?（新しい同僚と親しくなりましたか？）
2. Try to make a good impression on her.（彼女にいい印象を与えるようにしなさい）
3. It's a shame to waste all this food.（こんなに食べ物を無駄にするのはもったいない）

CDで発音の確認とリピート練習ができます。

耳練 4 Contract

Short Conversation ④

M: Have you gone through all the papers yet? What do you think?

W: Well, most of them look fine, but there's one problem with this contract. There's no clause to specify the consequences in case your people can't meet the project deadline.

M: I spoke with our chief engineer just this morning. He assured me that the software you've ordered will be ready on schedule at the end of this month.

W: That's all well and good, but if for some reason it's not ready on time, we're going to lose a lot of money. I think the contract needs to state that you people will take responsibility in that case.

M: All right. I'll draw up a new contract and fax it to you this afternoon.

W: Yes, that'd be great.

耳練-4

Comprehension Questions

1. Where do the man and woman work?
2. What does the woman want the man to do?
3. What will the man send the woman?

耳練チェックマトリックス 自分のリスニング力を判定しよう！

聴き取りCheck / Step	Situation（状況理解）	Vocabulary（語彙）	Expression（表現）	Pronunciation（発音）
1st Try				
2nd Try				
3rd Try				

【自己判定マーク】
◎パーフェクトに理解　○ほぼ理解　△半分ほど理解　×ほとんどわからない

［注］すべて◎になるまでトライしてみよう！

＊本マトリックス活用法については7ページを参照。

耳練ヒント

Situation Markers 状況・場面を把握しよう！

- one problem with this contract（契約に問題がある）⇒クライアントとの対話
- meet the project deadline
  （締切りに間に合う）⇒締切りのある商品の納入
- the software you've ordered（御社注文のソフトウェア）⇒商品はソフトウェア
- at the end of this month（月末には出来上がる）
- take responsibility in that case
  （その場合責任をとる）⇒責任問題に関する条項を追加すること

耳練-4 Contract

耳練ポイント

Vocabulary －単語の意味を確認しよう！

- go through ～／～に目を通す、調べる
- contract／契約(書)
- clause／条項
- specify／規定する
- consequence／結果
- in case ～／～の場合
- your people／あなたの部下
- meet the deadline／締切りに間に合う
- chief engineer／主任技師(=システムエンジニア)
- ready／出来上がっている
- on schedule／予定どおり
- on time／時間どおりに
- at the end of this month／月末に
- for some reason／何らかの理由で
- you people／「あなた方」すなわち「御社」
- responsibility／責任
- draw up ～／～を書き上げる
- fax／ファックスで送る

Key Expressions －重要フレーズを聴き取ろう！

01 **Have you gone through all the papers yet?**
「すべての書類に目を通しましたか？」⇒Useful Expressions

02 **What do you think?**「どうですか？」相手の意見を求める表現

03 **most of them look fine**「ほとんどはよさそうだ」

03 **there's one problem with this contract**
「この契約には一つ問題がある」with の用法に注意 ⇒Useful Expressions

04 **There's no clause to specify ～**「～を規定する条項がない」

10 **That's all well and good**「それはそれで結構だ」
通常 but/however と続く。That's all very good. とも言う

11 **we're going to lose a lot of money**
「多額の損失が出ることになります」予測を表す

12 **you people will take responsibility in that case**
「その場合は御社が責任をとる」⇒Useful Expressions

14 **All right**「わかりました」

14 **draw up a new contract**「新しい契約書を作成する」

16 **that'd be great**「それはありがたい」相手の申し出を受ける決まった言い方

Pronunciation －聴き取りポイントに注意しよう!

01 Have‿you, papers yet の連音
02 What‿do‿you でtとdが一つになっている
03 problem, contract のoのイギリス発音[ɔ]
05 can't [kɑːnt] のイギリス英語発音
05 meet‿the project‿deadline. の連音
07 with‿our chief‿engineer just‿this morning の連音
09 at‿the end‿of this month の連音
10 good のdが開放されたtと発音されている
11 lose‿a lot‿of の連音、lotの母音
14 fax‿it‿to you this‿afternoon の連音

日本語訳 －英文の内容を確認しよう!

契約

男：すべての書類に目を通していただきましたか？ どうでしょうか？
女：ほとんどはいいようですが、ただ、この契約には一つ問題があります。御社がプロジェクトの期限に間に合わなかった場合にどうなるのかを具体的に示す条項がありません。
男：今朝、主任技師と話をしたのですが、御社が発注されたソフトは間違いなく予定どおり今月末にはできるとのことでした。
女：それは大変結構ですが、もし何らかの理由で期日にできていなかった場合、わが社は多額の損失を被ります。契約書には、その場合には御社が責任をとる旨を明記しておく必要があると思います。
男：わかりました。新しい契約書を作って、今日の午後FAXで送ります。
女：そうしていただけると助かります。

Useful Expressions ❹ －このままそっくり暗記しよう!

1. Shall we go through all the details? （詳細をすべてチェックしましょうか?）
2. There's one problem with your proposal. （あなたの提案には一つ問題がある）
3. I will take the responsibility in that case. （その場合には私が責任をとります）

CDで発音の確認とリピート練習ができます。

5 A Commercial Property

Short Conversation ⑤

M: So, what we're looking for is a commercial property in a good location. Ideally, it would have a large display window on the ground floor so that people walking or driving by can get a good look at our suits and sportswear on display.
W: I know of three very good possibilities off hand, and I'm sure I can find several more after I check the listings. How soon are you hoping to buy?
M: As soon as possible, before interest rates go up. Actually, we'd like to start moving in early next month.
W: If you have time, I can drive you to a couple of places right now.
M: I've got to get back to my office by 5:30, but I have a couple of hours.
W: If we hurry, probably we could have a quick look at all of them. This way, please.

耳練-5

Comprehension Questions

1. What kind of business does the man want to open?
2. What is the woman's occupation?
3. Why is the man eager to make a deal quickly?

耳練チェックマトリックス 自分のリスニング力を判定しよう!

聴き取りCheck / Step	Situation (状況理解)	Vocabulary (語彙)	Expression (表現)	Pronunciation (発音)
1st Try				
2nd Try				
3rd Try				

【自己判定マーク】
◎パーフェクトに理解　○ほぼ理解　△半分ほど理解　×ほとんどわからない

[注] すべて◎になるまでトライしてみよう!
＊本マトリックス活用法については7ページを参照。

耳練ヒント

Situation Markers 状況・場面を把握しよう!

- looking for ... a commercial property ⇒男の人は商業地で物件を探している
- our suits and sportswear
  ⇒スーツやスポーツウェアを販売する場所を探している
- moving in early next month（来月早々引越したい）
- I have a couple of hours（2、3時間ある）
- This way, please. ⇒案内しているので一緒に出かける

耳練-5 A Commercial Property

耳練ポイント

Vocabulary －単語の意味を確認しよう！

- □ look for 〜／〜を探す
- □ commercial property／商業物件
- □ in a good location／好立地の
- □ Ideally／理想的には
- □ display window／ショーウィンドウ
- □ ground floor／１階
- □ so that 〜／〜であるように
- □ on display／陳列中の
- □ possibilities／可能性（この場合は条件に合いそうな物件のこと）
- □ off hand／即座に（手から直接渡せるの意）
- □ listings／登録物件（コンピュータなどのリストに載っている物件一覧のこと）
- □ How soon／どれほど早く
- □ interest rates／金利
- □ Actually／実のところ、本当は
- □ moving in／入居する
- □ have time／時間がある
- □ right now／今すぐに、これから
- □ a couple of hours／２、３時間

Key Expressions －重要フレーズを聴き取ろう！

01 **So,**「それで、だから」先行文脈と漠然とつなげる表現

01 **what we're looking for is a commercial property in a good location**
what を頭におき、we're looking for a commercial property in a good location を強調した表現 ⇒Useful Expressions

03 **people walking or driving by**「そばを車や徒歩で通り過ぎる人」walking 以下は後ろから people を限定している（後置修飾）。by は walking と driving の両方にかかっている

04 **get a good look at 〜**「〜をよく見る」⇒Useful Expressions

05 **know of 〜**「〜のこと／の存在を知っている」know だけだと詳しい知識があることになるが、know of とすると単に該当するものを知っているということになる

05 **I'm sure 〜**「きっと〜です」 Cf. I'm sure you'll like it.（きっと気に入りますよ）

08 **As soon as possible**「できるだけ早く」As soon as I can buy one. の意味だが、状況を問わずいつもこの形で使えるので便利

10 **drive you to 〜**「あなたを〜に車で案内する」
Cf. Can you drive me to the station?（車で駅まで送ってくれますか？）

12 **I've got to 〜**「〜しなければならない」

14 **have a quick look at 〜**「〜をざっと見る」⇒Useful Expressions

15 **This way, please.**「こちらへどうぞ」人を先導するときに使う

Pronunciation －聴き取りポイントに注意しよう！

01 is‿a commercial property in‿a good location の連音
02 have‿a large display window on‿the の連音
04 get‿a good look at‿our ［ゲラ…アラワ］のように聞こえる連音
05 possibilities‿off hand の連音、and‿I'm が［アンダイm］と聞こえること
08 As‿soon‿as possible の連音
09 moving‿in の連音
10 If‿you, drive‿you, couple‿of の連音
12 but‿I have‿a couple‿of‿hours ［バライハヴァカpラヴァワズ］の連音
14 have‿a quick look‿at‿all‿of them の連音

日本語訳 －英文の内容を確認しよう！

商業物件

男：つまり、立地のいい店舗を探しているのです。飾ってあるスーツやスポーツウェアが、歩行者や車で通りかかる人によく見えるように、1階に大きなショーウィンドウがある建物だと理想的です。

女：今、3軒、有力な物件がありますし、売り出し中の不動産のデータを調べれば他にも数軒は見つけられると思います。ご購入はどれくらいお急ぎですか？

男：できるだけ早く、金利が上がる前に。実は、来月早々に引越しを始めたいのです。

女：時間がおありなら、今から2、3の物件に車でご案内できます。

男：5時半に社に戻らなければなりませんが、2、3時間はあります。

女：急げば全部ざっと見ることはできるでしょう。こちらにどうぞ。

Useful Expressions ⑤ －このままそっくり暗記しよう！

1. What we need is a go-getter like you. (私たちが必要なのはあなたのような辣腕家です)
2. You should get a good look at this product. (この製品をよく見てみなさい)
3. Let's have a quick look at them now. (今はそれらをざっと見ておきましょう)

CDで発音の確認とリピート練習ができます。

耳練 6 Agenda

Short Conversation ❻

W: I was just looking at the agenda you've prepared for the staff meeting this afternoon. Do we really need to bring up the problem with the break room?

M: Well, the president did send out a memo on that, remember? He wants all the section leaders to make sure every single employee knows the rules about cleaning up after ourselves.

W: It's just that we have so many other items to deal with that are more important.

M: Trust me. I won't let the group get bogged down in a long discussion on it. The last thing I want is to have a twenty-minute argument about the break room.

W: Yeah. Just imagine the finger-pointing, with everybody blaming everybody else for the problem.

M: I give you my word that that's not going to happen.

Comprehension Questions

1. What are the speakers doing now?
2. What is probably the problem with the break room?
3. What does the man promise to do?

耳練チェックマトリックス 自分のリスニング力を判定しよう！

聴き取りCheck / Step	Situation（状況理解）	Vocabulary（語彙）	Expression（表現）	Pronunciation（発音）
1st Try				
2nd Try				
3rd Try				

【自己判定マーク】

◎パーフェクトに理解　○ほぼ理解　△半分ほど理解　×ほとんどわからない

[注] すべて◎になるまでトライしてみよう！

＊本マトリックス活用法については7ページを参照。

耳練ヒント

Situation Markers　状況・場面を把握しよう！

- agenda for the staff meeting
  （スタッフミーティングの議題）⇒同僚同士の会話
- the problem with the break room（休憩室の問題）⇒議題の一つ
- the president did send out a memo on that（社長からメモが出された）
  ⇒だから取り上げないわけにはいかない
- The last thing I want is ～（～はしたくない）
- that's not going to happen（そうはならない）⇒安心させている

耳練-6 Agenda

耳練ポイント

Vocabulary －単語の意味を確認しよう！

- □agenda／議題
- □prepare／作成する、準備する
- □staff meeting／スタッフミーティング（課長会議）
- □problem with ～／～の問題
- □break room／休憩室
- □memo／メモ、覚え書き
- □section leader／課長
- □item／事案
- □deal with ～／～に対処する、～を扱う
- □discussion／議論
- □argument／論争
- □finger-pointing／（罪、責任の）なすりあい

Key Expressions －重要フレーズを聴き取ろう！

02 **staff meeting this afternoon**
「今日の午後の課長会議」this afternoon は後ろから修飾（後置修飾）

02 **bring up ～**「～を取り上げる、話題にする」⇒Useful Expressions

04 **Well,** はっきり Yes というと角が立つので、少し緩和した言い方

04 **the president did send out a memo on that**「その件については社長がメモを実際出している」強勢を持つ did は実際そうだという強調を表す。つまり社長直々の指示だということ

04 **～, remember?**「（～を）覚えているでしょう？」

06 **rules about cleaning up after ourselves**「後片付けについての規則」

08 **It's just that ～**「ただ～なんです」先行文脈と部分的に矛盾対立することをつけ加えるときに使う

10 **Trust me.**「大丈夫ですよ」相手を安心させる表現

10 **I won't let ～**「～を放置しない」

10 **get bogged down ～**「～（という泥沼）の中で動きがとれなくなる」⇒Useful Expressions

11 **The last thing I want is ～**「～なんてごめんだ」the last thing とは「最もありそうもないもの」の意。したがって the last thing I want とは「最も（起こって）ほしくないこと」の意
⇒Useful Expressions

13 **with everybody blaming everybody else for the problem**「みんなが互いにその問題で非難しあう」with は付帯状況を表している。blame ～ for …「…について～を非難する」

15 **I give you my word that ～**「誓って～だ」この word は「請けあい、保障」の意味で、that 以下を保障する／約束するの意 ⇒Useful Expressions

15 **that's not going to happen**「そうはさせない」の意
that は直前の with everybody blaming everybody else for the problem をさす

Pronunciation －聴き取りポイントに注意しよう！

01 looking‿at‿the の連音と子音連続、you've‿prepared の語末語頭の子音連続
04 send‿out‿a memo の連音
06 rules‿about‿cleaning‿up‿after‿ourselves の子音連続と連音
10 Trust‿me の語頭語末の子音連続
10 bogged‿down‿in‿a long discussion‿on‿it の連音群
15 going‿to happen の語頭語末の子音連続

日本語訳 －英文の内容を確認しよう！

議題

女：今日の午後のスタッフミーティングのためにあなたが準備した議事録をちょうど見ていたところだけれど、休憩室の問題を持ち出す必要が本当にあるかしら？

男：いや、その件については社長が連絡メモを送ってきただろう、覚えてる？　社長は全セクションリーダーに、自分たちが使った後の片付けに関する規則を全社員に周知させてほしいんだ。

女：ミーティングではほかにもっと重要なことがあるから、言っただけよ。

男：大丈夫だよ。そのことで長い議論に落ち込まないようにするから。休憩室について20分も議論するなんてことはごめんだからね。

女：そうよ。その問題でだれが悪い彼が悪いと非難ごっこになったことを想像してみて。

男：誓ってそんなことにはしないよ。

Useful Expressions 6 －このままそっくり暗記しよう！

1. Let's bring it up at our next meeting. （次の会議でそれを話題にしましょう）
2. They got bogged down in a series of lawsuits.
   （彼らは一連の訴訟合戦に落ち込んだ）
3. The last thing I want is to have to do it all over again.
   （それを最初からやり直すなんてごめんだ）
4. I give you my word that I'm serious. （誓って本気だよ）

CDで発音の確認とリピート練習ができます。

Short Conversation 7

M: Aren't you attending the managers' conference this weekend?
W: No. I've just got too much piled up on my desk, what with all the personnel changes and the move to the new building in July. Besides, I went to the one last year in Phoenix and I didn't get much out of it.
M: But it's being held right here in town this year! And the guest speaker won the Nobel Prize for Economics!
W: Yeah, I know. But that was 20 years ago. I doubt that he has anything relevant to say about our firm's financial future.
M: I see what you mean. That makes me wonder if I should go or not. I've got a lot piled up on my desk, too.
W: I tell you what. You're not as behind as I am. Why don't you go and let me know if you hear anything useful.
M: Okay. I'll do that.

耳練-7

Comprehension Questions

1. Why won't the woman attend the conference?
2. What does the woman say about last year's conference?
3. What does the woman say about this year's guest speaker?

耳練チェックマトリックス 自分のリスニング力を判定しよう！

聴き取りCheck Step	Situation（状況理解）	Vocabulary（語彙）	Expression（表現）	Pronunciation（発音）
1st Try				
2nd Try				
3rd Try				

【自己判定マーク】
◎パーフェクトに理解　○ほぼ理解　△半分ほど理解　×ほとんどわからない

［注］すべて◎になるまでトライしてみよう！
＊本マトリックス活用法については7ページを参照。

耳練ヒント

Situation Markers 状況・場面を把握しよう！

- attending the managers' conference（管理職会議への出席）
  ⇒互いに管理職にある
- No. ⇒出席しない
- But it's being held right here in town this year!（今年は地元で開かれる）
  ⇒それでも出席しないのか？
- Yeah, I know. But（わかっているけど、でも）⇒やはり出席しない
- Why don't you go ⇒自分が行ったらどうか？
- Okay. ⇒男は行く

35

耳練-7 Managers' Conference

耳練ポイント

Vocabulary －単語の意味を確認しよう！

- □attend／出席する
- □piled up／山積している
- □what with ～ and …／～やら…やらで
- □personnel change／人事異動
- □move／引越し
- □in July／7月の（前の引越しを後ろから修飾する［後置修飾］）
- □Besides／それに（理由などを追加するときに使う）
- □in town／地元で（in town は問題となっている「当地」、たとえば電話で I'm in town. と言えば「今来ている」という意味）
- □guest speaker／ゲストスピーカー（招待講演者）
- □the Nobel Prize for Economics／ノーベル経済学賞
- □anything relevant／何か重要なこと（relevant は「関連した」の意）
- □behind／（仕事などが）遅れている

Key Expressions －重要フレーズを聴き取ろう！

02 **I've just got too much piled up on my desk**「仕事がうんとたまっている」
比喩的な表現で、文字どおり机の上に何かがなくても構わない ⇒Useful Expressions

04 **the one last year in Phoenix** 全体で「フェニックスであった去年のもの」
one は managers' conference のこと。last year, in Phoenix はいずれもこの one を後置修飾する

05 **(not) get much out of it**「そこから多くのものを得る（得ない）」「参考／勉強になる」
⇒Useful Expressions

06 **But it's being held right here**「ここで開かれる」
受身の進行形であるが、近い未来の予定を表している

08 **Yeah, I know. But**「わかっているけど」

08 **I doubt that ～**「～とは思わない」Cf. I suspect that he knows about this.
⇒Useful Expressions

11 **I see what you mean.**「なるほど」
相手の言ったことに同意する表現で、あいづちの一種。有用な表現なので暗記したい

11 **That makes me wonder if ～**「そうなると～かどうか迷う」

13 **I tell you what.**「じゃあこうしましょう」提案などをするときの言い出し方

13 **Why don't you ～?**「～したらどうですか？／しなさいよ」何かを提案・示唆するときの表現 ⇒Useful Expressions

Pronunciation —聴き取りポイントに注意しよう!

- 01 Ar‿en't‿you の連音と音変化［アンチュー］、短く発音される
- 02 piled‿up‿on my desk ［パイルダポンマイデsk］の連音、much‿out‿of‿it ［マッチアウラヴィt］の連音
- 06 But‿it's being ［バリツビン］の早い発音と音連続
- 09 firm's financial future の単語間の子音連続
- 11 what‿you ［ワチュ］の連音と音変化
- 11 me, I 対比のため強く発音されている
- 13 I tell‿you の子音連続
- 13 don't‿you の子音連続と対比のためyouが強く発音されている
- 14 let‿me, if‿you の子音連続

日本語訳 —英文の内容を確認しよう!

管理職会議

男：今週末の管理職会議に出席するの?
女：いいえ。あれこれの人事異動と7月の新社屋への引越しもあって仕事がたまっているの。それに、去年フェニックスで開かれた会議に出たけれど、大して得るところはなかったわ。
男：でも、今年は市内で開かれるんだよ! それに、ゲストスピーカーはノーベル経済学賞を受賞した人物だよ!
女：ええ、知っているわ。でも、受賞したのは20年前よ。彼がわが社の今後の財務状況について何か重要なことを言うとは思えないわ。
男：なるほど。そうなると僕もどうしようかと思ってしまうな。僕も仕事がたくさんたまっているし。
女：じゃあこうしましょう。あなたは私ほど仕事が遅れていないから、行って、何か有益なことがあったら教えてよ。
男：わかった、そうするよ。

Useful Expressions ❼ —このままそっくり暗記しよう!

1. (He can't help you.) He's got too much piled up on his desk.
   (［彼は助けてはくれない。］仕事がたまりすぎています)
2. You won't get much out of his book. (彼の本からはあまり得るものがない)
3. I doubt that he knows about this. (彼がこのことを知っているとは思わない)
4. Why don't you ask Bill? (ビルに聞いてみたらどうですか?)

CDで発音の確認とリピート練習ができます。 CD 1-48

8 A Telephone Sale Call

Short Conversation ⑧

W : Hello. I'm calling for GAC Telephone, and I was wondering if I could interest you in one of our long-distance calling plans. We have some wonderful bargains now that are available for a limited time only.

M : Actually, I'm very satisfied with the telephone service I have now, thank you.

W : Oh, but if I could just tell you some of our rates and some of our special plans for earning free bonus minutes...

M : Look, I understand what a tough job you have. In fact, I used to work in telephone sales myself when I was younger. That's why I'm cutting you some slack here.

W : Well, we have something in common, then! Would you mind telling me what service you're using now?

M : I'm just not interested. You'll have to excuse me now. I'm really quite busy.

耳練-8

Comprehension Questions

1. What is the purpose of the woman's call?
2. What aspect of her company's service does the woman emphasize?
3. Why does the man try to be polite to the woman?

耳練チェックマトリックス 自分のリスニング力を判定しよう!

聴き取りCheck Step	Situation (状況理解)	Vocabulary (語彙)	Expression (表現)	Pronunciation (発音)
1st Try				
2nd Try				
3rd Try				

【自己判定マーク】
◎パーフェクトに理解　○ほぼ理解　△半分ほど理解　×ほとんどわからない

[注] すべて◎になるまでトライしてみよう！
＊本マトリックス活用法については7ページを参照。

耳練ヒント

Situation Markers　状況・場面を把握しよう!

- Hello. I'm calling for GAC Telephone ⇒電話会社からの売込みの電話
- I'm very satisfied（満足している）⇒断っている
- Oh, if I could ⇒食い下がっている
- I'm just not interested.（関心がない）⇒さらに断っている

耳練-8 A Telephone Sale Call

耳練ポイント

Vocabulary －単語の意味を確認しよう！

- □long distance calling plans／長距離電話料金プラン
- □bargain／お買い得
- □available／買うことができる
- □rates／料金
- □earn／稼ぐ、貯める
- □bonus minutes／無料通話時間（分）
- □tough／大変な
- □In fact／実際
- □slack／たるみ（ここでは相手にいくぶんかの自由を与えること）
- □in common／共通の

Key Expressions －重要フレーズを聴き取ろう！

01 **I'm calling for～**「～のものですが」「～に代わって電話をかけている」の意

01 **I was wondering if I could ～**「～できるかどうかと思いまして」
過去進行形にして丁寧さを表す ⇒Useful Expressions

02 **interest you in ～**「あなたに～に関心を持たせる」

04 **available for a limited time only**「期間限定の」

05 **I'm very satisfied with the telephone service I have now**「今の電話サービスで大変満足しています」be satisfied with ～「～に満足している」⇒Useful Expressions

06 **thank you**「おかげさまで」このように文末に thank you をつけるのは、何かを断る際の言い方

07 **Oh, but**「でも」食い下がるときの決まり文句

09 **I used to work in telephone sales myself**「自分も電話の売込みの仕事をしていたことがある」used to ～「～したものだ」⇒Useful Expressions

11 **That's why ～**「だから～だ」 Cf. 耳練2の Useful Expressions 参照（p.16、17）

11 **cut you some slack**「あなたを大目に見る」ここではすぐに切らずにできるだけ丁寧に断っていることをさしている

12 **we have something in common**「私たちには共通点がある」

12 **Would you mind ～ing?**「～していただけますか？」
ここではしつこく食い下がる際に用いられているが、通常は丁寧な依頼をするときに使う

14 **I'm just not interested.**「まったく関心がありません」

14 **You'll have to excuse me now.**「もう電話を切ります」電話を切るときの決まり文句

14 **I'm really quite busy.**「本当はとても忙しい」この really は忙しい程度を述べているのではなく、「本当のところは」という意味

Pronunciation　−聴き取りポイントに注意しよう！

01　and⌣I was wondering if⌣I could⌣interest⌣you in one⌣of⌣our longdistance calling plans の連音群

04　for⌣a limited⌣time⌣only の子音連続と連音、特に limited の d が次の t と重なって聞こえないこと

05　satisfied⌣with⌣the の単語間の子音の融合

07　but⌣if⌣I could just tell you some⌣of⌣our rates⌣and some⌣of⌣our special plans の連音と強勢をおかれない部分の発音速度

日本語訳　−英文の内容を確認しよう！

売込み電話

女：もしもし、GAC テレフォンの者ですが、当社の長距離電話の料金プランのご紹介でお電話しています。現在、期間限定のとてもお得なプランがあるのですが。

男：今のところ、おかげさまで現在の電話のサービスにとても満足しています。

女：そうですか、でも当社の料金や無料通話時間がもらえるスペシャルプランについてご案内させていただければ…

男：あのね、あなたの仕事が大変なことはわかります。実際私ももっと若かった頃は電話の勧誘の仕事をしていたものです。だから、すこし大目に見ているんですよ。

女：じゃあ、私たちには共通点がありますね！　今どのようなサービスを使っていらっしゃるか教えていただけませんか？

男：まったく関心がありません。失礼しますよ。本当はとても忙しいんです。

Useful Expressions ⑧　−このままそっくり暗記しよう！

1. I was wondering if you could help me.（助けていただけないかと思いまして）
2. Are you satisfied with the job you have?（あなたの今の仕事に満足していますか？）
3. We used to come here to dine.（ここに食事に来たものだ）

CDで発音の確認とリピート練習ができます。

9 An Ambitious Young Man

Short Conversation 9

M: アメリカ
W: アメリカ

M: Karen, I haven't seen Jeffrey around here in ages. Do you have any idea what happened to him?

W: Oh, didn't you hear? He quit two months ago. He got accepted into a master's degree program at one of the best business schools on the East Coast.

M: Really? Well, good for him! I didn't know he had any such plans. I guess it's not that surprising, though, since he was always such a bright young man.

W: Yes, wasn't he? He always said he didn't want to stay in a large company his whole life. His dream is to start up a business of his own.

M: Now that you mention it, I remember hearing him talk about that. Something to do with search engines, wasn't it?

W: Right. He has this grand scheme to build a company that'll become the next Yahoo or Google.

耳練-9

Comprehension Questions

1. How does the man feel about the news about Jeffrey?
2. What is Jeffrey's long-term goal?
3. What field is Jeffrey especially interested in?

耳練チェックマトリックス 自分のリスニング力を判定しよう!

聴き取りCheck Step	Situation（状況理解）	Vocabulary（語彙）	Expression（表現）	Pronunciation（発音）
1st Try				
2nd Try				
3rd Try				

【自己判定マーク】
◎パーフェクトに理解　○ほぼ理解　△半分ほど理解　×ほとんどわからない

［注］すべて◎になるまでトライしてみよう!
＊本マトリックス活用法については7ページを参照。

耳練ヒント

Situation Markers 状況・場面を把握しよう!

- I haven't seen Jeffrey（ジェフリーを見かけていない）⇒共通の知合いである
- He quit two months ago.（2か月前に辞めた）
  ⇒このことから話をしている2人が会社の同僚であることがわかる
- He got accepted into a master's program（修士課程に合格した）
  ⇒大学院に行った
- His dream is to start up a business of his own.
  （彼の夢は自分の事業を起こすこと）

耳練-9 An Ambitious Young Man

耳練ポイント

Vocabulary －単語の意味を確認しよう！

- quit／（仕事などを）辞める
- get accepted／合格する、入学を許可される
- master's degree program／修士課程
- on the East Coast／東海岸の（前置詞 on に注意）
- surprising／意外な
- bright／頭のよい
- his whole life／一生
- business／事業、会社
- search engine／サーチエンジン、検索エンジン
- grand scheme／一大計画

Key Expressions －重要フレーズを聴き取ろう！

01 **see ～ around**「～を見かける」 ⇒ Useful Expressions

01 **in ages**「ずっと、長い間」誇張表現である。意味的には for a long time と同じであるが、for a long time は肯定文で、in ages は否定文で使われることが多い
  ⇒ Useful Expressions

01 **Do you have any idea?** 間接疑問文を従えて「わかりますか？心当たりはありますか？」
  Cf. I have no idea.「皆目わからない」 ⇒ Useful Expressions

03 **(Oh,) didn't you hear?**「（えっ）聞いてないの？」このまま覚えておきたい。意味上の目的語は後続の文の前に置くこともできる

06 **good for ～**「（～は）よくやったぞ、いいぞ」
  ほめるときに使う表現で、Good for you.「えらいぞ」などと言う

07 **I guess ～**「（考えてみれば）～だね」と人の意見に同意するときに用いる
  ⇒ Useful Expressions

07 **that surprising**「そんなに驚くべき」that は程度を表す

08 **was** 東部の学校へ行ってしまう前までの過去のことを表しているから。死んだわけではない

09 **Yes, wasn't he?**「ええ、そうよね」形は疑問であるが、同意を表す
  Cf. A: He passed the exam.（彼が試験に受かったよ）
     B: Did he? Good for him.（そうかい、よくやったね）

11 **start up a business**「起業する」

11 **of his own**「自分の」

12 **Now that you mention it**「そう言えば」定型表現。Now that ～で「（今）～だから」
  Cf. Now that you are here（あなたが来たので）

12 **I remember hearing him talk**「彼が話をしているのを聞いたおぼえがある」

15 **Yahoo or Google** 現在最も広汎に使われている検索エンジン

Pronunciation －聴き取りポイントに注意しよう！

02 what happened to him の語をまたぐ子音連続と音の融合
03 quit two months ago のquit twoでtが融合することと、monthsではthの音が聞こえないこと
05 best business schools on 語をまたぐ音連続。特にbestのtが明確に聞こえないこと
07 I guess it's not that surprising の語をまたぐ音連続、特にnot thatの語末のtが聞こえないこと
11 start up a business of his own の語をまたぐ子音－母音連続
12 Now that you mention it の連音と語をまたぐ子音連続

日本語訳 －英文の内容を確認しよう！

野心的な若者

男：カレン、このあたりでジェフリーを長い間見かけないけれど、彼がどうしたか知っているかい？

女：あら、聞いてなかったの？ 彼は2か月前に辞めたのよ。東海岸にある名門ビジネススクールの一つの修士課程に受かったのよ。

男：本当に？ それはよかった。そういうことを考えているとは知らなかったよ。でも、それほど驚くことではないかもしれないね、彼はすごく頭のいい若者だったから。

女：そうだったわね。一生ずっと大企業に勤めたくはないっていつも言っていたわ。起業するのが彼の夢ですものね。

男：そういえば、そんなことを彼が言っていたのを思い出した。検索エンジンと関係した何かじゃなかったかい？

女：そうよ。彼は次のヤフーかグーグルになるような会社を作るという大きな計画があるのよ。

Useful Expressions ⑨ －このままそっくり暗記しよう！

1. Did you see my cell phone around?（僕の携帯を見かけなかった？）
2. I haven't eaten beef in ages.（ずいぶん牛肉を食べていない）
3. Do you have any idea who he is?（彼がだれだかわかりますか？）
4. I guess you are right.（［考えてみれば］君の言うとおりだ）

CDで発音の確認とリピート練習ができます。

Faulty Product

Short Conversation ⑩

M: アメリカ
W: イギリス

W: Have a seat, Mr. Green. I appreciate your coming by on such short notice.
M: Not at all. We at Zeta Systems are always available to deal with our clients' problems. So what seems to be the matter?
W: The email filter your company provided has not been very effective. We're still receiving a lot of spam. To make matters worse, some email from our regular customers is getting blocked.
M: I assure you that we've given you the most up-to-date filtering system that's available.
W: Still, it's just not acceptable. If we don't see an improvement in the service soon, we'll have to give the contract to somebody else when it comes up for renewal next month.
M: Understood. I'll have our top engineer get right on it, and he'll install upgrades tomorrow morning.

耳練-10

Comprehension Questions

1. Why is the woman unhappy about the email filter?
2. What does the woman plan to do if the problem is not fixed?
3. How soon does the man promise to fix the problem?

耳練チェックマトリックス 自分のリスニング力を判定しよう！

聴き取りCheck / Step	Situation（状況理解）	Vocabulary（語彙）	Expression（表現）	Pronunciation（発音）
1st Try				
2nd Try				
3rd Try				

【自己判定マーク】
◎パーフェクトに理解　○ほぼ理解　△半分ほど理解　×ほとんどわからない

[注] すべて◎になるまでトライしてみよう！
＊本マトリックス活用法については7ページを参照。

耳練ヒント

Situation Markers 状況・場面を把握しよう！

- Have a seat, Mr. Green. ⇒グリーン氏は女性のところに来ている
- We at Zeta Systems... our clients' problems.
  ⇒グリーン氏はジータ・システムズの社員で、女性はクライアント
- The email filter... not very effective.
  （Eメールのフィルターがあまり有効でない）⇒これが来てもらった理由
- If we don't see an improvement... we'll have to give the contract to somebody else.（改善が見られないと他社と契約する）⇒女性の方がクライアントとして強い立場にある
- Understood.（了解しました）

耳練-10 Faulty Product

耳練ポイント

Vocabulary －単語の意味を確認しよう！

- □appreciate ／感謝する
- □come by ／立ち寄る（一時的であることを明確にした言い方）
- □notice ／予告
- □available ／用意ができている、待機している
- □deal with ～ ／～に対処する
- □client ／客、クライアント
- □provide ／提供する
- □effective ／有効な
- □spam ／スパム、迷惑メール
- □block ／ブロックする、阻止する
- □assure ／確約する
- □up-to-date ／最新の
- □available ／利用可能な、入手可能な（前述 available との意味の違いに注意）
- □Still ／それでも
- □acceptable ／受け入れられる
- □improvement ／改善
- □renewal ／更新
- □engineer ／技師、エンジニア
- □install ／インストールする
- □upgrades ／追加版、改良版（ここでは性能をよくするための追加プログラムのこと）

Key Expressions －重要フレーズを聴き取ろう！

01 **Have a seat**「お座りください、お掛けください」

01 **I appreciate your coming by on such short notice.**
「急に呼び出したのに（こんなに短時間の予告で）来ていただいてありがとうございました」
これは定型表現なのでこのまま覚えておきたい。
I appreciate your coming by は「あなたの来訪を感謝します」

03 **available to ～**「人が～する用意ができている」⇒Useful Expressions

04 **So what seems to be the matter?**「で、どういうことが問題なんでしょうか？」
これも定型表現。医者が患者に質問するときにも使う。seems を使うのは婉曲表現で、So what is the matter? は場合によっては詰問調になる

06 **To make matters worse**「もっと悪いことには」定型表現

07 **is getting blocked**「ブロックされて（しま）います」

09 **I assure you that ～**「～ですが」 文字どおりには「～を保証します」だが、「～」が事実であることを強調する言い方 ⇒Useful Expressions

13 **when it comes up for renewal**「更新の時期が来たときに」
it は the contract をさす ⇒Useful Expressions

14 **Understood**「了解」

14 **get right on it**「すぐに着手する」it は問題をさす

Pronunciation －聴き取りポイントに注意しよう！

01 Have a seat, appreciate your coming の連音
03 Not at all ［ナラロー］と聞こえる連音。Systems are always available の連音
04 clients' problems における語をまたぐ子音連結
06 lot of の連音と o の母音
07 matters イギリス英語の摩擦の多い t
07 some email from our regular customers is の連音
10 that's available の［ツァ］連音
11 it's just not acceptable. If we don't see an improvement in の連音
13 when it comes up の連音
14 have our top engineer get right on it の連音

日本語訳 －英文の内容を確認しよう！

欠陥品

女：お掛けください、グリーンさん。急に呼び出したのに来ていただいてありがとうございました。

男：どういたしまして。ジータ・システムズ社ではいつでも駆けつけてお客様の問題に対処いたします。で、どういったことが問題でしょうか？

女：御社の製品の電子メールのフィルターはあまり有効ではありません。まだたくさんのスパム（迷惑メール）が来ますよ。さらに悪いことに、うちの常連のお客様からのメールもいくつかブロックされています。

男：現在入手可能な最新のものをご提供させていただいておりますが。

女：そう言われても、あれでは問題になりません。すぐにサービスに改善がみられなければ、来月の契約更新時には他の会社と契約するしかありません。

男：承知しました。当社のトップエンジニアにすぐに取りかからせます。明日の朝、アップグレードしたものを彼がインストールします。

Useful Expressions ⑩ －このままそっくり暗記しよう！

1. Somebody will be available to assist you.（だれかお手伝いする者がいるでしょう）
2. I assure you that it will be delivered on time.（間違いなく期限内にお届けいたします）
3. His house will come up for sale next week.（彼の家は来週売りにでる）

CDで発音の確認とリピート練習ができます。

11 Crowded Airplane

Short Conversation 11

M: アメリカ
W: イギリス

M: I've never seen this flight so crowded. I think it's going to be full.

W: Oh, do you often fly this route? It's my first time.

M: Actually, I make this trip twice a month to supervise sales staff for my company. Sometimes I feel like I'm living out of my suitcase.

W: I know what that's like. I used to have to travel a lot in my previous job, but I don't anymore. It's kind of fun at first, but it gets really old after a while.

M: So you are not on business?

W: That's right. I'm changing planes in L.A. and going on to Christchurch, New Zealand, where my husband is joining me.

M: How nice! Any special occasion?

W: Yes, this is our 20th anniversary and we're celebrating it by trekking the Milford Track.

M: That's wonderful. I wish I could do something like that with my wife.

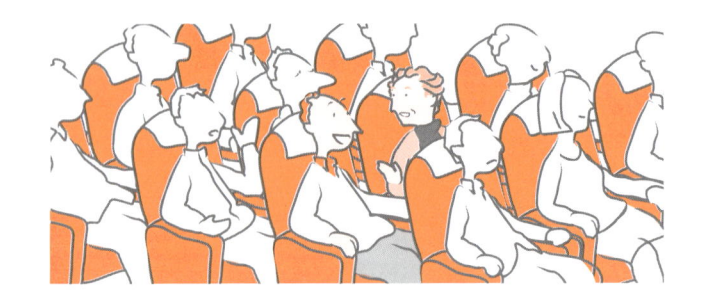

耳練-11

Comprehension Questions

1. What is the relationship of the speakers?
2. What did the woman dislike about her previous job?
3. What is the purpose of the woman's trip?

耳練チェックマトリックス 自分のリスニング力を判定しよう！

聴き取りCheck Step	Situation（状況理解）	Vocabulary（語彙）	Expression（表現）	Pronunciation（発音）
1st Try				
2nd Try				
3rd Try				

【自己判定マーク】
◎パーフェクトに理解　○ほぼ理解　△半分ほど理解　×ほとんどわからない

[注] すべて◎になるまでトライしてみよう！

＊本マトリックス活用法については7ページを参照。

耳練ヒント

Situation Markers　状況・場面を把握しよう！

- this flight ⇒ 機内での会話
- It's my first time. ⇒ この路線は初めて
- I make this trip twice a month to supervise sales staff for my company. ⇒ 月2回、販売部員の指導のために出張する
- I used to have to travel a lot.（過去にはよく出張した）
- I'm flying to Christchurch, New Zealand ⇒ ニュージーランドに行く

耳練-11 Crowded Airplane

耳練ポイント

Vocabulary －単語の意味を確認しよう！

- flight ／（飛行機の）便
- crowded ／混雑している
- route ／（空便の）路線、経路
- supervise ／監督、指導する
- sales staff ／販売（部）員
- previous job ／前の仕事
- old ／月並みな、いつもの
- So ／ということは
- on business ／商用
- special occasion ／特別な時（occasionとは普段とは異なることをする理由となる出来事のこと）
- 20th anniversary ／結婚20周年
- celebrate ／祝う

Key Expressions －重要フレーズを聴き取ろう！

01 **I've never seen this flight so crowded.**「この便がこんなに混んでいるのを見たことがない」訳が示すように this flight と so crowded の間には主語と述語の関係がある Cf. I've never seen him tired.（彼が疲れているところなど見たことがない）

02 **fly this route**「この路線を飛ぶ」
fly には路線、便、航空会社を目的語とする用法がある ⇒Useful Expressions

03 **make this trip**「この旅行をする」この便で飛ぶの意味 ⇒Useful Expressions

05 **live out of one's suitcase**「旅行かばんの中の身の回り品で生活する」
つまり「年中旅行している、各地を転々とする」ことを表す英語独特の表現

06 **I know what that's like.**「それがどんなだかよくわかる」の意味で「そうですよね」という程度のあいづちを打つ表現

06 **I used to have to travel a lot**「かつてはしょっちゅう旅行しなければならなかった」
⇒Useful Expressions

07 **I don't anymore.** ＝ I don't［have to travel a lot］anymore. の意味

07 **It's kind of fun at first**「最初は結構楽しい」
kind of は「まあまあ、ある程度」を表す緩和表現

08 **it gets really old after a while**「少しするとまったくつまらなくなる」
get old は「新鮮味を失う」

10 **That's right.**「そのとおりです」

10 **changing planes**「飛行機を乗り換える」常に planes と複数 ⇒Useful Expressions

15 **That's wonderful.**「それはすばらしい」これもあいづち表現として覚えておきたい

Pronunciation　−聴き取りポイントに注意しよう！

- 01　this flight の s-fl の子音連続、I think it's going to be full の連音
- 03　this trip の s-tr の子音連続、twice a month の連音
- 04　I feel like の同一子音連続、living out of my suitcase の連音
- 06　what that's like の3語にわたる子音連続
- 06　I used to have to の子音連続と d t、v f の子音連続の変化（無声化という）
- 07　kind of fun, but it gets, after a while の連音、not on business の連音、this is our の連音
- 15　That's wonderful の2語に渡る子音連続

日本語訳　−英文の内容を確認しよう！

混み合う機内

男：この便がこんなに混んでいるのは初めてです。満席になりそうですね。
女：この路線によく乗られるのですか？　私は初めてです。
男：会社の販売スタッフの指導で月に2度この旅行をしています。時には、旅行ばかりしている気分になりますよ。
女：わかります。私も前の仕事では出張が多かったんです。でも、今はなくなりました。出張も最初は面白いですが、しばらくするとすっかり飽きてしまうものです。
男：ということは、商用ではないということですね？
女：そうです。LAで乗り換えて、ニュージーランドのクライストチャーチまで行きます。そこで夫が合流してきます。
男：それはいいですね。何か特別な機会ですか？
女：はい、今年は私たちの結婚20周年なんです。だから、それを祝って、ミルフォード・トラックをトレッキングするんです。
男：それはすばらしいですね。私も妻とそんなことをしたいものです。

Useful Expressions ⓫　−このままそっくり暗記しよう！

1. He usually flies United.（彼は普段はユナイテッド航空で飛びます）
2. I used to have to make this trip every week.（私は毎週この旅行をしなければなりませんでした）
3. You have to change planes at JFK airport.（JFK空港で飛行機を乗り換えなければなりません）

CDで発音の確認とリピート練習ができます。

Headhunting

Short Conversation 12

M: Jennifer, I can speak for the vice president and the whole staff when I say how impressed we were with your presentation this afternoon. We could certainly use a real go-getter like you on our sales team.
W: It's kind of you to say so, Bob. Hmm, if I didn't know you better, I'd suspect that you were headhunting me.
M: Actually, my superiors wanted me to try to set up an informal meeting with you anytime you're free. No pressure, mind you. But I'm sure we could match the salary you're getting now, and the benefits here are really top-flight. What do you say?
W: I must admit that you have me intrigued. Can I get back to you on this next week?
M: That'd be fine. We can decide on the time and place then — if you agree to meet with my superiors, that is.
W: I see. Anyway, I'll send you an email.

Comprehension Questions

1. What does Bob want Jennifer to do?
2. How does Jennifer feel about Bob's request?
3. How will Jennifer contact Bob?

耳練チェックマトリックス　自分のリスニング力を判定しよう！

聴き取りCheck / Step	Situation（状況理解）	Vocabulary（語彙）	Expression（表現）	Pronunciation（発音）
1st Try				
2nd Try				
3rd Try				

【自己判定マーク】
◎パーフェクトに理解　○ほぼ理解　△半分ほど理解　×ほとんどわからない

[注] すべて◎になるまでトライしてみよう！

＊本マトリックス活用法については7ページを参照。

耳練ヒント

Situation Markers　状況・場面を把握しよう！

- on our sales team ⇒Bobは販促関係の仕事をしている
- your presentation this afternoon ⇒Jenniferがpresentationを行った
- you were headhunting me ⇒ヘッドハント[引き抜き]が問題となる
- Can I get back to you on this next week? ⇒このことで話をする

耳練-12 Headhunting

耳練ポイント

Vocabulary －単語の意味を確認しよう！

- □ speak for 〜／〜の意見を代弁する
- □ be impressed with 〜／〜に感銘を受ける、感心する
- □ presentation／プレゼンテーション、発表（いわゆるプレゼン）
- □ use／活用する
- □ go-getter／辣腕家、有能な人
- □ sales team／販売促進担当チーム
- □ suspect／（ではないか）と思う
- □ headhunt／引き抜く
- □ informal meeting／非公式の会談
- □ match 〜／〜に対抗する
- □ top-flight／一流の
- □ intrigued／（人が）何かに関心をもっている
- □ get back to 〜／（〜に）連絡する、返事する
- □ Anyway／どちらにしても（会うにしても、会わないにしても）

Key Expressions －重要フレーズを聴き取ろう！

01 **I can speak for 〜 when I say …**「〜も同感だけれど、…です」

01 **the vice president and the whole staff**「副社長とうちの部の社員」

02 **your presentation this afternoon**「今日の午後の君の発表」this afternoon は presentation を後ろから修飾（後置修飾）している

03 **We could certainly use 〜**「〜があるとよい」if we had one（もしいれば）が省略されていて「いれば使えるのに」ということから転じて「あればなあ」の意になる ⇒Useful Expressions

05 **It's kind of you to say so**「それはありがとうございます」ほめてもらったときに感謝する言い方

05 **if I didn't know you better** 実際はよく知っていて、引き抜きの話であることはわかっているが、気づいていない振りをしている（仮定法に注意）

07 **set up 〜 at/on** …「…に〜を計画／設定／手配する」⇒Useful Expressions

08 **No pressure, mind you.**「圧力を感じる必要はないんですよ」

10 **the benefits here**「ここ（＝わが社）の手当」

11 **What do you say?**「どうですか？」交渉の相手の積極的な対応を促す表現

12 **you have me intrigued**「あなたの話に大変興味を覚えた」me と intrigued とは主語と述語の関係にある

12 **Can I get back to you on this next week?**「この件の返事は来週でもいいですか？」
⇒Useful Expressions

14 **That'd be fine.**「それでいいですよ」同意、許可を表す

15 **if you agree … , that is**「私の上司に会ってくれると決めたらということですが」that is（つまり）をつけて、追加的に述べている

Pronunciation ー聴き取りポイントに注意しよう!

06 that‿you の子音連続

09 mind‿you でも子音連続がdʒ(ヂュ)となっている

11 What‿do では t-d の連続が l 音となり、さらに日本語のラ行の音に近い音に変わるため全体としては[ワルユセイ]のように聞こえる

12 must‿admit は t が後続の a とつながって[マスタ]となる

14 That'd‿be が[tha ルビ]のように聞こえる

16 send‿you でも子音連続がdʒ(ヂュ)となっている

日本語訳 ー英文の内容を確認しよう!

ヘッドハンティング

男:ジェニファ、わが社の副社長も、社員一同みんなそう思っていますが、今日の午後の君のプレゼンテーションには大変感心しました。あなたのような辣腕家がうちの営業部にいてくれると助かるんですが。

女:そう言ってくださるのはありがたいわ、ボブ。えーと、うっかりすると、私のことを引き抜こうとしているんじゃないかと思ってしまうわ。

男:実は、上司たちはあなたが暇な時にいつでもいいから、君とかしこまらない形で話し合いをする場を設定してくれと言っているんです。無理にというわけではないんですよ。でも、きっとわが社は今のあなたの給料に対抗することはできると思いますし、うちの諸手当はトップクラスです。どうですか?

女:確かに興味はありますね。この件に関しては来週連絡するということでいいですか?

男:いいですよ。時間と場所はその時に決めればよいでしょう、会ってくれるということになったらですが。

女:そうね。どちらにしろメールを送ります。

Useful Expressions ⑫ ーこのままそっくり暗記しよう!

1. I could certainly use a computer like this. (こんなコンピュータがあるといいな)
2. We've set up a meeting (on) next Monday. (次の月曜日に会議を設定しました)
3. Can I get back to you on this after the meeting? (この件は会議の後でいいですか?)

CDで発音の確認とリピート練習ができます。

13 A Million Messages

Short Conversation ⑬

W: Mr. Burton, I have about a million messages for you. I wrote them all down in the order that the people called.
M: I don't have time to look over this whole list, Molly. Which ones seem to be the most urgent?
W: Carl Fredericks from maintenance needs to know when he should start repairing the damage to the ceiling of the parking garage, the vice president wants you to send him your budget proposal, and Mrs. Burton called about a problem your son is having at school.
M: Get her on the line first, please. The vice president can wait.
W: You sure you don't want me to call him back first? He sounded very anxious to hear from you.
M: Yes, I'm sure. Our son's going through a difficult time right now. I've got to make sure it's nothing serious, or else I won't be able to concentrate on anything else.

耳練-13

Comprehension Questions

1. What is probably the woman's job?
2. Who will the man talk to first?
3. What is the matter with the man's son?

耳練チェックマトリックス　自分のリスニング力を判定しよう！

聴き取りCheck Step	Situation（状況理解）	Vocabulary（語彙）	Expression（表現）	Pronunciation（発音）
1st Try				
2nd Try				
3rd Try				

【自己判定マーク】
◎パーフェクトに理解　○ほぼ理解　△半分ほど理解　×ほとんどわからない

[注] すべて◎になるまでトライしてみよう！

＊本マトリックス活用法については7ページを参照。

耳練ヒント

Situation Markers　状況・場面を把握しよう！

- I have about a million messages for you.
  ⇒伝言を預かっていることからこの女性は秘書
- Which ones seem to be the most urgent?（どれが一番大事か）
- Mrs. Burton called（奥さんから電話があった）
- a problem your son is having at school ⇒息子が学校で問題があった
- Get her on the line first（まず彼女[＝奥さん]にかけてくれ）⇒息子の件が先

耳練-13 A Million Messages

耳練ポイント

Vocabulary －単語の意味を確認しよう！

- ☐ a million messages／
  文字どおり「100万の伝言」
  のこと。実際は「たくさんの」
  という意味の誇張表現
- ☐ maintenance／
  保守保全管理部
  （the maintenance department）
- ☐ repair／修理する
- ☐ damage／破損
- ☐ ceiling／天井
- ☐ parking garage／駐車場
- ☐ vice president／副社長
- ☐ budget proposal／予算書
- ☐ hear from ～／
  ～から連絡をもらう
- ☐ serious／深刻な
- ☐ or／そうでなければ

Key Expressions －重要フレーズを聴き取ろう！

01 **I wrote them all down**「それらをみんな書き留めた」them all の語順に注意
02 **in the order that people called**「電話があった順に」
　　the people は電話をかけてきた人で、わかっているから the が付いている
03 **look over this whole list**「リストに全項目を通す」go over the whole list と言っても同じ
04 **seem to be ～**「～でありそう」⇒Useful Expressions
05 **need to ～**「～する必要がある」⇒Useful Expressions
09 **a problem your son is having at school**
　　「息子さんが学校で抱えている／引き起こしている問題」
10 **Get ～ on the line**「～に電話をかける」
　　Cf. Mr. Smith is on the line.「スミスさんからお電話です」
10 **The vice president can wait.** この場合の The vice president は副社長その人ではなく「副社長の用件」なので、「副社長の件は後でよい」の意味
11 **You sure ～?**「本当に～ですか？」と念を押す表現。文頭の Are が省略されている
　　Cf. You coming? = Are you coming? ⇒Useful Expressions
12 **sounded anxious to ～**「（声や言葉から）～したがっているようだ」
13 **Yes, I'm sure.** その前の（Are）you sure ～? の質問に答えたもの
14 **make sure ～**「～であることを確認する」⇒Useful Expressions
14 **it's nothing serious**「深刻なことではない」it は息子の学校での問題をさす
15 **won't be able to concentrate on anything else**「ほかのことに集中できない」

Pronunciation　－聴き取りポイントに注意しよう！

01　have⌣about⌣a million の連音
02　wrote⌣them⌣all の子音連続と連音
03　look⌣over this whole⌣list の連音と同一子音連続
03　Which ones seem to be the most urgent? でwhichとurgentの間を一息で低い音調で弱く発音していること
05　Carl Fredericks で始まり、at school で終わる長い文全体における等間隔の強勢のリズムに注意
07　wants⌣you の子音連続の［ツュウ］への変化
08　called⌣about⌣a［call ダバウラ］の連音と音変化
10　Get⌣her の子音連続
11　don't⌣want⌣me の子音連続
12　from⌣you［fro ミュー］の子音連続

日本語訳　－英文の内容を確認しよう！

たくさんの伝言

女：バートンさん、すごくたくさんの伝言があります。電話がかかってきた順にすべて書いておきました。

男：このリスト全部に目を通している時間はないよ、モリー。一番緊急らしいのはどれだい？

女：メンテナンスのカール・フレデリクスさんは駐車場の屋根の傷んでいる部分の修理をいつ始めたらいいのかを知りたいそうです。副社長からは予算案を送るようにとのことです。それから、奥様からは息子さんの問題について電話がありました。

男：まず、家内に電話をつないでくれ。副社長は後でいい。

女：まず副社長に電話をかけなくて本当によろしいんですか？　電話をかけてほしがっていらっしゃる様子でしたが。

男：いいんだよ。息子は今難しい時期なんだ。深刻な問題でないことを確かめなければ、何にも手につかんよ。

Useful Expressions ⑬　－このままそっくり暗記しよう！

1. Who seems to be the best player on your team?（君のチームで一番の選手は誰だい？）
2. I need to talk to your boss.（あなたの上司に話がある）
3. (Are) you sure you don't want to come?（本当に来たくないのですね？）
4. Make sure you have everything.（忘れ物がないように確認しなさい）

CDで発音の確認とリピート練習ができます。

14 Weekend Plans

Short Conversation ⑭

W: Hello, Jeff?
M: Oh, hi, honey. I was hoping you'd call back. What happened?
W: Sorry I couldn't talk long when you called earlier. My supervisor dropped by and wanted to go over some details for the meeting with the legal department this afternoon. So, what did you decide about the weekend?
M: Since you left it up to me, I booked a cottage at the beach for two nights. So, what's this meeting going to be about?
W: The legal people are concerned about our new contract to supply Bittner Corporation with computers. They want to make sure the contract complies with the new federal law on exports.
M: I hope it'll turn out okay. I hear a lot of contracts will have to be revised because of the law.
W: I know. It's a major headache. Anyway, I'm sure it's not going to affect our plans, so there's no need to worry about it.

耳練-14

Comprehension Questions

1. What had the speakers been discussing earlier?
2. What happened to interrupt the conversation?
3. What will the woman do this afternoon?

耳練チェックマトリックス 自分のリスニング力を判定しよう！

聴き取りCheck Step	Situation（状況理解）	Vocabulary（語彙）	Expression（表現）	Pronunciation（発音）
1st Try				
2nd Try				
3rd Try				

【自己判定マーク】
◎パーフェクトに理解　○ほぼ理解　△半分ほど理解　×ほとんどわからない

［注］すべて◎になるまでトライしてみよう！
＊本マトリックス活用法については7ページを参照。

耳練ヒント

Situation Markers　状況・場面を把握しよう！

- Hello, Jeff? と Oh, hi honey. ⇒電話での夫婦の会話
- I was hoping you'd call back. What happened?
  ⇒前の電話での会話が中断された
- My supervisor dropped by（上司が立ち寄った）⇒中断の理由
- So, what did you decide about the weekend?（週末はどうするか）
  ⇒前の電話で週末の相談をしていた
- So, what's this meeting going to be about?（何の会議）
  ⇒このやりとりから2つの話題が交錯していることがわかる

耳練-14 Weekend Plans

耳練ポイント

Vocabulary －単語の意味を確認しよう！

- □honey／ここでは呼びかけの言葉。夫婦の間で使われることが多い
- □earlier／さっき
- □supervisor／上司
- □drop by／立ち寄る
- □detail(s)／細部、詳細
- □for the meeting／会議に備えて
- □legal department／法務部
- □Since ～／～だから
- □the weekend／(この)週末
- □book ～／～を予約する
- □a cottage at the beach／海辺の貸し別荘
- □the legal people／法務部の人たち(the people in the legal department の意味)
- □contract／契約
- □be concerned about ～／～を懸念する、～について心配している
- □supply ～ with…／～に…を供給する　Cf. provide ～ with …
- □comply with ～／～に適合する
- □federal law／連邦法（⇔ state law 州法）
- □on exports／輸出に関する
- □revised／改訂する

Key Expressions －重要フレーズを聴き取ろう！

02 **I was hoping ～**「～を望んでいた」　Cf. I was hoping you would say that.（君がそう言ってくれることを望んでいたんだ）

04 **go over ～**「～を(確認のため)見直す、ざっと見る、チェックする」
Cf. 耳練4 go through ～　参照(p.24、25)　⇒Useful Expressions

06 **So,**「それで」つまり前の電話での会話に話題を戻している

06 **So, what did you decide about the weekend?**「で、週末はどうすることにしたの？」つまり週末の計画を任せていた

07 **left ～ up to …**「～を…に任せた」⇒Useful Expressions

07 **book ～ for two nights**「～を2晩予約する」のつながりに注意。book の代わりに reserve も使う。Cf. we're fully booked.（満員です）

08 **So,**「それで」この So はすぐ前の会議の話題に戻ることを示している

08 **So, what's this meeting going to be about?** この this は日本語では「その」となるところ。is going to be は予定を尋ねている

13 **it'll turn out okay** it は漠然と会議のことをさす。turn out okay はここでは「うまくいく」の意　⇒Useful Expressions

16 **our plans** 週末の計画のこと

Pronunciation —聴き取りポイントに注意しよう！

03 when you called earlier の連音。特に you が直前の n のために [ニュウ] となっている点
04 wanted to の子音連続と音変化、wanted の部分は [ワネ] と聞こえる
05 with the と this afternoon と what did you の連音と子音連続。特に did you の部分
06 what did you decide about the weekend の子音連続と音変化および連音
07 Since you left it up to me 連音、特に it の t が次の up とつながって [ラp] となる
09 concerned about our でが [concern ダバウラワ] のようになる
13 turn out [tur ナウ t] の連音
15 going to affect our plans の連音
16 about it [アバウリ t] の音変化

日本語訳 —英文の内容を確認しよう！

週末の予定

女：もしもし、ジェフ？
男：やあ、電話をかけ直してくれないかなと思っていたところだよ。どうしたの？
女：さっき電話をもらった時にはゆっくり話ができなくてごめんなさい。上司が部屋に立ち寄って、午後の法務部との会議の細部を見直しておきたいということだったのよ。それで、週末はどうすることにしたの？
男：君が僕に任せるということだったので、ビーチのコテージを2泊予約したよ。それで、その会議って何についてなんだい？
女：法務部の人たちはビットナー社にコンピューターを供給する新規契約について心配しているのよ。その契約が輸出に関する新しい連邦法に違反していないことを確認したいのよ。
男：うまくいくといいね。あの法律のために修正しなければいけない契約が多くなるだろうって聞いているよ。
女：そうなのよ。頭の痛い話だわ。どっちにしても私たちの計画には影響はないから、心配しないで。

Useful Expressions 14 —このままそっくり暗記しよう！

1. Let's go over the list again（リストをもう一度確認しよう）
2. He left the decision up to us.（彼は決断をわれわれに任せた）
3. His idea didn't turn out okay.（彼の考えはうまくいかなかった）

CDで発音の確認とリピート練習ができます。

15 Shake-up

Short Conversation ⑮

M: There sure has been a big shake-up in top management these last few months, hasn't there?

W: Well, it wasn't exactly a big surprise that Marcia Waterston was named vice president. That was only a case of when, not if. So I don't know if I'd call it a big shake-up.

M: But that's not the only change. I wonder who's going to be the new Director of Human Resources.

W: What are you talking about? What happened to Miles Butterman?

M: Haven't you heard? The president found out that Miles was using company money to make improvements to his house. They gave him the choice of resigning or getting fired, and he agreed to quit. Yesterday was his last day.

W: Wow, that's really unbelievable! I always thought that Miles was so strict about following company rules. He's the last person I would have suspected of having bad ethics.

Comprehension Questions

1. What happened to Marcia Waterston?
2. Who is Miles Butterman?
3. How does the woman feel about what happened to Miles?

耳練チェックマトリックス 自分のリスニング力を判定しよう!

聴き取りCheck \ Step	Situation（状況理解）	Vocabulary（語彙）	Expression（表現）	Pronunciation（発音）
1st Try				
2nd Try				
3rd Try				

【自己判定マーク】

◎パーフェクトに理解　○ほぼ理解　△半分ほど理解　×ほとんどわからない

［注］すべて◎になるまでトライしてみよう!

＊本マトリックス活用法については7ページを参照。

耳練ヒント

Situation Markers 状況・場面を把握しよう!

- a big shake-up in top management

    （トップ経営陣の大刷新）⇒社内の人事異動の話をしていることから同僚同士の話

- What happened to Miles Butterman?

    ⇒マイルズ・バターマンの問題が出てきた

- Yesterday was his last day. ⇒彼は昨日で辞めた

- that's really unbelievable（信じられない、意外である）

耳練-15 Shake-up

耳練ポイント

Vocabulary ー単語の意味を確認しよう！

- □shake-up／人事の大刷新
- □top management／トップの経営陣
- □surprise／予想外の出来事
- □case／事例
- □Human Resources／人材管理部
- □resign／辞任、辞職する
- □getting fired／首になる
- □agree to～／～に同意する
- □quit／（仕事などを）辞める
- □Wow／へえ（驚きを表す）
- □unbelievable／信じがたい
- □strict／厳格な
- □follow／従う、守る

Key Expressions ー重要フレーズを聴き取ろう！

03 **Well,**「どうかしら」非同意の緩和表現

03 **it wasn't exactly a big surprise**「まったく意外なこととは言えない」not は exactly（まさしく）を否定している。it は that 以下をさす

04 **was named vice president**「副社長に指名された」name ～…で「～を…に指名する」 ⇒ Useful Expressions

04 **That was only a case of when, not if.**「あれは指名されるかどうかの問題ではなく、いつ指名されるかの問題だった」that はマーシア・ウォータストンの件をさす。when と if の後には she would be named vice president が省略されている

05 **I don't know if I'd call it ～**「それを～と呼んでいいかどうかわからない」婉曲にそうではないということ ⇒ Useful Expressions

07 **But that's not the only change.**「それが唯一の人事刷新ではない」that はマーシア・ウォータストンが副社長になった件をさす

07 **I wonder who ～**「だれが～かしら」自らが感じる疑問を表現する ⇒ Useful Expressions

09 **What are you talking about?**「いったい何のこと?」相手の言っていることがわからないことを表明する決まった表現

09 **What happened to Miles Butterman?**「マイルズ・バターマンはどうなったの?」What happened to ～? で「～はどうなったのか?」という便利な表現 ⇒ Useful Expressions

11 **Haven't you heard?**「聞いてないの?」about it がわかっているので省略されている

12 **make improvements to his house**「彼の家を改装する」

13 **gave him the choice**「彼に選択を与えた」選択の内容が次に or で結ばれている

17 **suspect(ed) ～ of …ing**「～が…すると怪しむ」

Pronunciation －聴き取りポイントに注意しよう!

01 has been a big shake-up in top management の連音とtopの母音
04 That was only a case of when, not if の連音。特にnot ifが[ナリf]と聞こえる
05 if I'd call it a big shake-up の連続した連音と子音連続
09 What are you は[ワラユ]と聞こえる
11 Haven't you で[Havenチュウ]となることに注意。heard [həːd]のイギリス発音
12 make improvements の連音

日本語訳 －英文の内容を確認しよう!

人事の大刷新

男：ここ数か月でトップの経営陣には一大人事刷新があったね。

女：でも、マーシア・ウォータストンが副社長に指名されたのは厳密には大して驚くにはあたらないわね。指名されるかどうかの問題ではなく、単にいつ指名されるかの問題だったから。だから、一大人事刷新と呼んでいいかどうかわからないわ。

男：でもそれだけの刷新じゃないんだよ。一体だれが人材管理部の新しい部長になるんだろう。

女：それってどういうこと？ マイルズ・バターマンはどうなったの？

男：聞いてないの？ マイルズは会社の金を自宅の改装に使っていたことが社長にばれたのさ。それで、辞めるかクビになるかといわれて、辞めることに同意したのさ。昨日が最後だったんだよ。

女：エーッ、それはまったく信じられないわ！ マイルズは会社の規則の遵守にすごく厳しいと思っていたもの。彼は倫理に反することを最もしそうにない人だと思っていたわ。

Useful Expressions ⑮ －このままそっくり暗記しよう!

1. They will name you chairman.（彼らはあなたを議長に指名するだろう）
2. I don't know if I would call him a genius.（彼を天才だと言っていいかどうかわからない）
3. I wonder what will happen next.（次に何が起こるのだろう）
4. What happened to your confidence?（君の自信はどうなったの?）

CDで発音の確認とリピート練習ができます。

16 Franchise Seminar

Short Conversation ⑯

M : アメリカ
W : カナダ

M : Hello. I'm calling about the seminar for new franchise owners in the greater Chicago area. Is it too late to sign up?

W : Actually, the deadline is this afternoon. If you have an application form, you can fax it to us.

M : Yes, I'll do that. Um, could you tell me how many new franchises Banky Burger is planning to open?

W : No, sorry. I'm not authorized to give out that information. I can tell you that the selection for new franchise owners is always very competitive at Banky Burger, though. After the seminar there'll be a series of tests for all the attendees. Usually less than a quarter of the applicants are accepted for the training course.

M : Wow... I knew it wouldn't be easy, but I didn't think it was that hard to get in. Anyway, what have I got to lose? I'll give it a shot.

W : Best of luck to you, and I'll look for your fax.

耳練-16

Comprehension Questions

1. What is probably the man's long-term career goal?
2. What information does the woman refuse to tell the man?
3. What will happen to all applicants after the seminar?

耳練チェックマトリックス 自分のリスニング力を判定しよう!

聴き取りCheck / Step	Situation (状況理解)	Vocabulary (語彙)	Expression (表現)	Pronunciation (発音)
1st Try				
2nd Try				
3rd Try				

【自己判定マーク】
◎パーフェクトに理解　○ほぼ理解　△半分ほど理解　×ほとんどわからない

[注] すべて◎になるまでトライしてみよう!
＊本マトリックス活用法については7ページを参照。

耳練ヒント

Situation Markers 状況・場面を把握しよう!

- Hello. I'm calling ... ⇒電話の会話である
- about the seminar for new franchise owners
  ⇒フランチャイズ店オーナーのセミナーについて
- Is it too late to sign up? ⇒申込みをしたい
- the deadline is this afternoon（今日の午後が締切り）
- could you tell me ⇒質問をしている
- I'm not authorized（権限がない）⇒答えられない
- I'll give it a shot. ⇒やってみる

耳練-16 Franchise Seminar

耳練ポイント

Vocabulary －単語の意味を確認しよう！

- □seminar／セミナー、説明会
- □franchise owners／フランチャイズ（系列）店のオーナー
- □the greater Chicago area／シカゴを中心とする都市圏
- □sign up／申し込む
- □deadline／締切り
- □application form／申込書
- □fax／ファックスで送る
- □Um／えーと
- □plan to ～／～する予定である
- □selection／選抜
- □competitive／競争が激しい
- □a series of／一連の
- □attendee／出席者、参加者
- □quarter／4分の1
- □applicants／申込者、志願者
- □accept／受け入れる
- □training course／トレーニングコース、研修
- □Anyway／どちらにしても

Key Expressions －重要フレーズを聴き取ろう！

02 **Is it too late to sign up?** 「申し込むには遅すぎますか？」 sign up は「申し込む」で、その対象は for で表す ⇒ Useful Expressions

05 **you can fax it to us** 「それをファックスで送ることができます」は「送れば間に合います」の意味

06 **Yes, I'll do that.** 「じゃあそうします」 that はファックスで申込書を送ること

06 **could you tell me ～** 「～を教えてもらえますか」 質問の定型版 ⇒ Useful Expressions

08 **No, sorry.** 「教えられない」

08 **I'm not authorized to give out that information.** 「その情報を伝える権限を与えられていない」 ⇒ Useful Expressions

11 **though** 「でも」 これは「質問には答えられないけれども」の意味で、先行文脈を受ける

13 **are accepted for the training course** 「合格して、研修を受けられる」

14 **I knew it wouldn't be easy** 「簡単でないことはわかっていた」

14 **it was that hard to get in** 「（フランチャイズに）加わるのがそれほど難しいとは」

15 **what have I got to lose?** 「何を失うものがあろうか、いやない」という反語で、今流に言えば「駄目もと」。このまま覚えたい

16 **I'll give it a shot.** 定型表現で「やってみます、トライしてみます」

17 **Best of luck to you** 「幸運を、うまくいけばいいですね」

17 **I'll look for your fax** ここでは「あなたのファックスを待っています」という意味

Pronunciation －聴き取りポイントに注意しよう!

02 Is it too late to sign up? の連音と子音連続
04 If you have an application form, you can fax it to us. の連音と子音連続
08 I'm not authorized to give out that information の子音連続と連音
09 that the では that の語末の t が聞こえないこと
13 accepted for の子音連続
14 but I didn't think it was that hard to get in の連音群。but I が［バライ］と聞こえる。that の語末の t が聞こえない
15 what have I got to lose, I'll give it a shot の連音群。what have が［ワラv］と聞こえる
17 Best of luck to you の連音と子音連続

日本語訳 －英文の内容を確認しよう!

フランチャイズ・セミナー

男：もしもし、グレーター・シカゴ・エリアのフランチャイズ店オーナーのためのセミナーについて電話しているのですが。申し込むにはもう遅いですか?

女：実は、締切りは今日の午後です。申込書をお持ちなら、こちらに FAX していただけます。

男：はい、そうします。あの、バンキー・バーガーが何店くらい新しいフランチャイズ店をオープンする予定なのか教えてもらえますか?

女：申し訳ありませんが、私にはその情報をお知らせする権限がありません。ただし、バンキー・バーガーでは新しいフランチャイズ店のオーナーの選抜はいつも競争が激しいということは申し上げられますが。セミナーの後、参加者全員に一連の試験があります。通常、申し込んだ方の 4 分の 1 以下しかトレーニングコースには合格しません。

男：へえ、易しくないとはわかっていましたが、加わるのがそこまで難しいとは思いませんでした。いずれにせよ、駄目もとですよね。試しにやってみます。

女：うまくいくといいですね。ファックスをお待ちしています。

Useful Expressions ⓰ －このままそっくり暗記しよう!

1. Are you signing up for the job?（その仕事に申し込みますか?）
2. Could you tell me what time it is now?（今何時でしょうか?）
3. I'm not authorized to make that decision.（そのような決定をする権限を与えられていない）

CD で発音の確認とリピート練習ができます。

Short Conversation ⑰

W: Bob, I wanted to talk to you about the tickets for the baseball game. You know, I've got those clients coming from out of town and I really need to show them a good time.

M: I'm afraid Wednesday's game was sold out, so I took the liberty of getting you four tickets for Thursday night's game.

W: What? You should have told me sooner. Now I'll have to rearrange the whole schedule.

M: Sorry, but Wednesday is opening day so tickets are impossible to get. Anyway, I got great seats in the front row for the Thursday game.

W: Thursday... Okay, let me think... Maybe it won't be that hard to pull it off, after all. If I can get the restaurant to change the dinner reservation to Wednesday, and persuade the engineers to postpone their presentation, everything might turn out all right.

M: Well, if you deal with the engineers, I'll call the restaurant for you.

Comprehension Questions

1. Why does the woman want tickets to a baseball game?
2. How does the woman feel about the man's first news?
3. What does the man say about the tickets that he got?

耳練チェックマトリックス 自分のリスニング力を判定しよう！

聴き取りCheck / Step	Situation (状況理解)	Vocabulary (語彙)	Expression (表現)	Pronunciation (発音)
1st Try				
2nd Try				
3rd Try				

【自己判定マーク】
◎パーフェクトに理解　○ほぼ理解　△半分ほど理解　×ほとんどわからない

[注] すべて◎になるまでトライしてみよう！

＊本マトリックス活用法については7ページを参照。

耳練ヒント

Situation Markers 状況・場面を把握しよう！

- tickets for the baseball game
  （[前に話題になっている]野球のゲームの切符）
- I've got those clients coming
  （顧客が訪ねてくる）⇒ここから2人が同僚であることが推測される
- Wednesday's game was sold out（水曜日は売切れ）⇒前述の切符は水曜日の切符
- getting you four tickets for Thursday（木曜の切符を買った）
- it won't be that hard to pull it off（うまくやれるかもしれない）

耳練-17 Baseball Tickets

耳練ポイント

Vocabulary －単語の意味を確認しよう！

- □sold out／（切符、座席などが）売切れ
- □liberty／自由（ここでは take the liberty of ~ing という熟語）
- □rearrange／組み替える、並び替える
- □opening day／開幕戦の日、初日
- □front row／最前列
- □pull it off／うまくやる
- □after all／結局
- □dinner reservation／ディナーの予約
- □persuade ~ to …／…するよう~を説得する
- □the engineers／（自分の会社の）エンジニア
- □postpone／延期する
- □turn out all right／うまくいく

Key Expressions －重要フレーズを聴き取ろう！

01 **I wanted to talk to you about ~**　「あなたに~の件で用事があった」過去形にしているのは、婉曲な言い方

01 **the tickets for the baseball game**　「例の野球の試合の切符」どちらにも the がついていることから、以前に購入を依頼したことがわかる

02 **You know** ここでは理由を説明する前置きになっている

02 **I've got those clients coming from out of town**　「例のクライアントが訪ねて来るの」I've got というのは「クライアントが訪ねて来るという状況がある」という意味。out of town は「市外／遠方から」

03 **show them a good time**　「彼らを歓待する」

05 **I'm afraid ~**　「残念ですが、~です」　⇒ Useful Expressions

05 **took the liberty of ~ ing**　「勝手に~する」「（僭越ながら）気を利かせて~する」という意味　⇒ Useful Expressions

08 **What?**　「何ですって?」驚きを表す

08 **You should have told me sooner.**　「もっと早く教えてくれなきゃ」should have ~ はすべきであったのにしなかったことを指摘する表現　⇒ Useful Expressions

10 **tickets are impossible to get**　「切符は買うのが不可能だ」impossible はこの用法があるが、possible ではこのような言い方はできない

13 **let me think**　「考えさせて」の意味だが、「うーん」と考えこむときに用いられる

14 **get the restaurant to change the dinner reservation**　「レストランにディナーの予約を変えさせる」get ~ to …で「~に…させる」

Pronunciation　ー聴き取りポイントに注意しよう！

01　I wanted to が［ワネto］のように聞こえる
02　I've got those clients coming from out of town. の子音連続と連音
05　was sold out の子音連続と連音
08　should have の連音とhaveの弱化、［シュダv］と聞こえる。have to の音変化
13　let me のtが聞こえない
14　pull it off の連音と［pulliロf］と聞こえること
17　turn out all right の連音、l-r の連音

日本語訳　ー英文の内容を確認しよう！

野球のチケット

女：ボブ、例の野球の試合の入場券について話があるの。あのね、遠くから来るクライアントがいて、ぜひ歓待しなければならないのよ。

男：残念ながら、水曜日の試合のチケットは売切れで、僕のほうで勝手に木曜日のナイターの入場券を4枚買っておいたよ。

女：何ですって？　もっと早く言ってくれなきゃ。これで予定をすべて組み直さなきゃならないじゃない。

男：申し訳ない。でも、水曜日は開幕戦だから入場券を手に入れるのは不可能だよ。とにかく、木曜日の試合では最前列のすごくいい席をとったから。

女：木曜ね…わかったわ、考えさせて。結局そんなに難しくないかもしれない。レストランにディナーの予約を水曜日に変えさせて、エンジニアたちにプレゼンを延期することを説得すれば、すべてうまくいくかもしれないわ。

男：あの、エンジニアと交渉してくれるなら、僕がレストランに電話をかけるよ。

Useful Expressions ⑰　ーこのままそっくり暗記しよう！

1. I'm afraid it's too late.（残念ながら間に合いません）
2. I took the liberty of reserving a room for you.（勝手ながら部屋を予約しておきました）
3. You should have come earlier.（もっと早く来るべきだった）

CDで発音の確認とリピート練習ができます。

Employee Orientation

Short Conversation 18

W: Jack, I hear that you're going to act as one of the trainers for the new employee orientation next month. Is that right?

M: Yes, it's my first time. I'm a little nervous about it. Evidently, I'll be conducting the unit on business manners: you know, how to talk to customers on the phone, how to introduce yourself to potential clients, that sort of thing.

W: I'm sure you'll do fine. It's just a suggestion, but I hope that you or one of the other trainers will emphasize the company dress code. Last year's new employees didn't seem to get the message. They needed a lot of warnings about improper clothing.

M: Is that right? I hadn't heard anything about that.

W: Oh, there were some cases that were just astonishing: men coming to work in jeans, women in miniskirts... I really think we need to give this some attention.

M: Okay, sure. I'll make a note of that right now, before I forget.

耳練-18

Comprehension Questions

1. What new assignment will the man begin next month?
2. What does the woman want the man to tell the new employees about?
3. What will the man do about the woman's suggestion?

耳練チェックマトリックス　自分のリスニング力を判定しよう！

聴き取りCheck / Step	Situation（状況理解）	Vocabulary（語彙）	Expression（表現）	Pronunciation（発音）
1st Try				
2nd Try				
3rd Try				

【自己判定マーク】
◎パーフェクトに理解　○ほぼ理解　△半分ほど理解　×ほとんどわからない

［注］すべて◎になるまでトライしてみよう！
＊本マトリックス活用法については7ページを参照。

耳練ヒント

Situation Markers　状況・場面を把握しよう！

- the new employee orientation
  （新入社員オリエンテーション）⇒同僚同士の話であることがわかる
- It's just a suggestion（提案がある）⇒提案の切出し
- emphasize the company dress code（社内の服装規定を強調する）
- Oh, there were some cases that were just astonishing
  （あきれかえるような例があったの）⇒以下はその具体例
- Okay, sure.（いいとも）⇒同意を表す

耳練-18 Employee Orientation

耳練ポイント

Vocabulary　―単語の意味を確認しよう！

- act as ～／～の役を務める
- new employee orientation／新入社員オリエンテーション（つまり研修）
- nervous about ～／～で緊張している
- Evidently／明らかに、どうも～らしい
- conduct／指揮をする、担当する
- unit／（プログラムなどの）部分
- how to ～／～の仕方
- potential client／クライアントになりそうな人
- that sort of thing／そういったこと、その類のこと
- suggestion／提案
- emphasize／強調する
- company dress code／社内服装規約
- message／ここでは「趣旨」
- improper clothing／不適切な服装
- astonishing／驚くべき、あきれた
- attention／注目、注意

Key Expressions　―重要フレーズを聴き取ろう！

01 **I hear that ～**「～だそうだね」⇒ Useful Expressions
02 **Is that right?**「そうなの？／そうでしょう？」確認を求める定型表現
04 **It's my first time.**「初めてです」これも定型表現
05 **I'll be conducting ～**「～を担当することになる」予定を表す
06 **you know** 以下にその例を挙げることを示す
07 **introduce yourself to potential clients**「クライアントになりそうな人への自己紹介の仕方」この yourself は一般的な人をさす
09 **I'm sure ～**「きっと～ですよ」⇒ Useful Expressions
09 **you'll do fine**「ちゃんとやる、うまくいく」fine は会話ではこのように副詞として使える
09 **It's just a suggestion, but**「単なる提案ですが」「だから聞き流してもいいけど」と押しつけがましくしない効果がある
11 **didn't seem to get the message**「趣旨が徹底しなかったようだ」not get the message とは趣旨がよく理解できていないことを表す ⇒ Useful Expressions
12 **They needed a lot of warnings**「何度も警告をしなければならなかった」they は去年の新入社員をさす
14 **Is that right?**「そうなんですか？」ここでは確認ではなく、驚きを表わす
14 **I hadn't heard anything about that.**「そのことについては何も聞いていなかった」去年の時点でのことなので過去完了になっている
16 **men coming to work in jeans, women in miniskirts**「男はジーンズで職場に来るは、女はミニスカートで職場に来るは」具体例を挙げている。coming to work が women の後に省略されている
18 **Okay, sure.**「いいですよ」女性の提案を受けての答え

Pronunciation　—聴き取りポイントに注意しよう！

01　that you're going to act as one of the trainers の子音連続と連音
04　I'm a little nervous about it. の連音
05　Evidéntly のアクセントに注意
06　how to が [ハウラ] と聞こえる
07　that sort of thing の連音と子音連続
09　It's just a suggestion の子音連続と連音
11　Last year's new の子音連続
11　They needed a lot of warnings about improper clothing の連音
14　Is that right? の子音連続、I hadn't heard anything about that. の連音
18　I'll make a note of that right now の連音群

日本語訳　—英文の内容を確認しよう！

新入社員オリエンテーション

女：ジャック、来月の新入社員のためのオリエンテーションであなたがトレーナーの1人を務めるって聞いたけど、そうなの？

男：そうだよ、初めてなんだ。それでちょっと緊張しているんだ。どうやら、僕がやるのはビジネスマナーに関するところらしいんだよ。ほら、顧客との電話の仕方とか、顧客になりそうな人にどういうふうに自己紹介するかとか、そういう類のやつさ。

女：あなたなら大丈夫よ。単なる提案なんだけれど、あなたでもほかのトレーナーの人でも、社内の服装規定を強調してくれるといいのだけれど。去年の新入社員には趣旨が徹底しなくて、不適切な服装について何度も警告しなければならなかったの。

男：そうなの？　それについては何も聞いていなかったな。

女：そうよ、あきれかえるような場合があったわ。男はジーンズ、女はミニスカートで出勤するとか…。この点に注意を払うべきだと本当に思うわ。

男：そうだね。忘れないうちにメモしておくよ。

Useful Expressions ⑱　—このままそっくり暗記しよう！

1. I hear that you've just been promoted（昇進したそうだね）
2. I'm sure this will work.（きっとこれでうまくいきますよ）
3. He didn't get my message.（彼は私の言っていることがよくわからなかった）

CDで発音の確認とリピート練習ができます。

19 Office Renovation

Short Conversation 19

W: I got your notice in my mailbox about painting the office and putting in new windows. I'm afraid next week just isn't going to work for me.

M: Sorry, but it's out of my hands. It has to be done next week. The order came down from the president herself.

W: Look, I understand that our offices need to be renovated. I'm totally in favor of that. My problem is, how am I supposed to get any work done for a week while I can't have access to my computer and my files? Can't you move them somewhere?

M: I hear what you're saying. You're not the first person to come to me with this problem. But even as we speak, the maintenance people are setting up cubicles on the second floor where you can hook up your computer and have your own private phone line.

W: Okay, that's fine for the computer. But what about my file cabinets?

M: I'm sorry, but we simply can't move the files back and forth. You'll just have to do without them for a week.

Comprehension Questions

1. How did the woman find out about the renovation of the offices?
2. What does the man say about the woman's complaint?
3. What does the man apologize for?

耳練チェックマトリックス　自分のリスニング力を判定しよう！

聴き取りCheck / Step	Situation（状況理解）	Vocabulary（語彙）	Expression（表現）	Pronunciation（発音）
1st Try				
2nd Try				
3rd Try				

【自己判定マーク】
◎パーフェクトに理解　○ほぼ理解　△半分ほど理解　×ほとんどわからない

［注］すべて◎になるまでトライしてみよう！

＊本マトリックス活用法については7ページを参照。

耳練ヒント

Situation Markers　状況・場面を把握しよう！

- I got your notice in my mailbox（メールボックスに連絡を受け取った）
  ⇒ここからおそらくは会社での話であることが推測される
- painting the office（オフィスを塗り替える）⇒これで会社の話であることが明確になる
- next week just isn't going to work（来週ではだめだ）
- The order came down from the president（社長命令だ）⇒だから変えられない
- But what about my file cabinets?（私のファイルキャビネットは？）⇒食い下がっている
- You'll have to do without them for a week.（1週間は、なしですまさなければならない）

耳練-19 Office Renovation

耳練ポイント

Vocabulary －単語の意味を確認しよう！

- □notice／連絡、通告
- □put in ～／～を取り付ける
- □renovate／改装する
- □totally／全面的に
- □access／利用（have access to ～「～を使う」）
- □maintenance people／施設課の人たち
- □set up／組み立てる
- □cubicle／デスクを囲む間仕切り
- □hook up／（コンピュータなどを）つなぐ
- □private phone line／個人用の電話

Key Expressions －重要フレーズを聴き取ろう！

02 **I'm afraid ～** 「残念ながら～です」Cf. 耳練17のUseful Expressions参照（p.76、77）

02 **next week just isn't going to work for me** 「来週ではまったく私の都合に合わない」 just は強調。work for ～ は「～に合う、うまくいく」 ⇒ Useful Expressions

04 **it's out of my hands** 「私の手を離れている」つまり私の権限外である
⇒ Useful Expressions

05 **the president herself** 「社長自身」社長はこの場合女性である

06 **Look** 「いい？」「あのね」相手の注意を促す表現。Listen も同様の働きがある

07 **I'm totally in favor of that.** 「それには大賛成よ」 be in favor of ～「～に賛成している」

07 **how am I supposed to ～?** 「どうやって～すればいいの？」 be supposed to ～は「～することになっている」 ⇒ Useful Expressions

11 **I hear what you're saying.** 「あなたの言っていることはわかります」この hear は understand の意味

11 **the first person to ～** 「～する最初の人」

12 **come to me with this problem** 「この問題を私に訴えてくる」

12 **even as we speak** 「こうして話している間にも」

16 **that's fine for the computer** 「コンピュータに関してはそれでいい」

18 **move ～ back and forth** 「～をあちこち動かす」

19 **do without ～** 「～なしですます」 Cf. How can we do without you?（君なしではやっていけない）

Pronunciation －聴き取りポイントに注意しよう！

01 I got‿your notice‿in‿my mailbox の連音、特にgot‿yourが［ガッチャ］のように聞こえること、mailがmileに近く聞こえること

04 Sorry, but‿it's‿out‿of my hands. の連音

07 how am‿I supposed‿to get‿any work done for‿a week の連音と子音連続

09 Can't‿you の［カーンチュ］

11 first‿person の語にまたがる子音連続

12 But even‿as の連音

16 what‿about［ホヮラバウt］の連音と音変化

19 You'll just have‿to do without‿them for‿a week.の子音連続と連音

日本語訳 －英文の内容を確認しよう！

オフィスの改装

女：オフィスの塗り替えと新しい窓の取り付けについての知らせをメールボックスに受け取ったわ。悪いけど、来週ではまったく都合が悪いわ。

男：悪いけど、僕ではどうしようもないんだよ。来週でなきゃならないんだ。社長自身からの命令なんだよ。

女：オフィスの改装が必要なことはわかるわ。それには全面的に賛成よ。ただ、コンピュータとファイルにアクセスできない1週間の間どうやって仕事をすればいいわけ？（コンピュータとファイルを）どこかに移動できないの？

男：君の言い分はわかるよ。この問題を僕に訴えてきたのは君が初めてではないんだ。でも、こうやって話をしている間も、施設課の職員は君たちが自分のコンピュータに接続したり専用の電話回線を使えるように、パーテイションで区切った仕事スペースを2階に設定しているよ。

女：コンピュータはそれで結構だけど、ファイルキャビネットはどうなの？

男：申し訳ないが、ファイルを移動させてまた戻すことはとにかくできないんだ。1週間はファイルなしでやってもらうしかないよ。

Useful Expressions ⑲ －このままそっくり暗記しよう！

1. Will this work for you?（こちらだとうまくいきますか？）
2. The matter is out of my hands now.（その件はもう私の手を離れました）
3. How am I supposed to find him?（どうやって彼を見つければいいんだろう？）

CDで発音の確認とリピート練習ができます。

20 Looking for a Job

Short Conversation ⓴

W: Darn it! This is really starting to get me down. There has to be something out there for me.

M: What on earth are you talking about? I see you peering into the newspaper every morning, and I've been meaning to ask you about that. What is it that you're trying to do?

W: I typed up a new resume, and I keep looking at the job openings in the newspaper and on the Internet every day, but I never find anything that matches my qualifications. All I see are data processing jobs and positions in the health care industry.

M: Oh, so you're looking for a new job? Well, I guess we couldn't really expect to keep you here as a receptionist forever. But it's a tough market these days for job-seekers. Anyway, what exactly are you looking for?

W: Well, a management job in retail sales would be ideal. But I'm realistic. I'd be willing to start out as a salesperson, or at this point, even as a cashier. I'm at the end of my rope!

M: I don't blame you for feeling that way. I'm surprised you haven't found anything yet. Anyway, just stay with it for a while and something will turn up — though I'm sure everyone here would be sorry to see you go.

耳練-20

Comprehension Questions

1. What does the woman say about the jobs that she finds?
2. What kind of job does the woman most hope to find?
3. What does the man advise the woman to do?

耳練チェックマトリックス　自分のリスニング力を判定しよう!

聴き取りCheck Step	Situation（状況理解）	Vocabulary（語彙）	Expression（表現）	Pronunciation（発音）
1st Try				
2nd Try				
3rd Try				

【自己判定マーク】
◎パーフェクトに理解　○ほぼ理解　△半分ほど理解　×ほとんどわからない

[注] すべて◎になるまでトライしてみよう!
＊本マトリックス活用法については7ページを参照。

耳練ヒント

Situation Markers　状況・場面を把握しよう!

- Darn it! ⇒怒っている

- What on earth are you talking about?

  ⇒わけを聞いている

- Oh, so you're looking for a new job?

  ⇒ここで女が職探しをしていることがわかる

- keep you as a receptionist

  ⇒ここで初めて、男が上司で、女がそのもとで受付をしていることがわかる

耳練-20 Looking for a Job

耳練ポイント

Vocabulary －単語の意味を確認しよう！

- □get ~ down／~の気を滅入らす、がっかりさせる
- □peer into ~／~をのぞき込む
- □type up／タイプして清書する
- □keep ~ing／~し続ける
- □opening／就職口、(職の)空き
- □on the Internet／インターネットで（定冠詞と前置詞 on に注意）
- □match／~に合う、~にふさわしい
- □qualifications／（複数形で）資格
- □data processing／データ処理、情報処理
- □health care industry／健康管理産業
- □look for a job／職を探す
- □market／= job market 求人市場
- □job-seeker／求職者
- □retail sales／小売販売
- □realistic／現実的
- □start out as ~／~として始める
- □at this point／ここに至っては、今となっては
- □turn up／姿を現す、ひょっこり見つかる（職、不動産物件など探しているものが見つかることをさす）

Key Expressions －重要フレーズを聴き取ろう！

01 **Darn it!** 女性が使う悪態で、男性の Damn it!（ちくしょう）に相当する

01 **This is really starting to get me down.** this は現在の状況をさし、文字どおりには「このことは私の気を滅入らせ始めている」つまり「だんだん気が滅入ってきた」の意

01 **There has to be something out there for me.**「世の中には何か私に合ったものがあるはずだ」この has to は「違いない」、out there は「広い世間には」の意味で、気持ちは「なのになぜ見つからないんだろう」

10 **All** = All the job openings の意味。all ~ is/are… は「~は…ばかり」
　⇒ Useful Expressions

12 **we couldn't really expect to keep you here as a receptionist forever**「永遠に君をここで受付としてとどめておくことは期待できない」つまり「君が新しい職に就きたいと思うのも無理ない」could となっているのは「たとえ望んでも」という意味

17 **I'd be willing to ~**「喜んで~する」⇒ Useful Expressions

18 **I'm at the end of my rope！**「万策尽きた」このまま覚えておきたい

20 **I don't blame you for ~ ing**「君が~するのも無理はない」文字どおりには「~してもそれを責めない」Cf. I don't blame you.（それも無理ないね）⇒ Useful Expressions

21 **stay with it**「頑張る」今の状態で頑張るの意味

23 **everyone here would be sorry to see you go**「ここのみんなは君が辞めるのを残念に思うでしょう」would になっているのは「もし君が辞めるなら」という仮定があるから

Pronunciation　—聴き取りポイントに注意しよう！

01　Darn it! の語末の t が明確に破裂音として開放されている
03　What on earth are you talking about? の連音
05　What is it that you're trying to do? の連音と音変化
07　I typed up a new resume, and I keep looking at the job openings in the newspaper の語をまたぐ子音連続と連音群。newspaper が newspiper に近く聞こえる
08　job [jɔb] の母音
16　start out as a salesperson の連音と音変化

日本語訳　—英文の内容を確認しよう！

職探し

女：もう、本当に気が滅入るわ。私に合ったものが何かあるに違いないのに。
男：一体何を言っているんだい。毎朝、新聞をのぞきこんでいるのには気づいていて、聞いてみようと思っていたんだ。何をしようとしているの？
女：新しい履歴書をタイプして、新聞とインターネットの求人欄を毎日ずっと見ているのに、私の資格に合う仕事がまったく見つからないのよ。出ているのはデータ処理の仕事とヘルスケア業界の求人ばかりよ。
男：ああ、新しい仕事を探しているんだね。君をここでずっと受付として働いてもらい続けるわけにもいかないね。でも仕事を探している人にとっては最近の求人市場は厳しいね。いずれにしろ、どんな仕事を探しているの？
女：小売販売の管理職が理想なの。でも夢を追いかけているわけじゃなくて、セールスの仕事でも、この際、レジ係からでも喜んで始めるつもりよ。もう万策尽きたのよ。
男：そう思うのも無理ないね。まだ仕事が見つかっていないなんて驚いたね。とにかく、しばらくそれを続けるしかないね、そうすれば何か出てくるよ。もっとも、ここにいるみんなは、君に行ってほしくはないと思うけど。

Useful Expressions ⑳　—このままそっくり暗記しよう！

1. All I have is just a few hundred dollars.（あるのは数百ドルだけだ）
2. I'd be willing to quit my job.（喜んで仕事を辞めますよ）
3. I don't blame you for quitting your job.（君が仕事を辞めるのも無理はない）

CDで発音の確認とリピート練習ができます。　CD 1-61

21 A Mountain Bike Prototype

Short Talk ❶

Hi, Larry. This is Shirley in Research and Development. Mr. Hendricks wanted me to get back to you about the mountain bike that his project team has been working on. The prototype is going to be ready about a week sooner than expected, so they're planning to take it out for a trial run on the 7th of next month. He wondered if you and some of the other folks there in Marketing would like to come along and watch. It'd give you a chance to offer suggestions on the design before they put the finishing touches on the bike. I'm at extension 5712, so give me a call anytime this afternoon or tomorrow.

耳練-21

Comprehension Questions

1. In what part of the company does Larry probably work?
2. What will Mr. Hendricks and his team do on the 7th?
3. What would Larry be able to do if he accepted the invitation?

耳練チェックマトリックス 自分のリスニング力を判定しよう!

聴き取りCheck Step	Situation (状況理解)	Vocabulary (語彙)	Expression (表現)	Pronunciation (発音)
1st Try				
2nd Try				
3rd Try				

【自己判定マーク】
◎パーフェクトに理解　○ほぼ理解　△半分ほど理解　×ほとんどわからない

[注] すべて◎になるまでトライしてみよう!

＊本マトリックス活用法については7ページを参照。

耳練ヒント

Situation Markers 状況・場面を把握しよう!

- Hi, Larry. This is Shirley
  ⇒電話で話している。一人でずっと話し続けているということは留守番電話のメッセージである
- in Research and Development（研究開発部）⇒シャーリーは研究開発部員
- the prototype ⇒試作品ができている
- trial run on the 7th（7日に試験走行）
- you and some of the other folks there in Marketing ⇒ラリーはマーケティング担当
- come along and watch（見学に来る）⇒見学に来ないかと誘っている

耳練-21 A Mountain Bike Prototype

耳練ポイント

Vocabulary －単語の意味を確認しよう！

- Research and Development ／研究開発部
- prototype／試作品、プロトタイプ
- work on 〜／〜に取り組む
- ready／出来上がっている
- a trial run／試験走行
- Marketing／マーケティング（部）
- come along／一緒に来る、同行する
- suggestion／提案
- finishing touches／最後の仕上げ
- extension／内線

Key Expressions －重要フレーズを聴き取ろう！

01 **This is Shirley**　「シャーリーです（が）」電話で名前を名のる定型表現

01 **Mr. Hendricks wanted me to get back to you on 〜**　「ヘンドリクスさんが〜に関してあなたに連絡してほしいということだった」⇒ Useful Expressions

03 **The prototype**　「その試作品」the がついているのは前文で言及しているマウンテンバイクの試作品であるから

04 **about a week sooner than expected**　「予定より約1週間早く」⇒ Useful Expressions

05 **they're planning to take it out for a trial run**　「試験走行のために（工場から、試験のための道路に）持ち出す計画だ」

06 **He wondered if 〜**　「〜ではないかと彼は思った」He は Mr. Hendricks
　⇒ Useful Expressions

06 **you and some of the other folks there in Marketing**　「あなたとマーケティングのほかの人たちの何人か」folks は「人たち」で、people より親しみを込めた言い方。there は「社内のそちらのマーケティング部門」という意味合い

08 **It'd give you a chance to 〜**　「（来れば）〜する機会を得られます」
　⇒ Useful Expressions

09 **put the finishing touches on the bike**　「バイクに最後の仕上げをする」最終的な手直しをすること

09 **I'm at extension 5712**　「私の内線番号は5712です」自分の内線番号に変えて、覚えておきたい

10 **give me a call**　「電話をください」後に内線番号を続けるなら、Give me a call at extension 5712. と言う

Pronunciation　−聴き取りポイントに注意しよう！

02　get‿back‿to の語にまたがる閉鎖音の連続
03　his‿project‿team の語にまたがる子音連続
05　take‿it‿out for‿a trial‿run の連音と子音連続
08　It'd‿give の複雑な子音連続

日本語訳　−英文の内容を確認しよう！

マウンテンバイクの試作品

こんにちは、ラリー。研究開発部のシャーリーですが、ヘンドリクスさんから、彼のプロジェクトチームが開発しているマウンテンバイクについてあなたに改めて連絡をとるように言われました。試作品は予定より1週間ほど早く出来上がる予定なので、チームでは来月7日に試験走行を計画しています。そこで、ヘンドリクスさんは、あなたをはじめマーケティング担当の方たちが一緒に来て見たいかもしれないと思っているの。あなたたちにとって、チームが最後の仕上げをする前に、デザインについての提案をする機会ができるでしょう。私の内線番号は5712です。今日の午後か明日、いつでもいいので電話をください。

Useful Expressions ㉑　−このままそっくり暗記しよう！

1. My boss wants you to get back to Mr. Smith on the new contract.
   （上司は、新しい契約についてあなたからスミスさんに連絡してほしいとのことです）
2. We're coming back about a week sooner than expected.
   （予定より約1週間早く帰ってきます）
3. So we wondered if you knew about it.
   （だからあなたがそのことを知っているかどうかと思ったのです）
4. It'd give you a chance to rub elbows with the board members.
   （役員と親しく話をする機会になりますよ）

CDで発音の確認とリピート練習ができます。

22 Radio Flea Market

Short Talk ❷

Now, the next item on Radio Flea Market: Lisa of Patterson City has a 1999 Honda Accord for sale. The car has an automatic transmission and a six-cylinder engine. The dark blue exterior is beautiful with no scratches or dents. This is a vehicle that gets very good gas mileage, with a functioning air conditioner, power windows and power locks, an AM/FM radio and a CD player, and a sun roof. The sound system may need replacing. All four tires and the transmission are less than a year old, and the owner can provide receipts as proof. The asking price is 4,000 dollars. If interested, call Lisa at 950-555-6599 between seven and ten p.m.

耳練-22

Comprehension Questions

1. Who is Lisa?
2. According to the announcement, what part of the car is not in top condition?
3. If someone wants to buy the car, what should he or she do?

耳練チェックマトリックス 自分のリスニング力を判定しよう！

聴き取りCheck　Step	Situation（状況理解）	Vocabulary（語彙）	Expression（表現）	Pronunciation（発音）
1st Try				
2nd Try				
3rd Try				

【自己判定マーク】
◎パーフェクトに理解　○ほぼ理解　△半分ほど理解　×ほとんどわからない

［注］すべて◎になるまでトライしてみよう！

＊本マトリックス活用法については7ページを参照。

耳練ヒント

Situation Markers 状況・場面を把握しよう！

- the next item on Radio Flea Market
  ⇒ラジオでのフリーマーケット、つまり中古品市場であることがわかる
- 1999 Honda Accord for sale ⇒1999年製のホンダのアコードが売りに出ている
- The car has 〜 ⇒以下がその車の説明

耳練-22 Radio Flea Market

耳練ポイント

Vocabulary －単語の意味を確認しよう！

- item／物、項目
- flea market／フリーマーケット、ノミの市
- automatic transmission／自動変速
- six-cylinder engine／6気筒エンジン
- dark blue／紺、紺青色
- exterior／外観、外装
- scratch／（こすった）キズ
- dent／へこみ
- vehicle／乗り物、車
- gas mileage／燃費
- functioning／正常に機能している
- air conditioner／エアコン
- power windows／電動ウインドウ
- power locks／電動ロック
- sound system／ステレオセット
- transmission／変速機
- owner／所有者
- receipt／領収書
- proof／証拠
- asking price／提示価格

Key Expressions －重要フレーズを聴き取ろう！

01 **Now the next item on Radio Flea Market**　「さて、ラジオ・フリーマーケットの次の出し物です」　文の形をとっていないが、議長や司会などが使う定型表現。
　Cf. Now the next item on the agenda.（では議題の次の項目に進みましょう）

02 **The car has an automatic transmission and a six-cylinder engine.**　なんでもないことであるが、日本語なら「オートマチック車で、6気筒エンジンです」というところを、英語では have を使うことが重要　⇒ Useful Expressions

05 **gets good gas mileage**　「燃費がよい」　走ってみるとよい燃費を出すの意であるが、get を使うことは覚えておきたい。make good mileage とも言う　⇒ Useful Expressions

07 **The sound system may need replacing.**　「ステレオセットは取替えが必要かもしれない」　need ～ ing で「～することを必要としている」　⇒ Useful Expressions

09 **the owner can provide receipts as proof**　「所有者はそれを証明するものとして領収書を見せることもできる」所有者というのは売りに出している人のこと。車を見に行った際に見せてくれるということ

10 **The asking price is 4,000 dollars.**　「言い値は4,000ドルです」　⇒ Useful Expressions

10 **If interested** = If you are interested　「関心があれば」

Pronunciation －聴き取りポイントに注意しよう！

02 has‿an‿automatic‿transmission の連音と閉鎖音連続
09 receipts‿as‿proof 連音と子音連続
10 If‿interested, call‿Lisa 連音と語をまたぐ同一子音連続
11 seven‿and‿ten‿p.m. 連音と子音連続の音変化

日本語訳 －英文の内容を確認しよう！

ラジオ・フリーマーケット

さて、ラジオ・フリーマーケットの次のアイテムはパターソンシティのリサさんが売りに出している1999年製ホンダ・アコードです。この車はオートマチック車で、エンジンは6気筒。濃いブルーのボディはきれいで、キズやへこみはありません。燃費は非常によく、エアコン、パワーウィンドウ、パワーロック、AM/FMラジオ、CDプレーヤー、そしてサンルーフがついています。カーステレオは交換する必要があるかもしれません。タイヤ4本すべてとトランスミッションは交換して1年も経っておらず、それを証明する領収書があります。希望売却価格は4,000ドルです。興味のある方は午後7時から10時の間にリサさんに電話をしてください。電話番号は950-555-6599です。

Useful Expressions －このままそっくり暗記しよう！

1. Our car has a navigation system.
   （うちの車はカーナビが付いている）
2. Japanese cars get good mileage.
   （日本車は燃費がいい）
3. This contract needs rewording.
   （この契約書は語句の修正が必要である）
4. What is your asking price?
   （あなたの言い値はいくらですか？）

CDで発音の確認とリピート練習ができます。

Short Talk ❸

And in business news, Avanti Incorporated has named Edward Klepp its new chief accounting officer, effective January first. Klepp has been serving as vice president and controller of Carson Health Services in Memphis, Tennessee, for the last five years, and he replaces George Hipple, who resigned at the end of the third quarter to take another position. Avanti CEO Elizabeth Carter announced the move through a press release yesterday. She expressed the hope that Klepp will play a key role in helping Avanti enter a new stage of growth. Klepp is a member of the Tennessee Society of Certified Public Accountants and began his career in 1992.

耳練-23

Comprehension Questions

1. What is Edward Klepp's current position?
2. Who is George Hipple?
3. According to the CEO, what is Avanti's goal?

耳練チェックマトリックス 自分のリスニング力を判定しよう!

聴き取りCheck Step	Situation (状況理解)	Vocabulary (語彙)	Expression (表現)	Pronunciation (発音)
1st Try				
2nd Try				
3rd Try				

【自己判定マーク】
◎パーフェクトに理解　○ほぼ理解　△半分ほど理解　×ほとんどわからない
[注] すべて◎になるまでトライしてみよう!
＊本マトリックス活用法については7ページを参照。

耳練ヒント

Situation Markers 状況・場面を把握しよう!

- And in business news（これからビジネスニュースが始まる）
  ⇒ラジオ（またはテレビ）のニュース
- Avanti Incorporated ⇒アヴァンティ社の話
- named Edward Klepp its new chief accounting officer
  （エドワード・クレップを最高会計責任者に指名した）
  ⇒以下はこのクレップ氏についてのことであると推測される

耳練-23 Business News

耳練ポイント

Vocabulary　—単語の意味を確認しよう！

- □ name／指名する、任命する
- □ chief accounting officer／最高会計責任者
- □ effective／有効な
- □ controller／管理者、業務担当者
- □ Carson Health Services／カーソン健康保険
- □ replace ～／～に取って代わる、～の後任となる
- □ resign／辞任する
- □ quarter／四半期
- □ CEO／= Chief Executive Officer　最高経営責任者
- □ announce／発表する
- □ move／（この場合は）決定
- □ press release／プレスリリース、報道機関への発表
- □ certified public accountant／CPA（公認会計士）
- □ career／キャリア、経歴、職歴、専門的職業

Key Expressions　—重要フレーズを聴き取ろう！

01 **And in business news**　「次にビジネス関連のニュースでは」

01 **Avanti Incorporated**　「アヴァンティ社」incorporated は法人化したという意味

01 **named ～ …**　「～を…に指名した、任命した」　⇒ Useful Expressions

02 **effective January first**　「1月1日付で」慣用的な表現で which will be effective on January first の省略。このような場合、前置詞 on は普通省略される
　　⇒ Useful Expressions

03 **serving as ～**　「～を務める」　⇒ Useful Expressions

05 **for the last (five) years**　「過去（5）年間」

06 **to take another position**　「転職のため」take は提供された地位、役職などに就くことを表す。Cf. He was offered several positions, and he took the best paying one.（彼はいくつもの仕事を提供され、最も給料のよいものに就いた）

07 **the move**　「動き、決断」クレップ氏を雇ったことをさす

08 **through a press release**　「プレスリリースで」つまり記者会見ではなくて書面で

09 **play a key role in helping Avanti enter a new stage of growth.**　「アヴァンティ社が新しい成長の段階に入る手助けをする上でカギとなる役割を果たす」play a key role in ～ ing で「～する上で重要な働きをする」　⇒ Useful Expressions

11 **began his career in 1992**　「1992年に公認会計士として仕事を始めた」

Pronunciation　－聴き取りポイントに注意しよう！

05　last five years の語をまたぐ子音連続
06　at the end of the third quarter の子音連続、連音など
10　stage of growth 連音と語をまたぐ複雑な子音連続

日本語訳　－英文の内容を確認しよう！

ビジネスニュース

さて、ビジネスニュースです。アヴァンティ社では1月1日付けでエドワード・クレップが最高会計責任者に就任します。クレップ氏はテネシー州メンフィスにあるカーソン・ヘルスサービスで過去5年間副社長および業務担当者を務めてきましたが、第3四半期末に他のポストに就くために辞任したジョージ・ヒップルの後任となります。アヴァンティ社のCEOエリザベス・カーターは、昨日プレスリリースでこの異動を発表しました。カーター氏はアヴァンティ社が新たな成長段階に入るために、クレップ氏が重要な役割を果たすだろうとの期待を表明しました。クレップ氏はテネシー州公認会計士協会のメンバーで、1992年から公認会計士をしています。

Useful Expressions　－このままそっくり暗記しよう！

1. They named Bill their new candidate.
   （彼らはビルを彼らの新しい候補者に指名した）
2. Mary will become our new department head effective September first.
   （メアリーは9月1日付で私たちの新しい部長になる）
3. Mr. Black will begin serving as the section chief.
   （ブラック氏は新しい課長を務めます）
4. This move will play a key role in solving the financial problem.
   （この決断は財政問題を解決する上でカギとなる働きをするでしょう）

CDで発音の確認とリピート練習ができます。

耳練 24 New Annex

Short Talk ④

The next item on the agenda is the naming of the new annex. Each department has been asked to submit any suggestions for a suitable name by the end of the day, and then by the early part of next month an executive committee will make the final decision. I'll run through some of the ideas that have already been proposed. One is "Murphy Annex," in honor of the former CEO whose idea it was to construct a second building. Then there is "West Annex," which simply describes where the new building is in relation to the main building. I'm not too wild about that name myself, since it seems to imply that we have other annexes — and of course, we don't. So, how about it? Any ideas come to mind?

耳練-24

Comprehension Questions

1. At what sort of event is this talk being given?
2. When will the name of the new annex be decided?
3. Why has "West Annex" been suggested as a name for the annex?

耳練チェックマトリックス 自分のリスニング力を判定しよう!

Step \ 聴き取りCheck	Situation（状況理解）	Vocabulary（語彙）	Expression（表現）	Pronunciation（発音）
1st Try				
2nd Try				
3rd Try				

【自己判定マーク】
◎パーフェクトに理解　○ほぼ理解　△半分ほど理解　×ほとんどわからない

[注] すべて◎になるまでトライしてみよう!

＊本マトリックス活用法については7ページを参照。

耳練ヒント

Situation Markers　状況・場面を把握しよう!

- The next item on the agenda
  ⇒会議の中での議長の発言である
- the naming of the new annex ⇒別館の命名が議題
- One is "Murphy Annex,"（一つは「マーフィー別館」）
- Then there is "West Annex,"（もう一つは「西別館」）
- Any ideas come to mind?（何か考えは?）

耳練-24 New Annex

耳練ポイント

Vocabulary －単語の意味を確認しよう！

- □ naming／命名
- □ annex／アネックス、別館
- □ submit／提出する
- □ suitable／ふさわしい
- □ an executive committee／執行委員会、役員会
- □ in honor of ～／～に敬意を表して、～を記念して
- □ describe／言葉で表す、～について説明する
- □ in relation to ～／～との関係で
- □ the main building／本館
- □ imply／暗示する、ほのめかす

Key Expressions －重要フレーズを聴き取ろう！

01 **The next item on the agenda is ～**「次の議題は～です」これも議長の定型表現
 ⇒ Useful Expressions

02 **Each department has been asked to submit ～**「各部には～を提出するよう依頼してあります」We've asked each department to submit ～と言うのと同じ
 ⇒ Useful Expressions

02 **any suggestions for a suitable name**「(何でも、いくつでもよいから) ふさわしい名前の提案」この場合の suggestion は個々の具体的な名前の案

03 **by the end of the day**「当日中に、今日中に」

03 **by the early part of next month**「来月の上旬までに」

04 **make the final decision**「最終決定をする」 ⇒ Useful Expressions

05 **run through ～**「～に一通り目を通す、～を一通り読み上げる」 ⇒ Useful Expressions

07 **the former CEO whose idea it was to construct a second building**「2番目の建物を建てようと言い出した前CEO」いわゆる関係代名詞の連続用法であるから whose の前にカンマを置いてもよい。Cf. It was his idea to construct a second building.（2番目のビルを建てることは彼の考えだった）

08 **which** これも連続用法

10 **I'm not too wild about ～**「～はあまり感心しない」よくないと思うということを緩和した表現。I'm not too excited about ～とも言う

12 **we don't** = we don't〔have other annexes〕

12 **So, how about it?**「ということでどうでしょうか？」改めて意見を聞いている

12 **Any ideas come to mind?**「何か考えはありませんか？」Do any ideas come to mind? の省略。come to mind は「思い浮かぶ」

Pronunciation　－聴き取りポイントに注意しよう！

01　The next item on the agenda　の連音と音変化
02　asked to submit any suggestions　子音連結と連音
04　next month　の語をまたぐ複雑な子音連続
10　wild about that name myself　連音と子音連結、および音変化

日本語訳　－英文の内容を確認しよう！

新しい別館

次の議題は新しい別館の名称です。各部には今日中にふさわしい名前を提案するよう要請してあります。来月の上旬までに重役会が最終的に決めます。すでに出されているいくつかのアイディアを一通り紹介したいと思います。一つは、2番目のビルを建てることを考えた前CEOに敬意を表した「マーフィー・アネックス」です。それから、単純にメインビルとの位置関係で新しいビルの場所を表す「ウェスト・アネックス」です。私自身はこの名前についてはあまりいいとは思いません。というのは、ほかにも別館があるような印象を与えますが、もちろんほかにはないからです。ということで、どうでしょうか。何かいい考えが浮かびましたか。

Useful Expressions 24 　－このままそっくり暗記しよう！

1. The next item on the agenda is the election of the new committee members.
   （次の議題は委員会の新委員の選挙です）
2. You have been asked to submit a proposal.
   （あなたは提案を提出することを求められています）
3. We have to make the final decision by the end of the day.
   （今日中に最終的な決定をしなければならない）
4. I will run through the candidates we have so far.
   （これまでに挙がっている候補［者］の名前を読みあげます）

CDで発音の確認とリピート練習ができます。

Short Talk ⑤

Banquet Hall Reservation

Hello, Mr. Jacobs. This is Wendy Chang calling from the Mandarin Restaurant. First of all, my apologies for not being here to take your call. The assistant manager doesn't have access to our banquet hall reservations, so he was not able to help you. I can now confirm that our central banquet hall is available for the night of December 15th. I'm not sure whether or not you're familiar with the central hall, but the room accommodates up to two hundred diners. There are twenty round tables that can seat up to ten diners each. There is also a raised dais with a podium. I can hold the room for you until this evening, so I hope you'll get back to me on this one way or the other. Again, I'm sorry for the inconvenience.

耳練-25

Comprehension Questions

1. Who is the speaker?
2. What does the speaker imply about the banquet hall?
3. What does the speaker want Mr. Jacobs to do?

耳練チェックマトリックス 自分のリスニング力を判定しよう！

聴き取りCheck / Step	Situation（状況理解）	Vocabulary（語彙）	Expression（表現）	Pronunciation（発音）
1st Try				
2nd Try				
3rd Try				

【自己判定マーク】
◎パーフェクトに理解　○ほぼ理解　△半分ほど理解　×ほとんどわからない

［注］すべて◎になるまでトライしてみよう！

＊本マトリックス活用法については7ページを参照。

耳練ヒント

Situation Markers　状況・場面を把握しよう！

- Hello, Mr. Jacobs.（もしもし、ジェイコブズさん）
  ⇒電話の会話
- This is Wendy Chang calling from the Mandarin Restaurant
  （こちらはマンダリン・レストランのウェンディ・チャンです）⇒レストランからの電話
- our central banquet hall is available
  （中央宴会場は空いています）⇒宴会場の予約に関することである
- I hope you'll get back to me（連絡ください）
  ⇒全体は留守番電話へのメッセージ

🔊 耳練-25 Banquet Hall Reservation

🔊 耳練ポイント

▮Vocabulary －単語の意味を確認しよう！

- □First of all／まず最初に（用件の最初にという意味）
- □apology／謝罪
- □access／アクセス、使う権限
- □banquet hall reservations／宴会場予約（リストのこと）
- □confirm／確認する
- □available／利用可能、空いている
- □accommodate／（部屋、ホテルなどが）収容する
- □up to ～／最大、最高～まで
- □diner／宴会参加者、お客様
- □a raised dais／高くなった台座、ステージ
- □podium／演台
- □inconvenience／不便

▮Key Expressions －重要フレーズを聴き取ろう！

01 **This is ～ calling from…**「こちらは…の～です」留守番電話のメッセージを残すときの定型表現 ⇒ Useful Expressions

02 **my apologies for ～**「～をおわびします」I offer my apologies. または Please accept my apologies. の意味。謝罪する対象がわかっているときは単に My apologies. と言う。常に複数で使う

02 **not being here to take your call**「不在であなたの電話に出られなかったこと」take your call は「あなたの電話を受ける」

03 **The assistant manager**「副支配人」the がついているのは「あなたの電話を受けた副支配人」という意味

03 **have access to ～**「～にアクセスする、～を入手できる、～に自由に出入りできる」ここでは宴会場予約のリストおよび、それを管理するプログラム

05 **I can now confirm that ～**「～ということを確認できる」から「確かに～である」

06 **available for ～**「～に利用可能である、空いている」 ⇒ Useful Expressions

07 **familiar with ～**「～をよく知っている、～に詳しい」 ⇒ Useful Expressions

10 **I can hold the room for you**「その部屋（＝宴会場）を押さえておくことができる」hold「仮に取っておく」

11 **get back to ～ on…**「…で～に連絡を取る、電話をかけ直す」Cf. 耳練12（p.56、57）および耳練21（p.92、93）の Useful Expressions 参照

12 **one way or the other**「どちらにしても」つまり予約するにしても、やめるにしても

12 **I'm sorry for the inconvenience**「ご不便をおわびします」最初の電話で用が済まなかったことを言っている。My apologies again for the inconvenience. とも言える

Pronunciation　−聴き取りポイントに注意しよう！

02　First of all の連音
08　accommodates up to two hundred diners の連音と子音連続
09　seat up to ten diners each の連音と子音連続
11　get back to me の閉鎖音を含む子音連続

日本語訳　−英文の内容を確認しよう！

宴会場の予約

もしもし、ジェイコブズさん。こちらはマンダリン・レストランのウェンディ・チャンです。まず、不在で直接お電話をお受けできなかったことをおわびします。当店ではアシスタント・マネージャーは宴会場の予約を扱うことができないため、彼はあなたの予約をお受けすることができませんでした。12月15日の夜、当店の中央宴会場は間違いなく利用可能です。この宴会場についてご存知かどうかわかりませんが、部屋の収容定員は200人です。最高10人が座れる円卓が20卓あります。また、高座には演台もあります。お部屋は今夜まで押さえておくことができますので、いずれにしてもこの件についてお返事をお待ちしております。ご不便をおかけしたことを改めておわび申し上げます。

Useful Expressions　−このままそっくり暗記しよう！

1. This is Dr. Yamada calling from the City Hospital.
   （こちらは市民病院の山田医師です）
2. Two seats are available for the 11 o'clock flight.
   （11時の便は2席空いています）
3. Are you familiar with this library?
   （この図書館のことはよくご存知ですか?）

CDで発音の確認とリピート練習ができます。

練26 Book Commercial

Short Talk ⑥

Do you think you could beat a professional basketball player at his own game? Most of us wouldn't even want to try. Think about that the next time you go to a used car dealership, where you are dealing with a professional salesperson. From the moment you enter a car dealership, you are behind in experience and behind in sales know-how. So what can you do to make the playing field level? Call now at our toll-free number and order Bob Anderson's new book "How to Get the Best Deal on a Used Car." Let Bob show you how to avoid common scams and rip-offs practiced by some dealers. Read how to find out when dealers are desperate to make a sale. Learn how to make an offer on a car that the dealer can't refuse! So get a pen and paper ready to write down this number now!

耳練-26

Comprehension Questions

1. What is the commercial for?
2. According to the commercial, what can we get if we buy this product?
3. What must we do in order to get the product?

耳練チェックマトリックス 自分のリスニング力を判定しよう！

聴き取り Check / Step	Situation（状況理解）	Vocabulary（語彙）	Expression（表現）	Pronunciation（発音）
1st Try				
2nd Try				
3rd Try				

【自己判定マーク】
◎パーフェクトに理解　○ほぼ理解　△半分ほど理解　×ほとんどわからない

［注］すべて◎になるまでトライしてみよう！

＊本マトリックス活用法については7ページを参照。

耳練ヒント

Situation Markers　状況・場面を把握しよう！

- Do you think you could beat a professional basketball player at his own game?（プロのバスケットボールの選手を負かすことができると思いますか？）
  ⇒この段階では話がどのような状況で、何が話題であるのかわからない。プロということが関係しているかも知れない

- the next time you go to a used car dealership（中古車販売業者の所へ行った時に）⇒中古車販売に関係しているが、どのように関係しているかは不明

- Call now at our toll-free number and order Bob Anderson's new book（今すぐ無料電話をかけて、ボブ・アンダーソンの新しい本を注文しましょう）
  ⇒ここで本の宣伝であることがわかり、おそらくラジオかテレビのコマーシャルであることがわかる

111

耳練-26 Book Commercial

耳練ポイント

Vocabulary －単語の意味を確認しよう！

- ☐ beat／勝つ、やっつける
- ☐ used car dealership／中古車販売業者
- ☐ salesperson／販売員、セールスマン
- ☐ behind／遅れている
- ☐ sales know-how／販売のコツ
- ☐ level／水平
- ☐ toll-free number／フリーダイヤル
- ☐ common／よく起こる、目にする、日常的な
- ☐ scam／悪徳商法
- ☐ rip-off／不当に高い値段(の商品)、暴利(をむさぼる行為)
- ☐ practice／実行される
- ☐ find out／見つける、見抜く
- ☐ desperate／必死
- ☐ make a sale／販売する、商談を成立させる

Key Expressions －重要フレーズを聴き取ろう！

01 **you could beat a professional basketball player at his own game**「プロバスケットボール選手に勝てる」could になっているのは、もし試合をしたらという仮定が含まれているから。at his own game「〜の得意の分野で」この場合はバスケットボールのゲームでの意

03 **Think about that**「そのことを考えてみなさい」つまり「プロに太刀打ちしようとするのは無謀だということを考えてみなさい」

05 **From the moment you enter a car dealership**「中古車販売店に入った時から」
　⇒ Useful Expressions

06 **behind in experience and behind in sales know-how**「経験でも、売込みのノウハウでも遅れをとっている」 ⇒ Useful Expressions

07 **make the playing field level** = level the playing field「条件を平等／公平にする、ハンディをなくす」

07 **Call now at our toll-free number**「今すぐこのフリーナンバーに電話をかけてください」コマーシャルの常套文句。前置詞 at が使われることに注意。toll-free とは「料金無料」の意味。アメリカでは 800 で始まるので our 800 number とも言う

09 **"How to Get the Best Deal on a Used Car"**「中古車をどこよりも安く買う、一番得をする」 ⇒ Useful Expressions

09 **Let Bob show you 〜**「ボブが〜を説明します」 文字どおりには「ボブに〜を説明させてください」

11 **(be) desperate to**「〜しようと必死である、躍起になっている」 ⇒ Useful Expressions

12 **make an offer on 〜**「〜について買値を提示する」

13 **So get a pen and paper ready...** get a pen and paper ready (so as) to write down this number で「この番号を書き留めるために」の意。this number はこれから言う番号ともとれるが、ここで終わっているので画面に番号が出ていると考えられる

Pronunciation －聴き取りポイントに注意しよう！

01 you could beat a professional basketball player の閉鎖音がかかわる子音連続と連音
02 Most of us の連音
03 Think about that the next time 連音と語にまたがる閉鎖音がかかわる子音連続
06 behind in experience and behind in sales know-how の連音
07 what can you do to make the playing field level の子音連続
09 How to Get the Best Deal on a Used Car の連音と閉鎖音がかかわる子音連続

日本語訳 －英文の内容を確認しよう！

本の宣伝

あなたはプロのバスケットボール選手を負かせると思いますか？　たいていの人は試してみたいとも思わないでしょう。今度中古車ディーラーに行った時にそのことを考えてみましょう。あなたの相手はプロのセールスマンです。店に入った瞬間から、あなたは経験とセールスのノウハウの点で負けているのです。では、ハンディをなくすためにはどうすればいいでしょうか。今すぐこのフリーダイヤルに電話してボブ・アンダーソンの新しい本『中古車をどこよりも安く買う方法』を注文しましょう。本の中で、著者は一部のディーラーによる、よくある悪徳商法や不当に高い値段に引っかからない方法を説明しています。ディーラーがなんとか車を売りたいと思っているかどうかの見分け方も書いてあります。ディーラーが断れないようなオファーの仕方も教えてくれます！　では紙と鉛筆を用意してこの番号を書き留めてください！

Useful Expressions －このままそっくり暗記しよう！

1. Everybody was tense from the moment the president entered the office.
   （社長がオフィスに現れた時から、みんなは緊張していた）
2. Our company is behind in household electrical appliances.
   （わが社は家電で遅れをとっている）
3. I got the best deal on my computer.（コンピュータを安く手に入れた）
4. She is desperate to find another job.（彼女は別の仕事を探すのに必死だ）

CDで発音の確認とリピート練習ができます。

27 Condominium Association Meeting

Short Talk ❼

At our last meeting, we on the condominium board announced our plan to upgrade the building security system, so I'd like to begin tonight by giving you all an update on that. We've tentatively decided to ask a company called Quintomex to install a new telephone access system at the front door of the building. With this system, nobody can get into the building without punching in an access code, and nobody will be able to call your unit without knowing your number in advance. The system has a concealed video camera, so that when somebody does call your unit you'll be able to confirm who it is. Quintomex is pretty well known in this field and they have references from other owners in the area. We'll pass out their brochure so you can look it over before we take a vote.

耳練-27

Comprehension Questions

1. Who is being addressed?
2. What is Quintomex?
3. Why does the speaker mention a video camera?

耳練チェックマトリックス 自分のリスニング力を判定しよう!

聴き取りCheck / Step	Situation（状況理解）	Vocabulary（語彙）	Expression（表現）	Pronunciation（発音）
1st Try				
2nd Try				
3rd Try				

【自己判定マーク】
◎パーフェクトに理解　○ほぼ理解　△半分ほど理解　×ほとんどわからない

[注] すべて◎になるまでトライしてみよう!

＊本マトリックス活用法については7ページを参照。

耳練ヒント

Situation Markers 状況・場面を把握しよう!

- at our last meeting ⇒ 何らかの会議の席である
- we on the condominium board
  （マンション管理組合理事会のわれわれ）⇒ マンションの管理組合の総会である
- upgrade the building's security system
  （建物のセキュリティ・システムのアップグレード）⇒ セキュリティ・システムが議題
- We've tentatively decided to ask a company called Quintomex
  （暫定的にクイントメックス社にした）
- before we take a vote（投票・採決をする前に）
  ⇒ これから採決する

耳練-27 Condominium Association Meeting

耳練ポイント

Vocabulary －単語の意味を確認しよう！

- □ condominium board／マンション管理組合理事会
- □ announce／発表する
- □ update／最新情報、経過報告
- □ tentatively／暫定的に、仮に
- □ install／設置する、取り付ける
- □ telephone access system／ドアフォン、有線システム
- □ front door／正面玄関
- □ punch in／打ち込む、入力する（punch in～と punch～in の両方が可能）
- □ access code／暗証番号
- □ call／呼び出す
- □ unit／ユニット、住戸
- □ in advance／前もって、事前に
- □ concealed video camera／隠しビデオカメラ
- □ so that ～／だから～（その結果～だという意味）
- □ pretty well known／かなり知られている
- □ field／分野
- □ reference／推薦状、紹介状
- □ brochure／パンフレット、説明書
- □ pass out／配布する（これも pass ～ out でも可）
- □ take a vote／採決する、決をとる

Key Expressions －重要フレーズを聴き取ろう！

01 **we on the condominium board** このように理事会などの組織に加わっていることを表すのには on を用いることが重要。Cf. two players on the team（チームの2人の選手）

02 **our plan to upgrade the building security system**「建物の警備システムを新しくするわれわれの計画」We plan to upgrade the building security system. の名詞化

03 **I'd like to begin tonight by ～ ing**「今夜は～することから始めたいと思います」会議を開会するときの議長の定型表現 ⇒ Useful Expressions

04 **decided to ask ～ to do** …「～に…することを依頼することにした」⇒ Useful Expressions

08 **your number**「あなたの番号」それぞれの部屋に部屋番号とは違った番号が割り当てられている

10 **when somebody does call**「だれかが実際に呼び出したときに」この does は「実際に」という強調を表す。これは、「まず各住戸の番号を知らなければならないが、それがわかって実際に呼び出してきた場合でも」という意味

12 **they have** の they は Quintomex をさす

13 **look it over**「それにざっと目を通す」look over このように目的語が代名詞のときはこの語順しかないが、代名詞でない場合には look over ～と look ～ over の2通りの語順がある ⇒ Useful Expressions

Pronunciation　−聴き取りポイントに注意しよう！

01　**At_our last_meeting** の連音と子音連続
03　**giving_you all_an_update_on_that** の連音
06　**With_this_system** 語末と語頭で同じ音が連続し、切れ目がないことに注意
13　**look_it_over** の連音

日本語訳　−英文の内容を確認しよう！

マンション管理組合の総会

前回の会議で、私たちマンション理事会の理事たちはマンションのセキュリティ・システムのアップグレードに関する私たちの計画を発表しましたので、今夜はそれに関する現状報告から始めたいと思います。理事会としましては、正面玄関に新しいドアフォンを設置する工事をクイントメックスという会社に依頼することにとりあえず決めました。このシステムでは、暗証番号なしにはだれも建物内に入ることはできません。また、各戸の番号を事前に知らなければドアフォンで部屋を呼び出すこともできません。このシステムには隠しビデオカメラがあるので、部屋のドアフォンが鳴った場合、だれが来たのかを確認することができます。クイントメックス社はドアフォン業界ではかなりよく知られており、近隣の他のオーナーからの推薦状もあります。同社のパンフレットを配りますので、決をとる前に目を通してください。

Useful Expressions　−このままそっくり暗記しよう！

1. I would like to begin by introducing our new board members.
   （新しい役員を紹介することから始めたいと思います）
2. We decided to ask you to reconsider.（あなたに考え直すことを求めることにしました）
3. Please look over the documents before we begin.
   （始める前に書類に目を通してください）

CDで発音の確認とリピート練習ができます。

Short Talk 8

We are now going to begin the Test of Proficiency in Spanish. In just a moment, the staff will begin to pass out the test booklets and answer sheets. Please do not open the test booklet or make any marks on these materials until you are instructed to do so. The test will consist of sections on listening, reading, and writing. All listening and reading questions will be multiple choice items. In the writing section, you will translate sentences from English into Spanish by hand-writing your answers in spaces provided on the answer sheet. Your desk should be cleared of all items except pencils and erasers. No dictionaries or electronic devices are allowed at any time during the test. Now, if there are no questions, we will begin to distribute the test materials.

耳練-28

Comprehension Questions

1. What is the main topic of the talk?
2. How is the writing section different from other sections of the test?
3. What will happen next?

耳練チェックマトリックス 自分のリスニング力を判定しよう！

聴き取りCheck / Step	Situation (状況理解)	Vocabulary (語彙)	Expression (表現)	Pronunciation (発音)
1st Try				
2nd Try				
3rd Try				

【自己判定マーク】
◎パーフェクトに理解　〇ほぼ理解　△半分ほど理解　×ほとんどわからない

［注］すべて◎になるまでトライしてみよう！

＊本マトリックス活用法については7ページを参照。

耳練ヒント

Situation Markers 状況・場面を把握しよう！

- We are now going to begin the Test of Proficiency in Spanish
 （スペイン語のテストを始めます）⇒試験を実施する側の説明
- the staff will begin to pass out the test booklets and answer sheets
 （係員が問題と解答用紙を配布します）
 ⇒発言している人は係員ではなく、おそらく一斉放送をしている

耳練-28 Spanish Test

耳練ポイント

Vocabulary　−単語の意味を確認しよう！

- ☐proficiency／熟練、習熟
- ☐Test of Proficiency in Spanish／スペイン語検定試験
- ☐staff／係員、職員（担当者全員をさす）
- ☐test booklets／試験冊子
- ☐answer sheet／解答用紙
- ☐instruct／指示する
- ☐multiple choice／選択肢
- ☐translate／翻訳する、訳す
- ☐hand-write／手書きする
- ☐provided／与えられた
- ☐eraser／消しゴム
- ☐electronic device／電子機器（電子辞書、携帯電話など）
- ☐distribute／配布する

Key Expressions　−重要フレーズを聴き取ろう！

01 **We are going to begin ～**「～をこれから始めます」テストなどの開始を告げる定型表現

02 **In just a moment**「すぐに、間もなく」

02 **the staff**「係員」複数の会場にいる係員全員をさしている

03 **Please do not ～ until …**「…まで～しないでください」典型的な指示文
　⇒ Useful Expressions

04 **these materials**「これらのもの」問題冊子と解答用紙のこと

05 **consist of ～**「～からなる、～で構成される」　⇒ Useful Expressions

07 **multiple choice items**「選択式のもの」questions を繰り返すのを避けて items と言った

08 **you will ～**「～していただきます」これも試験などにおける指示文の典型
　⇒ Useful Expressions

08 **by hand-writing ～**「～を手書きで記入することによって」handwriting は「筆跡」という名詞であるが、この hand-writing は hand-write という動詞の動名詞形である

10 **Your desk should be cleared of ～**「机の上からは～を取り除いてください」You should clear your desk of ～ の受け身形

11 **No dictionaries or electrical devices** 否定を含む主語で始まる否定文に注意

12 **at any time**「いかなる時点でも」文頭の否定の No があるため、any が使われている

12 **if there are no questions**「質問がなければ」通常このように複数扱いされる

13 **test materials** = booklets and answer sheets

Pronunciation　−聴き取りポイントに注意しよう！

01　Test⌣of⌣Proficiency 連音と語にまたがる子音連続
02　pass⌣out⌣the test⌣booklets 連音と語にまたがる子音連続
05　consist⌣of sections⌣on listening の連音
09　your answers⌣in⌣spaces provided⌣on⌣the answer sheet の連音と語にまたがる子音連続
10　cleared⌣of⌣all⌣items except⌣pencils⌣and⌣erasers の連音と子音連続

日本語訳　−英文の内容を確認しよう！

スペイン語検定試験

ではスペイン語の検定試験を始めます。まもなく、係員が試験問題と解答用紙を配り始めます。指示があるまで試験問題を開けたり、配られたものに印をつけたりしないでください。試験はリスニング、リーディング、ライティングのセクションからなっています。リスニングとリーディングの解答は選択式です。ライティングでは、解答用紙の与えられた空欄に英語からスペイン語への翻訳を手書きします。机の上には鉛筆と消しゴム以外のものは置かないように。試験中はいかなるときも辞書や電子機器の使用は認められません。質問がないようでしたら、試験問題と解答用紙の配布を始めます。

Useful Expressions　−このままそっくり暗記しよう！

1. Please do not open the booklet until I tell you to do so.
   （指示をするまで冊子を開かないでください）
2. The committee consists of ten members.（委員会は10人の委員からなる）
3. Next you will fill out the questionnaire.（次にアンケート調査に答えていただきます）

CDで発音の確認とリピート練習ができます。

Short Talk ❾

Good afternoon. This is my third time to attend this conference on behalf of the Association of Small Publishers. We're a non-profit group that your company can join for a small annual membership fee. These are difficult times for small publishers, as you know, with overall sales of books decreasing year by year. However, we can help you to get through these tough times by offering a wealth of services. For example, we can give advice on how to reduce editorial and design costs and how to get huge discounts on shipping — that is, not only shipping books, but practically anything. You can also advertise your books free on our online bookstore once you become a member. Now that I've given you a general idea of what we're about, let me begin my slideshow presentation.

Comprehension Questions

1. What is the speaker's goal?
2. According to the speaker, what can his group do for the audience?
3. What will the speaker do next?

耳練チェックマトリックス 自分のリスニング力を判定しよう!

聴き取りCheck Step	Situation（状況理解）	Vocabulary（語彙）	Expression（表現）	Pronunciation（発音）
1st Try				
2nd Try				
3rd Try				

【自己判定マーク】
◎パーフェクトに理解　○ほぼ理解　△半分ほど理解　×ほとんどわからない
[注] すべて◎になるまでトライしてみよう!
＊本マトリックス活用法については7ページを参照。

耳練ヒント

Situation Markers 状況・場面を把握しよう!

- Good afternoon. This is my third time to attend this conference on behalf of the Association of Small Publishers.
  ⇒集会に出席した人の冒頭の挨拶、出版関係者の集会
- We're a non-profit group ⇒非営利団体の代表である
- let me begin my slideshow presentation
  ⇒スライドをつかったプレゼンテーションをする前の自己紹介であった

耳練-29 Association of Small Publishers

耳練ポイント

Vocabulary －単語の意味を確認しよう！

- □non-profit group／non-profit organization 非営利団体
- □annual membership fee／年会費
- □as you know／ご存知のように
- □overall／全般的な、全部の
- □give advice on ～／～について助言（アドバイス）する
- □reduce／削減する
- □editorial／編集の
- □shipping／配送、出荷
- □practically／事実上、実質的に、ほとんど
- □advertise／広告する、宣伝する
- □on-line bookstore／ネット上の書店

Key Expressions －重要フレーズを聴き取ろう！

01 **This is my ～ time to …**「…するのは～度目です」 ⇒ Useful Expressions

02 **on behalf of ～**「～を代表して、～の代わりに」 ⇒ Useful Expressions

04 **These are difficult times**「今は多難な時期です」 difficult times は tough times とも言う。複数扱いすることに注意 ⇒ Useful Expressions

05 **with overall sales of books decreasing year by year**「全体の本の売上げ部数が年々減少して」 with に導かれた付帯状況を表す表現で、overall sales of books が decreasing の主語の働きをしている

06 **year by year**「毎年、年々」 Cf. day by day「日ごとに」 hour by hour「刻々と」

06 **we can help you to get through these tough times**「この困難な時期を乗り越えるために手助けをすることができます」 we can help you get through these tough times のように to を使わないと「乗り越える手助けをすることができます」で、より責任が伴う。get through ～「～を乗り切る、やり過ごす」

07 **by offering a wealth of services**「さまざまな／豊富なサービスを提供することにより」

09 **shipping — that is, not only shipping books, but practically anything.** that is「つまり」は shipping の中身の追加説明の導入で、not only shipping books, but (shipping) practically anything の意味。「本だけでなく、事実上何でも」ということ

11 **advertise your books free**「無料で本を宣伝できる」 このように free は単独で「無料で」の意味で使える

13 **what we're about** ここでは「私たちの業務内容」の意

13 **let me begin ～**「～を始めます」 話を進行させる際の常套表現

Pronunciation －聴き取りポイントに注意しよう！

01 third time to attend this conference 語にまたがる子音連続と音変化
03 a non-profit group that your company can join の子音連続と音変化
06 get through these tough times の子音連続
09 how to get huge discounts on shipping の連音と音変化

日本語訳 －英文の内容を確認しよう！

小規模出版社協会

こんにちは。私が小規模出版社協会の代表としてこの会議に参加するのは今回が3度目です。私どもの協会は、皆様の会社が小額の年会費でメンバーになれる非営利団体です。ご存知のように、毎年書籍の販売は減少しており、昨今小規模出版社にとっては厳しい時代です。しかしながら、私どもはさまざまなサービスを提供することで皆様がこの困難な時期を乗り越えるお手伝いをすることができます。たとえば、編集やデザインのコスト削減や運送費―書籍のみならず実質的にあらゆるものを含みますが―を大幅に削減する方法についてのアドバイスをすることができます。また、メンバーになられますと、私どものオンライン書店で御社の書籍の宣伝を無料で行うこともできます。これで当協会についての概略はおわかりいただけたと思いますので、ここでスライドショーによる説明を始めさせていただきたいと思います。

Useful Expressions －このままそっくり暗記しよう！

1. This is my first time to visit your company.（御社を訪れるのは初めてです）
2. On behalf of President Morrison, it is my pleasure to welcome you all to our company.（モリスン社長に代わって当社への来訪を歓迎いたします）
3. The 1990s were difficult times for Japan economically.
   （1990年代は経済的に日本にとっては大変な時代でした）

CDで発音の確認とリピート練習ができます。

30 Factory Tour

Short Talk ⑩

Hello, everyone. My name is Kathy Koenig, and I'll be conducting your tour of the factory this morning. Let me just give you a brief preview of what to expect before we get started. This is Nordstrom Aircraft's main production facility. A complete product line of commercial aircraft is produced here. As part of the tour, you'll be able to see four models of airplanes in various stages of manufacture. All of this takes place within this single building, which is one of the four largest buildings in the world in terms of the volume of open space. Obviously, you won't be able to walk this tour. In a few minutes, we'll be boarding a shuttle bus. The tour itself takes a little more than an hour. At the end, we'll return here to the cafeteria, where you are welcome to stay for lunch if you choose.

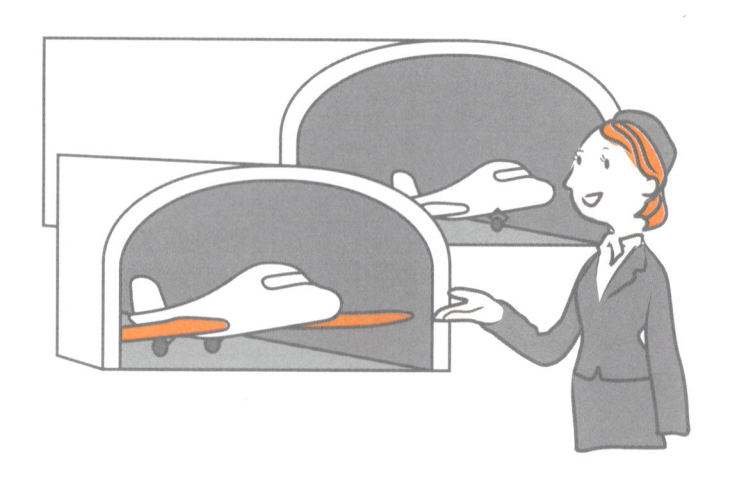

耳練-30

Comprehension Questions

1. Who is the speaker?
2. What will the tour group be able to watch?
3. Why will the tour be conducted by bus?

耳練チェックマトリックス 自分のリスニング力を判定しよう!

聴き取りCheck / Step	Situation (状況理解)	Vocabulary (語彙)	Expression (表現)	Pronunciation (発音)
1st Try				
2nd Try				
3rd Try				

【自己判定マーク】
◎パーフェクトに理解　○ほぼ理解　△半分ほど理解　×ほとんどわからない

[注] すべて◎になるまでトライしてみよう!

＊本マトリックス活用法については7ページを参照。

耳練ヒント

Situation Markers 状況・場面を把握しよう!

- I'll be conducting your tour of the factory this morning.
  (私は今朝みなさんの工場見学の案内をします)⇒工場見学のガイドである
- This is Nordstrom Aircraft's main production facility.
  (これはノードストローム航空機社の主要施設です)⇒航空機製造会社である
- The tour itself takes a little more than an hour.
  (1時間強で済む)⇒これからツアーに出かける

127

耳練-30 Factory Tour

耳練ポイント

Vocabulary －単語の意味を確認しよう！

- □conduct／案内する、引率する
- □tour／見学ツアー
- □preview／予告編、概要
- □main production facility／主要生産施設
- □a complete product line／全製品品目（つまり全機種）
- □commercial aircraft／（軍用ではなく）民間航空機（集合名詞として単数で用いられる。airplaneは可算名詞）
- □stages of manufacture／生産段階
- □take place／起こる、行われる
- □in terms of ～／～に関して、～の点から見ると
- □volume／量
- □walk／歩いてカバーする
- □board／乗車する、乗り込む
- □at the end／最後に、終わりに、終わったときに

Key Expressions －重要フレーズを聴き取ろう！

01 I'll be ～ ing「これから～します」これからしばらくの間～をするという予告
　⇒ Useful Expressions
02 conducting your tour of ～「あなたが～を見学するのを案内する」つまりこれから始まる工場見学のガイドを務める
02 Let me just ～「～いたします」これもガイドなどの決まった表現 ⇒ Useful Expressions
03 what to expect「どういうものか」文字どおりには「どのようなものを予想すべきか」
03 before we get started「出発する前に」get started「始める」⇒ Useful Expressions
05 is produced here「ここで製造されています」単数の is に注意
06 As part of the tour「見学の一部として」つまり「見学には次のものが含まれます」の意
06 see four models of airplanes in various stages of manufacture「さまざまな生産段階にある4機種の飛行機を見る」したがって4機種の何倍分かを見ることになる
07 All of this「そのすべて」つまり4機種の生産全体
09 the volume of open space「空間の広さ」volume はここでは音量ではなく空間の量
10 Obviously「当然ですが」くらいの意味。文字どおりには「明らかに」
10 walk this tour「見学ツアー全体を徒歩で行う」walk が他動詞として使われている
11 The tour itself「見学ツアー自体」
13 you are welcome to ～「～してください」
13 if you choose「よければ」

Pronunciation －聴き取りポイントに注意しよう！

02 **Let me just give you** 語にまたがる子音連続
03 **what to expect before we get started** 語にまたがる子音連続
04 **Nordstrom** の語中の新連続
05 **A complete product line** の語にまたがる子音連続
06 **models of airplanes in various stages of manufacture** の連音と子音連続
11 **The tour itself takes a little more than an hour** の連音と子音連続

日本語訳 －英文の内容を確認しよう！

工場ツアー

みなさん、こんにちは。私はキャシー・コーニッグで、今朝の皆様の工場ツアーの案内をさせていただきます。さて、ツアーを始める前にツアーの概要をお話しておきたいと思います。ここはノードストローム・エアクラフト社の主要生産施設で、商業用航空機のすべての機種がここで生産されています。ツアーでは、さまざまな製造工程にある4機種をご覧になれます。これらすべてがこの建物一棟の中で行われており、この建物は広さの点で世界の4大ビルの一つです。もちろん、このツアーは徒歩では行えませんので、間もなくシャトルバスに乗ります。ツアーの所要時間は1時間強です。ツアーの最後にはこのカフェテリアに戻りますので、よろしければ昼食をお召し上がりください。

Useful Expressions －このままそっくり暗記しよう！

1. I'll be showing you the important features of the museum in a minute.
   （すぐにこの博物館の重要な特色を案内します）
2. Let me first take you to the main entrance.（まず正面玄関にお連れします）
3. If you are all ready, let's get started.（準備がよければ始めましょう）

CDで発音の確認とリピート練習ができます。

練31 Pet Lovers Incorporated

Short Talk ⓫

M 🇬🇧 イギリス

It's a great pleasure to be able to talk to the new staff about the founder of our company, Janet Huffington. After obtaining a degree in education in 1973, Ms. Huffington turned her attention to the field of dog training, working part-time as a trainer of guide dogs for the blind while taking graduate courses in animal behavior. Then in 1981, she established Pet Lovers Incorporated right here in Houston, in a small office on the first floor of the building next door to us. Over the years, her reputation grew, and Pet Lovers became a name associated with the training of pets to serve people with various physical challenges and to help on rescue missions. Her emphasis on gentle and humane treatment has won her several awards from the American Society for the Prevention of Cruelty to Animals.

耳練-31

Comprehension Questions

1. What is the purpose of the talk?
2. What does Pet Lovers Incorporated do?
3. What aspect of the treatment of animals does Ms. Huffington emphasize?

耳練チェックマトリックス 自分のリスニング力を判定しよう！

聴き取り Check Step	Situation （状況理解）	Vocabulary （語彙）	Expression （表現）	Pronunciation （発音）
1st Try				
2nd Try				
3rd Try				

【自己判定マーク】
◎パーフェクトに理解　○ほぼ理解　△半分ほど理解　×ほとんどわからない

［注］すべて◎になるまでトライしてみよう！

＊本マトリックス活用法については7ページを参照。

耳練ヒント

Situation Markers 状況・場面を把握しよう！

- It's a great pleasure to be able to talk to the new staff about the founder of our company
  ⇒新入社員に対して会社の創設者の話をしている
- Janet Huffington
  ⇒創設者の名はジャネット・ハフィントン
- Then in 1981, she established Pet Lovers Incorporated
  ⇒会社の名前はペットラバーズ社

131

耳練-31 Pet Lovers Incorporated

耳練ポイント

Vocabulary －単語の意味を確認しよう！

- ☐ founder／創設者、創始者
- ☐ obtain／取得する
- ☐ degree／学位
- ☐ working ～／
  ～として働いた（分詞構文で、結果を表す）
- ☐ guide dogs for the blind／
  盲導犬
- ☐ graduate courses／
  大学院の授業
- ☐ animal behavior／
  動物行動学
- ☐ establish／
  設立する、創設する
- ☐ reputation／評判、名声
- ☐ physical challenge／
  身体的障害のこと
- ☐ rescue missions／（災害などの際の）救助活動
- ☐ emphasis／強調（点）
- ☐ humane treatment／
  人道的な扱い
- ☐ prevention／予防、防止
- ☐ cruelty／残酷（な仕打ち）

Key Expressions －重要フレーズを聴き取ろう！

01 **It's a great pleasure to be able to ～**「～するのは大きな喜びです」 典型的なスピーチの前置き ⇒ Useful Expressions

01 **new staff**「新入社員」 staff は集合名詞で単数扱いすることに注意

02 **the founder of our company, Janet Huffington** 同格表現

02 **After obtaining a degree in education**「教育学で学位を取った後」

03 **turned her attention to ～**「～に関心を移した」

04 **working part-time as a trainer of guide dogs for the blind**「盲導犬の訓練士としてパートタイムで働く」 ⇒ Useful Expressions

05 **while taking graduate courses in animal behavior**「動物行動学の大学院の授業を取りながら」 つまり大学院に行きながら ⇒ Useful Expressions

08 **the building next door to us**「わが社の隣の建物」 next door to us は後置修飾

08 **Over the years**「年月を重ねるにつれて」 ⇒ Useful Expressions

09 **and Pet Lovers became a name associated with the training of ～** 文字どおりには「ペットラバーズは～の訓練と結び付いた名前になった」であるが「～の訓練と言えば、ペットラバーズということになった」の意味になる

10 **pets to serve ～**「～に仕えるペット、～の役に立つペット」

10 **people with various physical challenges**「身体にさまざまな障害を持つ人たち」 最近は障害（handicap）と言わず挑戦（challenge）と言う

12 **Her emphasis on gentle and humane treatment**「彼女が（ペットの）優しい、人道的な扱いを強調したこと」

12 **～ won her several awards**「～が原因となって、彼女はいくつもの賞を得た」 her が間接目的語、several awards が直接目的語

Pronunciation　—聴き取りポイントに注意しよう！

01　It's‿a great‿pleasure　連音と子音連続
04　working‿part-time‿as‿a trainer of guide‿dogs　の連音と子音連続
06　Then‿in‿1981　の連音と子音連続
07　in‿a small‿office‿on‿the first‿floor　の連音と子音連続

日本語訳　—英文の内容を確認しよう！

ペットラバーズ社

わが社の創業者ジャネット・ハフィントンについて、新人スタッフの皆さんに話ができることをうれしく思います。1973年に教育学の学位を取得した後、ハフィントン女史は犬の訓練の分野に関心を持ち、大学院で動物行動学の授業を取るかたわら、盲導犬の訓練士としてパートタイムで働きました。その後、1981年に彼女はここヒューストンで、わが社の隣のビルの1階にある小さなオフィスで、ペットラバーズ社を創設しました。長年の間に彼女の評判は広まり、ペットラバーズの名前は身体にさまざまな障害を持った人々や救助活動のためのペットの訓練と結び付けられるようになりました。優しさと人道的な扱いを大事にすることによって彼女はアメリカ動物愛護協会から何度か賞を受けています。

Useful Expressions ㉛　—このままそっくり暗記しよう！

1. It's a great pleasure to be able to make an opening speech for this conference.
   （会議の開会の挨拶をするのは大きな喜びです）
2. Then he worked part-time as a salesperson at a convenience store.
   （それから彼はコンビニの販売員としてパートタイムで働いた）
3. He attended graduate school while working part-time for an on-line broker.
   （彼はオンラインブローカーでアルバイトをしながら、大学院に行った）
4. Over the years he gradually became more and more short-tempered.
   （年を経るにしたがって彼はますます短気になった）

CDで発音の確認とリピート練習ができます。

練32 Outsourcing

Short Talk ⑫

I've been asked to lay out for this committee the pros and cons of outsourcing. More specifically, I'll address the question, "What benefits and drawbacks can we expect if we outsource our software development projects?" On the plus side, there are of course the economic advantages. Software engineering is a highly competitive field, so we should be able to find a competent firm to meet our needs at a reasonable price. In addition, outsourcing frees up a good part of our own staff so that they can work on more crucial projects. On the down side, there is, of course, a certain loss of control. It is important that we strive to keep management control and high standards even while the work is being done elsewhere, but it is inevitable to lose control to some extent. I'll pause now for any questions.

Comprehension Questions

1. What is the purpose of the talk?
2. What does the speaker say about the software engineering industry?
3. What does the speaker recommend doing, if the company outsources projects?

耳練チェックマトリックス　自分のリスニング力を判定しよう!

聴き取りCheck / Step	Situation（状況理解）	Vocabulary（語彙）	Expression（表現）	Pronunciation（発音）
1st Try				
2nd Try				
3rd Try				

【自己判定マーク】
◎パーフェクトに理解　○ほぼ理解　△半分ほど理解　×ほとんどわからない

[注] すべて◎になるまでトライしてみよう!

＊本マトリックス活用法については7ページを参照。

耳練ヒント

Situation Markers　状況・場面を把握しよう!

- I've been asked to lay out for this committee the pros and cons of outsourcing. ⇒アウトソーシングについての委員会への報告である
- "What benefits and drawbacks can we expect if we outsource our software development projects?" ⇒ソフトウェアの外注のよい点と悪い点
- I'll pause now for any questions. ⇒ここから質問を受け付ける

耳練-32 Outsourcing

耳練ポイント

Vocabulary　－単語の意味を確認しよう！

- ☐lay out／明確に述べる、明らかにする、説明する
- ☐committee／委員会
- ☐pros and cons／よい点と悪い点
- ☐address／（問題を）扱う、論じる
- ☐benefits and drawbacks／よい点と悪い点（pros and cons と同じ）
- ☐outsource／外注する、外部委託する
- ☐plus side／よい面、プラスの面
- ☐advantage／利点
- ☐competitive／競争の激しい
- ☐firm／企業、会社
- ☐reasonable price／安価、適正価格（at a reasonable price「手ごろな値段／適正価格で」）
- ☐in addition／加えて、さらに
- ☐free up／使えるようにする、自由にする、解放［して他の目的に使えるように］する（free up ～の形でも free ～ up の形でも使える）
- ☐crucial／不可欠な
- ☐down side／悪い面、マイナスの面
- ☐strive to ～／～するよう努力する
- ☐inevitable／避けられない
- ☐to some extent／ある程度は
- ☐pause／中断する

Key Expressions　－重要フレーズを聴き取ろう！

01 **I've been asked to ～**「～することを依頼されました」⇒Useful Expressions

01 **lay out for … ～**「…に対して～を説明する」ここでは～部分が長いのでこの語順になっているが、本来は lay out ～ for … ⇒Useful Expressions

02 **More specifically**「すなわち、もっと正確に言えば、さらに具体的に言うと」

02 **the question** 次の疑問文と同格

06 **we should be able to find a competent firm**「有能な会社を見つけられるはずだ」
should be able to ～「～できるはずだ」⇒Useful Expressions

07 **a competent firm to meet our needs** = a competent firm that meets our needs
to 以下が a competent firm を限定している

08 **a good part of our own staff**「わが社の社員のかなりの部分」
staff は集合名詞で通常は単数扱い。ただし、ここではこの表現を受ける代名詞として they が使われていることにも注意

12 **elsewhere**「他所で」つまり社外で

13 **I'll pause now for any questions.**「ここで一旦終えて、質問があれば答えます」
any questions の any は「もし質問があれば」という気持ちを表している。このまま覚えておきたい表現

Pronunciation　—聴き取りポイントに注意しよう！

01　I've been asked to の子音連続と連音
03　What benefits and drawbacks の子音連続と連音
04　development projects 語にまたがる複雑な子音連続
07　competent firm 閉鎖音を含む子音連続
08　frees up a good part of our own staff の連音と子音連続
13　but it is inevitable の連音

日本語訳　—英文の内容を確認しよう！

アウトソーシング

この委員会のためにアウトソーシングのよい点と悪い点を説明するのが私の仕事です。より具体的には、「わが社のソフトウェア開発プロジェクトを外注した場合、どのような利益と不利益が予想されるか」という疑問に答えたいと思います。プラスの面としては、もちろん経済的な利点があります。ソフトウェア工学（エンジニアリング）はとても競争が激しい分野ですから、手ごろな価格でわが社のニーズを満たせる能力のある会社を見つけることができるはずです。さらに、アウトソーシングによってわが社のかなりのスタッフの手が空きますから、彼らはもっと重要なプロジェクトの作業をすることができます。マイナスの面としては、当然のことながら、いくぶんコントロールできなくなるということがあります。外部で仕事がなされる場合でも、運営上のコントロールと高い水準を維持すべく努力することが重要ですが、いくらかのコントロールを失うことは避けられません。ここで質問があればお受けしたいと思います。

Useful Expressions　—このままそっくり暗記しよう！

1. I've been asked to make a proposal. （提案をするように頼まれました）
2. Will you lay out the project for this committee? （この委員会に企画を説明してくれますか?）
3. You should be able to get there by ten. （10時までにはそこに着くことができるはずだ）

CDで発音の確認とリピート練習ができます。

耳練 33 Ellis Island

Short Talk ⑬

Before we begin our tour of Ellis Island I'd like to provide a little background information. As you know, Ellis Island was the gateway to America for immigrants from a great many European countries. During the years from 1892 until its closure in 1954, over 12 million immigrants went through immigration procedures on this island. The Main Building, which we are standing in front of, was converted into a museum and reopened to the public in 1990. During our walk through the facility we'll be seeing a variety of photos and exhibits which should allow you to get a feel for what the immigration process was like for the people who went through it. Our tour should take about 45 minutes. There is also a 30-minute documentary film showing on the second floor which is well worth viewing after our tour ends.

耳練-33

Comprehension Questions

1. Where does this talk take place?
2. What purpose does the Main Building serve today?
3. What does the speaker recommend doing at the end of the tour?

耳練チェックマトリックス 自分のリスニング力を判定しよう！

聴き取りCheck Step	Situation（状況理解）	Vocabulary（語彙）	Expression（表現）	Pronunciation（発音）
1st Try				
2nd Try				
3rd Try				

【自己判定マーク】
◎パーフェクトに理解　○ほぼ理解　△半分ほど理解　×ほとんどわからない
［注］すべて◎になるまでトライしてみよう！
＊本マトリックス活用法については7ページを参照。

耳練ヒント

Situation Markers 状況・場面を把握しよう！

- Before we begin our tour of Ellis Island I'd like to provide a little background information.
  ⇒エリス島の見学ツアーのガイドの言葉、したがって以下はツアーに関するもの
- As you know, Ellis Island ⇒以下はエリス島の歴史の説明
- Our tour should take about 45 minutes. ⇒所要時間は45分
- 30-minute documentary film ⇒30分のドキュメンタリーがある

耳練-33 Ellis Island

耳練ポイント

Vocabulary －単語の意味を確認しよう！

- ☐ Ellis Island／エリス島（ニューヨークにあり、かつて入国管理事務所があった）
- ☐ background information／背景知識
- ☐ gateway／入り口、玄関
- ☐ a great many ～／非常に多くの～（不定冠詞 a を使用することが重要）
- ☐ immigrants／移民
- ☐ closure／閉鎖
- ☐ immigration procedure／移民手続き、入国管理手続き
- ☐ Main Building／本館
- ☐ convert／変換する
- ☐ walk／見学コース
- ☐ facility／施設
- ☐ a variety of ～／さまざまな～
- ☐ exhibit／展示物、陳列物

Key Expressions －重要フレーズを聴き取ろう！

01 **I'd like to provide a little background information**「いくらかの背景知識をお話しします」ガイドの発言であるが、さまざまな場面で使える ⇒Useful Expressions

03 **the gateway to America**「アメリカへの入り口、玄関」にあたるものという比喩的な用法

05 **went through immigration procedures**「入国の審査の手続きを踏んだ」
go through ～で「～の（しかるべき）手続きを踏む」⇒Useful Expressions

06 **The Main Building, which we are standing in front of**
「本館は、その前に今私たちが立っていますが」関係節の連続用法

07 **was converted into a museum**「博物館になった」
convert ～ into …「～を…に変える」⇒Useful Expressions

08 **(was) reopened to the public**「再び一般に公開された」博物館に改装する前は一般公開されており、改装中は休館していたが、再び公開するようになったという意

08 **During our walk through the facility**「施設の見学ツアーの間に」施設とは博物館のこと

09 **which should allow you to get a feel for what the immigration process was like for the people who went through it**「移民手続きを臨む人たちにとって、それがどんなものであったかを味わうことができるはずです」長い複雑な文だが、全体を頭から聞いていきながら問題なく理解できるまで練習することが重要。get a feel for ～「～の感触をつかむ／気分を味わう」what the immigration process was like は間接疑問文

12 **should take about 45 minutes**「45分ほどかかるはず」should の用法に注意

13 **showing on the second floor**「2階で上映している」show は自動詞で「(映画などが)かかっている」の意味

13 **which is well worth viewing** 前にカンマはないがこの関係代名詞も連続用法で「それは大いに見る価値がある」という意。worth ～ing「～する価値がある」
⇒Useful Expressions

Pronunciation －聴き取りポイントに注意しよう！

01 Ellis⌣Island I'd⌣like⌣to の連音と子音連続
03 immigrants⌣from 語にまたがる複雑な子音連続
04 until⌣its⌣closure の連音と子音連続
09 of⌣photos⌣and⌣exhibits の子音連続と連音
10 you⌣to get⌣a feel⌣for の連音、子音連続と音変化

日本語訳 －英文の内容を確認しよう！

エリス島

エリス島のツアーを始める前に、少し予備知識をお教えしましょう。ご存知のように、エリス島は非常に多くのヨーロッパの国々からの移民にとって、アメリカへの玄関口でした。1892年から1954年に閉鎖されるまでの間、1200万人以上の移民がこの島で移民の手続きを行いました。現在私たちが正面に立っているのはメイン・ビルディングで、博物館になり1990年に再び一般に公開されるようになりました。施設を歩いて見ていく中で、さまざまな写真や展示があり、移民手続きに臨む人たちにとってそれがどのようなものだったかを感じることができるでしょう。ツアーの所要時間はおよそ45分です。また、2階では30分のドキュメンタリー映画も上映されており、それはツアーの後に見る価値があるものです。

Useful Expressions －このままそっくり暗記しよう！

1. Before we begin our presentation I would like to provide a little background information on space science.
   （発表の前に宇宙科学についての背景知識を少し述べておきます）
2. Please go through registration procedures before going to your rooms.
   （各人の部屋へ行く前に登録の手続きをしてください）
3. We are planning to convert this into our second guest house.
   （これを2つ目のゲストハウスにする予定です）
4. The museum is well worth visiting.（その博物館は訪れる価値が大いにあります）

CDで発音の確認とリピート練習ができます。

Short Talk ⑭ — Sunburst Coffee

It's a great honor for me to be able to introduce today's guest speaker. I doubt that there's anyone here today who has never enjoyed a cup of coffee in a Sunburst Coffee shop. Today, we'll hear from the man who gained control of the company when it was a small family business in Seattle, consisting of just three locations. Today, Sunburst is a household word, with over seven hundred shops in the United States alone, and over three hundred more in twelve foreign countries. And new shops are opening at the rate of two per week. I think it's safe to say that our guest has a lot to offer us regarding how to break into new markets in different countries and cultures, and that's precisely why we invited him here today. Without further ado, then, please join me in welcoming our guest speaker, Mr. Charles Finkleman.

Comprehension Questions

1. Why is Charles Finkleman well known?
2. How many Sunburst Coffee shops are there in the world?
3. According to the speaker, what is Mr. Finkleman's outstanding talent?

耳練チェックマトリックス　自分のリスニング力を判定しよう！

聴き取りCheck / Step	Situation（状況理解）	Vocabulary（語彙）	Expression（表現）	Pronunciation（発音）
1st Try				
2nd Try				
3rd Try				

【自己判定マーク】
◎パーフェクトに理解　○ほぼ理解　△半分ほど理解　×ほとんどわからない

［注］すべて◎になるまでトライしてみよう！
＊本マトリックス活用法については7ページを参照。

耳練ヒント

Situation Markers　状況・場面を把握しよう！

- It's a great honor for me to be able to introduce today's guest speaker. ⇒講演会の講師の紹介
- Sunburst Coffee ⇒講師はサンバースト・コーヒーと関係がある
- we'll hear from the man who gained control of the company ⇒サンバースト・コーヒーの社長が講師
- please join me in welcoming our guest speaker, Mr. Charles Finkleman ⇒紹介がこれで終わる。講師はチャールズ・フィンクルマン

耳練-34 Sunburst Coffee

耳練ポイント

Vocabulary －単語の意味を確認しよう！

- □honor／名誉
- □guest speaker／講師、講演者
- □family business／家族(同族)経営の事業(会社)
- □locations／所在地
- □a household word／よく知られた人(物)、だれでも知っているもの
- □rate／率
- □regarding／関して
- □ado／大騒ぎ

Key Expressions －重要フレーズを聴き取ろう！

01 **It's a great honor for me to be able to introduce ～**「～を紹介できるのは私にとって光栄の至りです」講演会などでの紹介の常套表現。It's a great honor and pleasure と言うこともある

02 **I doubt that～** = I don't think ～「～とは思わない」と内容が否定なので、there's anyone と any が用いられている

03 **a Sunburst Coffee shop**「サンバースト・コーヒーの店」Sunburst Coffee は固有名詞だが、店の一つであるので a がついている

04 **gained control of ～**「～の支配権を得る」つまり「買収して経営する」

04 **the company**「その会社」つまり Sunburst Coffee。これ以前にどこにも company という語は出ていないが、Sunburst Coffee が company であることはわかっているため

06 **three locations**「3店舗」

07 **in the United States alone**「米国だけで」このように alone は後ろから限定する

08 **three hundred more**「あと／さらに300店舗」

09 **new shops are opening at the rate of two per week**「新店舗が1週間に2店舗の割合で開店している」利用価値の高い表現形式。無冠詞複数名詞を主語にとって、後に at the rate of ～「～のペースで／割で」を続ける ⇒Useful Expressions

10 **I think it's safe to say that ～**「～であると言ってよい／言って間違いない」
⇒Useful Expressions

10 **has a lot to offer**「価値のあるものをたくさん持っている」⇒Useful Expressions

12 **that's precisely why ～**「まさにそのような理由で～」

13 **Without further ado**「前置きはそのくらいにして」と紹介などを切り上げるときに使う常套表現。このまま覚えておきたい

13 **please join me in welcoming ～**「～さんです」文字どおりには「私と一緒に～さんを歓迎してください」これも紹介の最後の常套文句

Pronunciation　－聴き取りポイントに注意しよう！

- 01　guest‿speaker　語にまたがる複雑な子音連続
- 03　enjoyed‿a cup‿of‿coffee　の連音と子音連続
- 03　Sunburst‿Coffee　の語にまたがる複雑な子音連続
- 07　hundred‿shops in the United‿States　の閉鎖音を含む子音連続
- 12　that's‿precisely　の語にまたがる複雑な新連続

日本語訳　－英文の内容を確認しよう！

サンバースト・コーヒー

本日のゲストスピーカーをご紹介させていただきます。今日ここにいらっしゃる方の中にサンバースト・コーヒーの店でコーヒーをおいしく飲んだことがない方はいないのではないかと思います。今日は、同社がまだシアトルでわずか3店の小さな家族経営の会社だった時に経営権を掌握した人物の話を伺います。今ではサンバーストはアメリカだけでも700店以上、さらに海外12か国にも300店以上あり、よく知られています。しかも、毎週2か所のペースで新しい店がオープンしています。さまざまな国や文化の中で新しい市場にどのように参入するのかということについて、きっと私たちのためになる話をしてくださることでしょう。また、それだからこそ今日ここにお招きしたわけです。それでは、前置きはそのくらいにして、ここでゲストスピーカーのチャールズ・フィンクルマン氏を盛大にお迎えしましょう。

Useful Expressions　－このままそっくり暗記しよう！

1. New businesses are joining the field at the rate of three per month.
   （新規事業が月に3社の割合で参入しています）
2. I think it's safe to say that our company is the first to adopt this system.
   （わが社がこのシステムを導入した最初であると言っても差し支えない）
3. This area has a lot of attractive features to offer.
   （この地域には魅力的な点がたくさんある）

CDで発音の確認とリピート練習ができます。

練35 Paper Reduction

Short Talk ⑮ イギリス

Before we get into the agenda, I've been asked to remind all you department heads about the vice president's campaign to reduce expenditures on paper. We want everyone to use the cheaper, lower-grade paper when using the printers and please do use the printers as much as possible instead of the photocopying machines. Be sure to make no more copies than are necessary, and whenever possible, make double-sided copies. Any leftover copies or other papers that can't be used should be dropped into the recycle boxes, which are clearly labeled. The only exception to this rule is documents containing any type of sensitive information, which should be shredded, of course. Also, please be sure that staples and clips have been removed from papers before recycling them. Please pass these tips on to your subordinates and associates.

耳練-35

Comprehension Questions

1. To whom is the talk addressed?
2. What is the main purpose of the talk?
3. What does the speaker say about documents containing sensitive information?

耳練チェックマトリックス 自分のリスニング力を判定しよう!

聴き取りCheck Step	Situation (状況理解)	Vocabulary (語彙)	Expression (表現)	Pronunciation (発音)
1st Try				
2nd Try				
3rd Try				

【自己判定マーク】
◎パーフェクトに理解　○ほぼ理解　△半分ほど理解　×ほとんどわからない
［注］すべて◎になるまでトライしてみよう!
＊本マトリックス活用法については7ページを参照。

耳練ヒント

Situation Markers 状況・場面を把握しよう!

- Before we get into the agenda (議題に入る前に)
  ⇒会議の議長の発言であること
- all you department heads
  ⇒部長会議であることがわかる
- the vice president's campaign to reduce expenditures on paper
  ⇒紙の経費を削減する副社長のキャンペーン
- Please pass these tips on to your subordinates and associates.
  ⇒これでこの話題には区切りがついた

耳練-35 Paper Reduction

耳練ポイント

Vocabulary －単語の意味を確認しよう！

- remind／思い出させる
- reduce／減らす、削減する
- expenditures／支出、(〜)費
- low-grade paper／低質紙
- photocopying machine／コピー機
- double-sided copy／両面コピー
- leftover／残り
- exception／例外
- documents／文書、書類
- contain／含む
- sensitive／機密の
- shred／シュレッダーにかける
- be sure that 〜／〜であることを確かめる
- staple／ホッチキスの針
- tip(s)／［チップの tip と同じ綴りであるがこちらは］（ためになる）助言、情報
- subordinates／部下
- associates／同僚

Key Expressions －重要フレーズを聴き取ろう！

01 **Before we get into the agenda**「議題に入る前に」つまり「予定されている議事に入る前に」これは次に続く I've been asked... の時間を述べているのではなく、I've been asked... と述べている今の時間が we get into the agenda の前であるということ

01 **I've been asked to remind you about 〜**「〜について念を押すよう頼まれました」他の人からの連絡を伝える際の定型表現。remind 〜 about/of…「〜に…のことを思い出させる」 ⇒ Useful Expressions

01 **all you department heads**「部長全員」remind の目的語。この you は all the department heads の the と同じような働きをしている

05 **do use the printers as much as possible**「できるだけプリンターを使ってください」この do は強調の do で、必ず強勢をともなって使われる

06 **Be sure to 〜**「必ず〜しなさい、〜するように気をつけなさい」 ⇒ Useful Expressions

06 **make no more copies than are necessary**「必要以上のコピーをしない」つまり「必要な数だけのコピーをする」than はこのように関係代名詞として働くことに注意

07 **whenever possible** = whenever it is possible「可能な場合はいつでも」

09 **which (= and they) are clearly labeled**「それにははっきりとラベルが貼ってある」

10 **The only exception to this rule**「この決まりの唯一の例外」前置詞 to を使用することに注意

11 **which (= and they) should be shredded**「それらはシュレッドしなければならない」

14 **pass 〜 on (to…)**「（情報など）〜を（…に）伝える、回覧する」 ⇒ Useful Expressions

Pronunciation　—聴き取りポイントに注意しよう！

01　we get into の連音、［ゲリン to ］となる
01　I've been asked to remind の連音と子音連続
08　that can't be の閉鎖音を含む子音連続

日本語訳　—英文の内容を確認しよう！

紙の費用削減

議題に入る前に、副社長が進めている紙の費用を削減する運動のことを部長の皆さんに再度確認するよう要請がありました。全員がプリンターには廉価な低質紙を使うこと。また、なるべくコピー機ではなくプリンターを使うようにしてください。ただし、必要以上に印刷しないこと。また、可能な場合は必ず両面コピーにしてください。コピーの残りやほかに使えない紙はリサイクルボックスに入れてください。リサイクルボックスははっきりわかるようにラベルが貼られています。この決まりの唯一の例外はあらゆる機密情報を含む文書で、もちろんシュレッダーにかけてください。また、リサイクルする前に、紙からホッチキスの針やクリップを外してあることを確認してください。これらの情報を部下や同僚に伝えてください。

Useful Expressions　—このままそっくり暗記しよう！

1. I've been asked to remind you about the new law on copyrights.
（著作権に関する新しい法律について皆さんに念を押すよう言われています）
2. Be sure not to inform any more people than necessary.
（必要な人にだけ知らせてください）
3. Please pass this information on to your direct subordinates.
（この情報を直属の部下に伝えてください）

CDで発音の確認とリピート練習ができます。

耳練 36 Job Fair

Short Talk ⑯

It's nice to see so many of you seniors here today. It was only a few years ago that I myself was about to graduate with my bachelor's degree in business and no idea what I might end up doing with my life. Then I attended a job fair very much like this one, where I met a recruiter from Cosmos Consultants, and it was an event that changed my life — for the better, I hasten to add. For those of you not already familiar with the name, Cosmos deals mainly with event planning, advertising, public relations — the whole range of general consulting. Our clients include all kinds of companies from multinational corporations to small start-up firms. We also provide services for individuals, including politicians and prominent private citizens. I'll be here all day today and tomorrow morning, so please do drop by our booth if you have any questions.

Comprehension Questions

1. What is the purpose of the talk?
2. To whom is the talk addressed?
3. Why does the speaker mention politicians?

耳練チェックマトリックス 自分のリスニング力を判定しよう！

聴き取りCheck\Step	Situation（状況理解）	Vocabulary（語彙）	Expression（表現）	Pronunciation（発音）
1st Try				
2nd Try				
3rd Try				

【自己判定マーク】
◎パーフェクトに理解　○ほぼ理解　△半分ほど理解　×ほとんどわからない

［注］すべて◎になるまでトライしてみよう！

＊本マトリックス活用法については7ページを参照。

耳練ヒント

Situation Markers 状況・場面を把握しよう！

- It's nice to see so many of you seniors here today.
  （こんなにたくさんの4年生に会えてうれしい）⇒聴衆が大学4年生であることはわかるが、話し手がどのような人かは、これだけではわからない
- Then I attended a job fair very much like this one
  ⇒就職説明会の会場であることがわかる。話し手はおそらくは求人側
- Cosmos Consultants
  ⇒これが求人側の会社名
- so please do drop by our booth if you have any questions
  ⇒Cosmos Consultants の説明担当者であること

耳練-36 Job Fair

耳練ポイント

Vocabulary　—単語の意味を確認しよう！

- □ seniors／大学4年生（高校・大学の最終学年）
- □ I myself／私自身も
- □ graduate／卒業する
- □ bachelor's degree／学士号
- □ attend／出席、参加する
- □ job fair／就職説明会
- □ recruiter／リクルートする人、新人採用係
- □ for the better／いいように、よい方向に
- □ familiar with ～／～をよく知っている
- □ planning／企画
- □ advertising／広告
- □ public relations／広報、PR
- □ multinational corporation／多国籍企業
- □ start-up firm／新興企業
- □ prominent／著名な
- □ private citizen／個人

Key Expressions　—重要フレーズを聴き取ろう！

- 01 **it's nice to do ～**「～してうれしい」自己紹介の出だしの文句
- 01 **It was only a few years ago that ～**「～はほんの数年前のことだった、ほんの数年前に～だった」（強調構文）
- 02 **was about to graduate**「卒業しようとしていた、卒業するところであった」
- 02 **with my bachelor's degree in business and no idea ～**「経営学士は取れるものの、～のことは一向にわからない状態で」a bachelor's degree と no idea 以下はともに with の目的語
- 03 **no idea what I might end up doing with my life**「自分の人生がどのようなことになるかわからず」つまり「将来の見通しなどなく」⇒ Useful Expressions
- 04 **very much like this one**「ちょうどこのような」
- 06 **it was an event that changed my life**「それは私の人生を変えた出来事だった」it は先行文脈の内容をさす
- 07 **I hasten to add**「あわてて（急いで）付け加えますが」挿入的に使われている
- 07 **For those of you ～**「～の皆さんに言いますが」
- 08 **deals with ～**「～を専門とする、扱う」⇒ Useful Expressions
- 09 **the whole range of general consulting**「つまりコンサルティング全般です」
- 12 **provide services for ～**「～に対してサービスを提供する」
- 14 **do drop by our booth**「私どものブースにぜひ立ち寄ってください」do は強調。drop by ～「～に立ち寄る、顔を出す」⇒ Useful Expressions

Pronunciation　―聴き取りポイントに注意しよう!

- 01　It was‿only a few years‿ago の連音
- 03　what‿I might end‿up doing の連音と音変化
- 06　it was‿an‿event‿that‿changed my life の連音と子音連続
- 08　with‿event‿planning の連音と子音連続
- 14　if‿you have‿any questions の連音

日本語訳　―英文の内容を確認しよう!

就職説明会

今日はこんなにたくさんの4年生に来ていただきうれしく思います。私自身、ビジネスの学士号を取得しての卒業を控え、自分が人生において結局何をすることになるのか、まったく何もわからない状態だったのはほんの数年前のことでした。そんな時、今回のものによく似た就職説明会に参加し、そこでコスモス・コンサルタンツ社の新人採用担当者と会ったのですが、それは私の人生を変える出来事でした。もちろん、よい方向に変わったということを急いで付け加えておきます。当社の名前をまだあまり知らない方もいるでしょうが、コスモス社は主にイベント企画、広告、PR など一般的なコンサルティング業務を幅広く行っています。当社のクライアントには多国籍企業から小規模な新興企業まで、あらゆる企業がいます。また、政治家や著名な個人をはじめとする個人の方々にもサービスを提供しています。今日と明日の午前中、私はずっとここにいますので、何か質問がありましたら、当社のブースに立ち寄ってください。

Useful Expressions　―このままそっくり暗記しよう!

1. I had no idea what he was talking about.
   （彼が何のことを話しているのかわかりませんでした）
2. Our section deals with customer complaints and product improvement.
   （この課は顧客の苦情処理と製品改良を行います）
3. I will drop by your office late this afternoon.（午後遅くに御社に立ち寄ります）

CDで発音の確認とリピート練習ができます。

耳練 37 Election Report

Short Talk ⑰

It is now six o'clock. The polls closed exactly one hour ago and we have the first election returns. With five percent of the vote counted, incumbent senator Bill Harkin leads challenger Helen Klosterman, 52 percent to 46 percent, with the remaining 2 percent of the vote going to candidates from minor parties. Now, at this stage most of the votes that have been counted are from urban areas, mainly Cleveland, where Senator Harkin was expected to do very well. We have not had any reports yet from the rural areas of the state, which is where Klosterman is expected to get most of her support. Therefore, it is a bit surprising that Harkin's lead is only 6 percentage points, since his campaign manager had hoped to do much better in Cleveland. Still, the vote count has only begun, and there is a long night ahead of us. Stay tuned for more results.

Comprehension Questions

1. Who are Harkin and Klosterman?
2. What does the reporter say about the vote counting?
3. What does the reporter say about the outcome of the election?

耳練チェックマトリックス 自分のリスニング力を判定しよう!

聴き取りCheck / Step	Situation（状況理解）	Vocabulary（語彙）	Expression（表現）	Pronunciation（発音）
1st Try				
2nd Try				
3rd Try				

【自己判定マーク】
◎パーフェクトに理解　○ほぼ理解　△半分ほど理解　×ほとんどわからない

[注] すべて◎になるまでトライしてみよう!

＊本マトリックス活用法については7ページを参照。

耳練ヒント

Situation Markers 状況・場面を把握しよう!

- It is now six o'clock. The polls closed exactly one hour ago and we have the first election returns.
（6時である。投票が1時間前に終わって、最初の集計がでた）
⇒ラジオかテレビの選挙速報である

- With five percent of the vote counted
⇒開票率は5パーセントである

- Stay tuned for more results.
⇒選挙速報は一旦終わり

耳練-37 Election Report

耳練ポイント

Vocabulary －単語の意味を確認しよう！

- poll／投票
- election return／開票結果、選挙結果
- the vote／（単数で）投票総数
- incumbent senator／現職上院議員
- challenger／対立候補
- remaining／残った、残りの
- candidate／候補者
- minor parties／弱小政党
- urban areas／都市部
- reports／選挙結果報告、得票数報告
- rural areas／農村部
- support／支持
- surprising／意外、予想外
- campaign manager／選挙運動本部長、選対部長
- vote count／開票

Key Expressions －重要フレーズを聴き取ろう！

02 **With five percent of the vote counted**「投票総数の5パーセントが開票された段階で」付帯状況を表す with の用法

03 **incumbent senator Bill Harkin leads challenger Helen Klosterman, 52 percent to 46 percent**「現職上院議員ビル・ハーキンが対立候補ヘレン・クロスターマンを52パーセント対46パーセントでリードしています」lead 〜 X to Y「X対Yで〜をリードする」⇒ Useful Expressions

04 **with the remaining 2 percent of the vote going to candidates from minor parties**「残りの2パーセントは弱小政党の候補者の得票です」これも付帯状況を表す with の用法

06 **most of the votes that have been counted**「開票された票のほとんど」この場合は vote はそれぞれの票をさす

07 **where 〜 = and there 〜**「そしてそこでは」

08 **Senator Harkin was expected to do very well**「ハーキン上院議員が善戦することが予想されていた」⇒ Useful Expressions

09 **which is where**「そしてそこは」これも関係節の連続用法

11 **it is a bit surprising that 〜**「〜であるとは少し意外である」⇒ Useful Expressions

11 **Harkin's lead is only 6 percentage points**「ハーキンのリードはわずか6パーセントポイント」文にすると Harkin leads only by 6 percentage points. と by が必要

14 **there is a long night ahead of us**「今夜は長い夜になります」この場合の long「長い」は心理的に長いという意味で、実際の夜の長さが変わるわけではない
Cf. We had a long day.（長い一日だった）

14 **Stay tuned for 〜**「チャンネル／局を変えずに〜を見て／聞いてください」Stay tuned はラジオ局、テレビ局が他の局に変えないように言う決まった表現

Pronunciation　—聴き取りポイントに注意しよう！

01　The polls closed exactly one hour ago の語にまたがる複雑な子音連続と連音
06　at this stage 同種の子音連続
07　urban areas の連音
08　was expected to do very well の連音と同種の子音連続
14　there is a long night ahead of us の連音

日本語訳　—英文の内容を確認しよう！

開票速報

現在午後6時。投票はちょうど1時間前に締め切られ、最初の開票結果が出ました。開票率5%で、現職のビル・ハーキン上院議員が52%対46%で対立候補のヘレン・クロスターマン氏をリードしています。残りの2%は弱小政党の候補者に投じられました。さて、現在のところ、集計済みの票の大半は都市部、すなわちもっぱらクリーブランドのもので、ここはハーキン上院議員が優勢と予想されている地域です。クロスターマン票の大半を占めると予想される州内の農村部からはまだ報告がありません。というわけで、ハーキン氏の選挙運動本部長はクリーブランドでもっと善戦することを期待していたので、リードがわずか6%というのは少々驚きです。とはいえ、開票作業はまだ始まったばかりで、結果が判明するにはまだまだ時間がかかるでしょう。この後もチャンネルはそのままで開票速報をご覧ください。

Useful Expressions ㊲　—このままそっくり暗記しよう！

1. The Red Sox lead the Yankees 5 to 3.（レッドソックスがヤンキーズを5対3でリードしています）
2. Our new flat screen TV is expected to do well in the next quarter.
　（わが社の新しい薄型テレビは次の四半期に健闘するものと期待されています）
3. It's a bit surprising that exports increased despite the rise in yen.
　（円高にもかかわらず輸出が増えたのはやや意外です）

CDで発音の確認とリピート練習ができます。

練38 Enterprise Zone Program

Short Talk ⑱

The purpose of the Illinois State Enterprise Zone Program is to attract your businesses to the areas of the state that can get the most benefit from new economic activity. Naturally, I'm talking about economically depressed areas. At present, there are 95 such zones in the state of Illinois. In order to attract new businesses to these zones, the state offers you a number of tax incentives. These incentives include an exemption on the tax paid on building materials and a tax credit for each economically disadvantaged employee you hire. I'll explain exactly what we mean by "economically disadvantaged" a little later. In order to qualify for the exemptions, you have to make an application to us at the state Department of Commerce. The entire state government will make every effort to simplify your application process, since the Enterprise Zone Program is one of our highest priorities.

耳練-38

Comprehension Questions

1. What is the purpose of the talk?
2. What does the speaker promise to do soon?
3. Who is the audience for this talk?

耳練チェックマトリックス 自分のリスニング力を判定しよう！

聴き取りCheck Step	Situation（状況理解）	Vocabulary（語彙）	Expression（表現）	Pronunciation（発音）
1st Try				
2nd Try				
3rd Try				

【自己判定マーク】
◎パーフェクトに理解　○ほぼ理解　△半分ほど理解　×ほとんどわからない

［注］すべて◎になるまでトライしてみよう！

＊本マトリックス活用法については7ページを参照。

耳練ヒント

Situation Markers　状況・場面を把握しよう！

- The purpose of the Illinois State Enterprise Zone Program is to attract your businesses
  ⇒イリノイ州政府関係者が話をしている
- the state offers you a number of tax incentives
  ⇒税制上の優遇措置がある
- make an application to us at the state Department of Commerce
  ⇒州の商務省の人が話をしている

耳練-38 Enterprise Zone Program

耳練ポイント

Vocabulary －単語の意味を確認しよう！

- □enterprise zone／企業誘致地域、企画事業地域
- □attract／誘致する
- □benefit／恩恵
- □economic activity／経済活動
- □naturally／当然
- □economically depressed area／経済的に落ちこんでいる地域
- □at present／目下のところ
- □tax incentives／税制上の優遇措置
- □qualify for ～／～の資格を得る
- □exemption／免税、課税控除
- □building materials／建材
- □tax credit／税額減免、税額控除、税還付
- □economically disadvantaged／経済的に恵まれない
- □Department of Commerce／商務省
- □simplify／簡素化する
- □application process／応募手続き
- □priorities／優先物

Key Expressions －重要フレーズを聴き取ろう！

01 The purpose of … is to ～ 「…の目的は～することです」
02 attract your businesses to the areas of state ～ 「～のような州の地域に皆さんの企業を誘致する」 attract ～ to… 「～を…に引きつける」
02 that can get the most benefit from new economic activity 「新しい経済活動から最も恩恵を受けるであろう」 new economic activity は企業の誘致をさす
05 In order to attract new businesses to these zones 「これらの地域に新たな企業を誘致するために」 In order to ～ 「～するために（は）」 ⇒ Useful Expressions
06 the state offers you a number of tax incentives 「州は皆さんにいくつかの税制上の優遇措置を提供する」
08 exemption on the tax paid on building materials 「建材に支払った税金の減免」 前置詞 on の用法に注意
09 economically disadvantaged employee 「経済的に恵まれない従業員」 ～ ly disadvantaged で「～の点で恵まれていない」 Cf. physically disadvantaged （身体的に障害がある）
10 what we mean by ～ 「～がどういうことか」 ⇒ Useful Expressions
12 make an application to ～ = apply to ～ 「～に応募する、～に応募書類を提出する」
14 make every effort to ～ 「～をするためにあらゆる努力をする」 ⇒ Useful Expressions
15 one of our highest priorities 「われわれの最優先事項の一つです」

Pronunciation　−聴き取りポイントに注意しよう！

03　I'm‿talking‿about economically depressed‿areas. の連音
04　At‿present, there are 95 such zones‿in the state‿of‿Illinois の子音連続と連音
06　offers‿you a number‿of tax‿incentives の連音
08　tax‿credit の語にまたがる複雑な子音連続
15　highest‿priorities の語にまたがる複雑な子音連続

日本語訳　−英文の内容を確認しよう！

企業誘致地域プログラム

イリノイ州企業誘致地域プログラムの目的は、皆様のような事業所を新たな経済活動の恩恵を最も受けるであろう地域に誘致することです。当然のことながら、そのような地域というのは経済的に落ち込んでいる地域です。現在、イリノイ州にはそのような地域が95か所あります。これらの地域に新しい企業を誘致するために、州としては皆様に数々の税制上の優遇措置を用意しています。その中には建築資材に対する課税の免除や、皆様が経済的に恵まれない人たちを従業員として雇用した場合、その人数に比例した税額控除などがあります。「経済的に恵まれない」ということについては、もう少し後で詳しくご説明いたします。免税を受けるためには州の商務省に申請をしなければなりません。企業誘致地域プログラムはわれわれの最優先課題の一つですから、州政府全体で申請手続きの簡素化に全力をあげるつもりです。

Useful Expressions　−このままそっくり暗記しよう！

1. In order to apply for the job, you have to be an experienced system engineer.（その仕事に応募するためには、経験のあるシステムエンジニアである必要があります）
2. My boss didn't tell me exactly what he meant by "major shake-up."
（「大人事異動」が一体何であるのか上司ははっきり教えてくれなかった）
3. We make every effort to keep our customers satisfied.
（当社はお客様に満足いただくためにあらゆる努力を行います）

CDで発音の確認とリピート練習ができます。

39 Conflict Resolution

Short Talk ⑲   オーストラリア

Thank you, Ms. Jenkins, for that very kind introduction. It's an honor to be invited to Simmons Corporation to talk to you executives about the art of conflict resolution. Since the publication of my second best-selling book, "The Corporate Jungle," I've been asked to speak at over a hundred corporations, as well as a few dozen colleges and universities, and even in the locker rooms of some professional sports teams. In the highly competitive world that we live in today, it is difficult for any organization to survive. Even if all of a company's resources are used for maximizing that company's potential, survival is still a difficult struggle. And yet, we see that inside most companies, so much energy is wasted on internal struggles. You know what I'm talking about: petty competitions among managers, jealousy, and envy. I'm here today to help you to transfer all that negative energy into more positive channels by learning how to work together for the good of the company as a whole.

耳練-39

Comprehension Questions

1. Who is the speaker?
2. Who is the audience for this speech?
3. What does the speaker hope to teach the audience?

耳練チェックマトリックス 自分のリスニング力を判定しよう！

聴き取りCheck / Step	Situation（状況理解）	Vocabulary（語彙）	Expression（表現）	Pronunciation（発音）
1st Try				
2nd Try				
3rd Try				

【自己判定マーク】
◎パーフェクトに理解　○ほぼ理解　△半分ほど理解　×ほとんどわからない

［注］すべて◎になるまでトライしてみよう！

＊本マトリックス活用法については7ページを参照。

耳練ヒント

Situation Markers 状況・場面を把握しよう！

- Thank you, Ms. Jenkins, for that very kind introduction.
  ⇒紹介されて、これから講演が始まる
- It's an honor to be invited to Simmons Corporation to talk to you executives about the art of conflict resolution.
  ⇒シモンズ・コーポレーションズという会社で講演をしている
- Since the publication of my second best-selling book, "The Corporate Jungle,"
  ⇒"The Corporate Jungle"という本の著者である

耳練-39 Conflict Resolution

耳練ポイント

Vocabulary ―単語の意味を確認しよう！

- ☐ introduction／紹介
- ☐ executive／役員、管理職
- ☐ art／方法、技術
- ☐ conflict resolution／対立解消、紛争解決
- ☐ publication／出版
- ☐ best-selling book／ベストセラー
- ☐ ～ as well as…／～も…も、…に加えて～も
- ☐ a few dozen／数十（の）
- ☐ organization／組織
- ☐ survive／生き残る
- ☐ Even if ～／たとえ～であっても
- ☐ resources／資源（ここでは人的資源 human resources のこと）
- ☐ maximize／最大限にする
- ☐ potential／潜在能力、可能性
- ☐ survival／生き残り
- ☐ struggle／奮闘
- ☐ internal struggle／内部抗争
- ☐ petty／つまらない、けちな
- ☐ jealousy／嫉妬
- ☐ envy／ねたみ
- ☐ transfer／転換する、方向を変える
- ☐ channel／道筋、方向
- ☐ for the good of ～／～の（利益の）ために
- ☐ as a whole／全体として

Key Expressions ―重要フレーズを聴き取ろう！

01 **Thank you, Ms. Jenkins, for that very kind introduction.**「ジェンキンズさん、身にあまるご紹介ありがとうございました」紹介されたあとの講演の最初に言う常套表現。kind は「事実以上に好意的な」という意味

01 **It's an honor to be invited to talk to ～ about …**「～に…についてお話するようご招待いただいたのは名誉なことです」これも講演の出だしの常套表現 ⇒ Useful Expressions

02 **you executives**「役員の皆さん」

03 **the art of conflict resolution**「対立解消法」art はこのように「方法」の意味がある。Cf. the art of cooking（料理［法］）

04 **The Corporate Jungle**「企業ジャングル」企業の中も生存競争が激しいジャングルであるという意味が込められている

05 **over a hundred corporations**「100社以上の企業」

08 **In the highly competitive world that we live in**「私たちが住む、きわめて競争的な世界では」関係代名詞 that は in の目的語

09 **it is difficult for ～ to …**「～が／にとって…することは難しい」⇒ Useful Expressions

11 **we see that ～**「～という状況が見受けられる」

12 **so much energy is wasted on ～**「多くのエネルギーが～に浪費されている」
⇒ Useful Expressions

13 **You know what I'm talking about**「私の言っていることがおわかりになるでしょう」相手に理解の確認を求める定型表現

15 **help you to ～**「皆さんが～するのを手伝う」直接的に手伝う場合は help you ～となり、to を使わない。to を用いると「～できるように手伝う」という意味合いになる

Pronunciation　―聴き取りポイントに注意しよう！

01　It's‿an‿honor to be invited‿to Simmons Corporation の連音。また invited の t がラ行の音になることに注意
03　art‿of conflict‿resolution の連音と、語にまたがる複雑な子音連続
05　I've been‿asked‿to speak‿at‿over‿a hundred corporations の連音と子音連続
09　Even‿if‿all‿of‿a company's resources の連音
11　difficult‿struggle の語にまたがる複雑な子音連続

日本語訳　―英文の内容を確認しよう！

対立解消

大変結構なご紹介にあずかりありがとうございます。対立解消の方法について重役の皆様方に話をするために、シモンズ社にお招きいただき光栄です。私にとって2冊目のベストセラーとなった『企業ジャングル』の出版以来、100社以上の企業、また数十校の大学、そしてプロスポーツチームの選手控え室でも講演することを依頼されています。今日私たちが生きる競争の厳しい世界では、いかなる組織にとっても生き延びるのは大変なことです。ある企業が自社の潜在的な力を最大化するためにすべての資源を使ったとしても、生き延びることは依然として必死の努力が必要です。それにもかかわらず、ほとんどの企業の内部では、非常に多くのエネルギーが内部抗争のために浪費されています。私の言っていることがおわかりになりますね。課長同士のつまらない競争や嫉妬や羨望などです。皆様が会社全体のために力を合わせる方法を学び、そのネガティブなエネルギーすべてをもっとポジティブな方向に転換するお手伝いをするために、私は今日ここにいるのです。

Useful Expressions ―このままそっくり暗記しよう！

1. It's an honor to be invited to Sunburst Coffee to talk about tea production around the world.（サンバースト・コーヒーに招かれて、世界のお茶の生産についてお話するのは名誉なことです）
2. In the field of flat screen TVs it is difficult for any company just to survive.（薄型テレビの分野では、どの会社も生き残るだけでも難しい）
3. We should not waste our energy on such trivial things.
   （われわれはそのような些末なことにエネルギーを浪費すべきではない）

CDで発音の確認とリピート練習ができます。

40 Clean Electricity

Short Talk ⑳

オーストラリア

Thanks for inviting us here today to talk to you about Blue Sky Energy Company. As you may know, our company is the largest retail provider of so-called "clean" electricity in the United States. We've been chosen by nearly 600,000 consumers and businesses throughout the country as their energy provider. Now, one of the first questions that always comes up is, "Will our electricity supply be stopped when we switch from our current electricity provider to Blue Sky Energy?" The answer to that is "No." Your business will continue to get its electricity without interruption. The only thing that changes is the way that your electricity is generated. And Blue Sky's electricity is always less polluting than the typical power system, because it's generated from cleaner sources. Moreover, depending on the product you choose, you may actually save money on your power bill. How is all this possible, you ask? I'm going to turn things over to my colleague, John Barnes, who will get into the details.

Comprehension Questions

1. What does the speaker's company provide?
2. What do some of the customers of the speaker's company worry about?
3. What will the speaker do next?

耳練チェックマトリックス 自分のリスニング力を判定しよう！

聴き取りCheck Step	Situation（状況理解）	Vocabulary（語彙）	Expression（表現）	Pronunciation（発音）
1st Try				
2nd Try				
3rd Try				

【自己判定マーク】
◎パーフェクトに理解　○ほぼ理解　△半分ほど理解　×ほとんどわからない
［注］すべて◎になるまでトライしてみよう！
＊本マトリックス活用法については7ページを参照。

耳練ヒント

Situation Markers 状況・場面を把握しよう！

- Thanks for inviting us here today to talk to you about Blue Sky Energy Company.
  ⇒Blue Sky Energy Companyから複数の人間が説明に来ている

- As you may know, our company is the largest retail provider of so-called "clean" electricity in the United States.
  ⇒電力会社の人間である

- I'm going to turn things over to my colleague, John Barnes, who will get into the details.
  ⇒ここで同僚に交代する

耳練-40 Clean Electricity

耳練ポイント

Vocabulary —単語の意味を確認しよう！

- retail／小売（Cf. wholesale「卸売り」）
- provider／提供企業（retail provider「小売業者」）
- so-called／いわゆる
- consumers and businesses／一般家庭と事業所
- energy provider／エネルギー供給企業（源）
- come up／出てくる、聞かれる
- supply／供給
- switch／代わる、転換する（switch from 〜 to…「〜から…に乗り換える」）
- current／現在の
- interruption／中断
- generate／発電する
- polluting／汚染源となる
- typical／典型的な、従来の
- cleaner sources／よりクリーンなエネルギー源
- moreover／さらに、その上に
- depending on 〜／〜により、〜次第で
- bill／請求書（power bill「電気料金」）
- colleague／同僚
- details／詳細（get into the details「詳細を説明する」）

Key Expressions —重要フレーズを聴き取ろう！

01 **Thanks for inviting us here**「私たちをお招きいただきありがとうございました」説明をするために呼ばれて話をするときの冒頭の定型表現 ⇒ Useful Expressions

03 **"clean" electricity**「クリーンな電気」発電の際に、他より排出する汚染物質が少ない電気の意味

05 **throughout the country**「国中で」前の largest にかかる

06 **one of the first questions that always comes up**「最初に聞かれる質問の一つ」that の先行詞は one of the first questions であり、そのために comes と単数になっている。現代英語では the first questions を先行詞とするよりこの方が一般的

09 **Your business**「御社」

10 **without interruption**「引き続いて、途切れることなく」

10 **The only thing that changes is 〜**「変わるのは〜だけだ」⇒ Useful Expressions

11 **the way that your electricity is generated**「御社の電気が発電される方法」

13 **typical power system**「典型的発電システム、通常の発電」

14 **product you choose**「お選びになる電力の種類」

15 **save money on 〜**「〜のお金を節約する」⇒ Useful Expressions

15 **How is all this possible, you ask?**「どうしてそんなことが可能かとお尋ねですか？」相手の思っている疑問を先取りして話を展開する方法

16 **turn things over to 〜**「（仕事、責任などを）〜に委譲する」⇒ Useful Expressions

Pronunciation －聴き取りポイントに注意しよう！

01 **Thanks␣for** の語をまたぐ子音連続
03 **largest␣retail␣provider** の語をまたぐ子音連続
04 **We've␣been** のまぎらわしい子音連続
10 **get␣its␣electricity without␣interruption** の連音と音変化

日本語訳 －英文の内容を確認しよう！

クリーンな電気

今日は私どもブルースカイ・エネルギー社について話す機会をいただきありがとうございます。ご存知の方もいらっしゃるかも知れませんが、当社は米国におけるいわゆる「クリーン」エネルギーの最大の小売業者で、全米60万の家庭や事業所からエネルギー会社として選ばれています。さて、常に一番最初に出てくる疑問の一つは「電気を今の電力会社からブルースカイ・エネルギーに替えたら電力供給は止まってしまうのか？」ということですが、答えは「ノー」です。御社への電力供給は中断することなく続きます。変わるのは発電方法だけですが、ブルースカイの電気は従来の発電方法に比べよりクリーンなエネルギー源を使っているため、従来よりも常に汚染が少ないのです。さらに、お使いいただく製品によっては電気料金が節約できるものもあります。どうしてそんなことができるのかと思われることでしょう。ここで、同僚のジョン・バーンズにバトンタッチしたいと思います。彼が詳細をご説明します。

Useful Expressions －このままそっくり暗記しよう！

1. Thanks for inviting us to your managers' conference.
   （管理職会議に私どもを招待いただきありがとうございます）
2. The only thing that changes is the way you make your payment.
   （唯一変わるのは支払いの方法です）
3. We can save money on office paper.（会社で使う紙のお金を節約できる）
4. I'm going to turn things over to our next speaker.
   （では次の講演者にバトンタッチします）

CDで発音の確認とリピート練習ができます。

英語
徹底耳練

耳練41−50 [一般長文編]

41 Workplace Burnout

Long Passage ❶

   Susan is an emergency room doctor. After five years at her hospital, she still feels that the other doctors don't keep her in the loop for important decisions. She believes she is not consulted on important decisions regarding patients, and feels left out of the cheerful banter among the other ER doctors and nurses. As a result, she feels tired at the end of the day — not just physically tired, but tired of her job itself, as if she no longer cares about the valuable work she is doing.

   How might we define this type of problem? Workers like Susan are not merely stressed out: they are *burned* out. Burnout is a chronic problem in all kinds of workplaces. Workers who are burned out aren't just feeling blue or having a bad day. These are workers who constantly feel overwhelmed and tend to suffer from doubt or anxiety.

   Burnout reflects an uneasy relationship between people and their work. And just like when two people — say, a married couple — don't get along well, the blame usually can't be pinned entirely on one side or the other.

   So, how can a valuable but burned-out worker like Susan be helped? Susan realized she had to help herself. First, she sat down and tried to figure out the causes of her burnout. She identified the main cause as a sense of isolation, of not being included in the group. Once she had identified the problem, she began to deal with it. By speaking privately with other doctors and letting them know how isolated she felt, she was gradually able to get more involved with the group. In fact, her colleagues may have appreciated the fact that she brought up the issue of isolation directly with them, instead of making a formal complaint to higher-ups in the organization.

   Susan's case had a happy ending, but most burned-out workers are unable to work out solutions to their own problems. Ultimately, the burden for decreasing workplace burnout must fall upon the employers. It is impossible to expect burned-out workers to work

耳練-41 Workplace Burnout

things out on their own. It is all such workers can do to cope with their day-to-day anxieties — a classic case of "can't see the forest for the trees."

Fortunately, more and more companies are recognizing the value of helping workers cope with workplace burnout. Many have adopted in-house programs to improve job satisfaction.

日本語訳 －英文の内容を確認しよう！

仕事で燃え尽き症候群

スーザンは救急担当(ER)医師だ。この病院に来て5年になるにもかかわらず、今もほかの医師たちは自分を重要な決定の輪に入れてくれないと彼女は感じている。彼女は患者に関する重要な決定について相談されないと思い、ほかのERの医師や看護師たちの楽しい冗談の言い合いから仲間外れにされていると感じている。その結果、彼女は一日が終わると疲れを感じる。それは肉体的に疲れているだけでなく、まるで彼女の価値のある仕事についてもうどうでもいいと思っているかのように、仕事そのものにうんざりするのだ。

こういうタイプの問題はどう定義すればよいのだろうか？ スーザンのような人たちはただストレスで参っているだけでなく、彼らは燃え尽きているのだ。燃え尽きはどのような職場にもある慢性的な問題だ。職場で燃え尽きた人たちは落ち込んだり、気分がすぐれないだけではない。彼らは常に仕事に圧倒されていると感じ、不安や心配に苦しむ傾向がある。

燃え尽きは人と仕事の不安定な関係を反映している。そして、2人の人間、たとえば夫婦がうまくいかないときとまったく同じように、責任はどちらか一方だけにあるとはたいてい言えない。

それでは、スーザンのように大事な仕事を担いながらも燃え尽きてしまった人を救うにはどうすればいいのだろうか？ スーザンは自分で立ち直るしかないことに気がついた。まず、彼女は座って、自分が燃え尽きた原因を突き止めようとした。彼女は、主因は仲間に入れられていないという孤独感にあることを突き止めた。一度問題がわかると、彼女はそれに対処し始めた。他の医師たちと個人的に話をし、自分がどれほど孤独を感じていたかを彼らに知らせることで、彼女は徐々に仲間と関われるようになった。実際、彼女の同僚たちは、彼女が孤立の問題を組織の上層部に正式に苦情の申し立てをせず、直接自分たちにぶつけてくれたことを喜んだだろう。

スーザンの場合はハッピーエンドになったが、職場で燃え尽きた人のほとんどは自分自身の問題の解決策を見つけ出すことができない。結局のところ、職場での燃え尽きを減らす責任は雇用主が担うことになる。燃え尽きた人たちに、自分でものごとを解決することを期待するのは不可能だ。燃え尽きた人たちは「木を見て森を見ることができない」典型的なケースで、その日その日の不安に対処するのが精一杯だ。

幸いにも、労働者が職場での燃え尽きに対処できるよう、手助けすることの価値を認識する企業が増えている。多くが仕事の満足感を改善する社内のプログラムを採用している。

耳練ポイント

Vocabulary & Key Expressions　—重要語句とフレーズを聴き取ろう！

- 01 **emergency room** = ER「救急室、緊急治療室」
- 02 **don't keep her in the loop for important decisions**「重要な決定に関して彼女を蚊帳の外におく」この場合 the loop とは組織などの権力の中枢のこと
- 03 **is not consulted on ～**「～について相談されない」
- 04 **important decisions regarding ～**「～についての重要な決定」
- 04 **left ～ out of …**「～を…からのけ者にする、…の仲間に入れない」
- 05 **banter**「冗談の言い合い、気さくな冗談」　05 **As a result**「その結果」
- 06 **tired**「疲れた、うんざりした」この場合は両方の意味を兼ねている
- 06 **not just physically tired, but tired of her job itself**「単に肉体的に疲れているだけでなく、自分の仕事そのものにうんざりしている」not jut ～ but …の構文　07 **as if**「あたかも」
- 07 **no longer～**「もはや～でない」　07 **cares about ～**「～を気にする、～を大事に思う」
- 07 **valuable**「大事な」　09 **How might we define this type of problem?**「このような問題を（もし定義するとすれば）何と定義すればいいでしょうか？」　10 **not merely ～** = not only / just ～「単に～でない」
- 10 **stressed out**「ストレスで参っている」　10 **burnout**「燃え尽き（状態）」burnout syndrome「燃え尽き症候群」ともいう　10 **chronic problem**「慢性的な問題」Cf. acute（急性の）
- 12 **having a bad day**「気分がすぐれない、（その日の）調子が悪い」　13 **constantly**「絶えず」
- 13 **feel overwhelmed**「圧倒される思いがする」　13 **tend to ～**「～する傾向がある」
- 13 **suffer from doubt or anxiety**「不安や心配に苦しむ」
- 14 **uneasy**「ぎこちない、不安定な、ぎくしゃくした」　15 **just like when ～**「ちょうど～のときのように」
- 16 **get along**（well）「うまくいく」
- 16 **the blame can't be pinned entirely on one side or the other**「どちらか一方に全面的に責任があるとは言えない」pin ～ on … 口語で「～を…のせいにする」
- 19 **help herself**「自分で解決する」　20 **figure out**「（考えて）解明する」
- 20 **identified ～ as …**「～を…であると判定する／断定する」　21 **sense of isolation**「孤立感」
- 21 **of not being included in the group**「グループの仲間に加えてもらっていない（という感覚）」
- 22 **Once ～**「一旦～すると」　22 **identified** ここでの意味は「発見する、見つける、わかる」
- 22 **deal with ～**「～に対処する」　23 **privately**「個人的に」
- 23 **how isolated she felt**「（自分が）どれほどの孤立感を感じているか」know の目的語
- 24 **gradually**「徐々に」　24 **get more involved with ～**「～により深く関わる」
- 25 **may have ～**「～したかもしれない」推測を表す
- 25 **appreciated**「（積極的に）評価する、感謝する」
- 27 **higher-ups in the organization**「組織の上層部」higher-ups は通常複数で「上役、お偉方」
- 29 **work out solutions**「解決法を考え出す」　29 **Ultimately**「究極的には」
- 30 **burden for ～ing**「～のための負担、責任」　30 **fall upon ～**「～に落ち着く」
- 31 **work things out**「事態を打開する」　32 **on their own**「独力で」
- 32 **It is all such workers can do to cope with their day-to-day anxiety**「その日その日の不安に対処するのが、そのような労働者ができる精一杯のことである」it は to cope 以下をさす
- 33 **classic case of ～**「典型的な～の例」
- 33 **"can't see the forest for the trees"**「木のために森が見えない（木を見て森を見ず）」個々の事柄にとらわれて全体が把握できないたとえ
- 36 **helping workers cope with workplace burnout**「労働者が職場での燃え尽きに対処する助けをする」
- 36 **adopted**「採用する」　37 **job satisfaction**「仕事の充実感」

Compulsive Hoarding

Long Passage ❷

　Recently there have been a number of Japanese TV programs featuring people who live in what are called "garbage mansions." These people fill their homes with old newspapers, junk mail, old clothes, furniture, and various other useless things, posing public health problems and fire hazards. Their neighbors complain, but they do not listen to such complaints and claim that what they have collected is not trash.

　Such behavior is called compulsive hoarding, and is known to exist widely. Compulsive hoarders are jokingly referred to as "pack rats," and they are regarded as eccentrics. There are similar TV shows in the U.S. such as *Clean Sweep* and *How Clean Is Your House*. Such TV shows are popular perhaps because people can laugh at the strange behavior of compulsory hoarders and maybe even enjoy a sense of superiority: "I'm messy too, but not that messy."

　However, compulsive hoarding is not a laughing matter. Many psychologists consider compulsive hoarding to be a type of Obsessive Compulsive Disorder (OCD) and to be driven by the individual's need to manage the sense of anxiety raised by obsessive doubts. These people cannot help having "what if" worries. For instance, they cannot throw away old newspapers and books because they worry, "What if I need to know something and don't have the information?"

　The hoarding habit can even become dangerous. In 2003 a New York City man named Patrice Moore became trapped in his own apartment after his collection of magazines, newspapers, and books collapsed on top of him. Apart from a small bed, his room, only three meters by three meters, was completely filled with the publications, which he had been hoarding for more than a decade. The materials fell upon Moore in such a way that he was buried in a standing position. For two days he called for help until a neighbor happened to hear him. In addition to his neighbors, firefighters, the police, health

耳練-42))) Compulsive Hoarding

workers and officials from the city's emergency management authority were involved in the rescue operation, which took over three hours.

People like Moore share many traits. They are indecisive — unable to make decisions about what to throw away and what to keep. They are perfectionists and thus want to do things perfectly, which is impossible, so they instead procrastinate and avoid making decisions. In any case, getting angry about them or making fun of them does not solve the problem. These people need professional as well as community help.

日本語訳 —英文の内容を確認しよう！

ものを捨てられない人たち

最近日本のテレビでは「ごみ屋敷」と呼ばれる家に住む人たちを取り上げた番組がたくさんある。彼らは新聞やダイレクトメール、古着、家具をはじめとするさまざまな無用のものを家中にため込んで、公衆衛生や防火上の問題を引き起こしている。近隣の住民が苦情を言うが、彼らは聞く耳を持たず、自分が集めているものはごみではないと主張する。

こういう行為は蓄積癖と呼ばれ、広く存在することが知られている。蓄積癖のある人は冗談めかして「モリネズミ」と呼ばれ、変わり者として笑いの種になっている。アメリカにも *Clean Sweep* や *How Clean Is Your House* といった同様のテレビ番組がある。こういうテレビ番組に人気があるのは、蓄積癖のある人たちの奇妙な行動を笑い、「私もだらしがないけれど、あれほどじゃない」と優越感さえ覚えることができるからかもしれない。

しかし、蓄積癖は笑いごとではすまない。多くの精神科医が蓄積癖は強迫性障害（OCD）の一つだとみなしており、疑い深さからくる不安感をコントロールする必要からおこるものと考えている。これらの人々は「もし…」という不安から逃れられないのだ。たとえば、彼らは「もし何かについて知る必要があって、その情報が（手元に）なかったらどうしよう」と不安なため新聞や本を捨てられないのだ。

蓄積癖は危険になることさえある。2003年に、ニューヨーク市に住むパトリス・ムーアという男性は、自宅で自分が集めた雑誌や新聞や本の山が崩れ、その下敷きになって身動きできなくなった。幅3メートル、奥行き3メートルしかない彼の部屋は、ベッドを除けば、彼が過去10年以上の間にため込んだ出版物で完全に埋まっていた。これらが崩れ落ちた時、彼は立ったままその中に埋もれてしまった。近所の人がたまたま彼の声を聞きつけるまで、2日間にわたり彼は助けを求めて叫び続けた。3時間以上かかった彼の救出には、近所の人のほかに消防士、警察官、保健所の人、そして市の緊急事態に対応する部署の人たちも加わった。

ムーア氏のような人たちには多くの性格上の共通点がある。優柔不断で、捨てるものと取っておくものを決めることができない。完璧主義者であるため、ものごとを完璧にやりたいと思っているが、それはだれもできないことなので、彼らはぐずぐずと引き延ばし、決断することを避ける。いずれにしろ、彼らのことを怒ったり、笑い物にしても問題の解決にはならない。彼らには地域の支援だけでなく専門家の助けも必要なのだ。

耳練 42 おわり

🔊 耳練ポイント

Vocabulary & Key Expressions　−重要語句とフレーズを聴き取ろう!

01 a number of 〜「いくつかの〜」多数を表す場合と、複数あることだけを表す場合とある
02 featuring「特集する」　03 junk mail「ダイレクトメール」　04 posing「(危険、問題)を引き起こす」
04 public health problems and fire hazards「公衆衛生上の問題や火災の危険」
05 Their neighbors「そのような人たちの隣人たち」　05 complain「苦情を言う」
06 listen to 〜「〜に耳を貸す」　07 trash「ごみ、無用のもの」　08 behavior「行動」
08 compulsive hoarding「蓄積癖」compulsive は「強迫観念に駆られた」という意味。hoardingは意味もないものを収集する行動　09 jokingly「冗談で、からかって」
09 are referred to as 〜「〜と呼ばれている」refer 〜 as … で「〜を…と呼ぶ」
09 pack rats「モリネズミ(ふくらんだ頬に物を入れて巣の中にためる習性がある)」
10 eccentrics「奇人、変人」形容詞としては「変わっている」
11 *Clean Sweep* 番組名「(いらないものの)一掃、総ざらい」
13 enjoy a sense of superiority「優越感にひたる」
14 "I'm messy too, but not that messy."「私も散らかし屋だけど、あれほどひどくはない」優越感の中身を表している　15 not a laughing matter「笑いごとではない」a laughing matter は日本語の「笑いごと」と同じように常に否定形で用いられて、ことの深刻さを強調する
15 psychologists「心理学者」　16 a type of「一種の」
16 Obsessive Compulsive Disorder (OCD)「強迫性障害」※
17 be driven by 〜「〜によって決定される、動かされる」　17 the individual's need to 〜「その人の〜することの必要性」　18 manage「対処する」　18 the sense of anxiety「不安、心配」
18 raised by 〜「〜に起因する」
18 obsessive doubts「脅迫的疑念」カギをかけたか心配になったり、手を洗ったのにきれいになっていないと思ったりする疑念
19 cannot help 〜ing「〜しないではいられない、どうしても〜してしまう」Cf. I could not help laughing.(笑わずにはいられなかった)
19 "what if" worries「もし〜ならどうしよう」という類の心配　19 For instance「たとえば」
21 What if I need to know something and don't have the information?「何か調べる必要があって、見つけることができなければどうしよう?」
24 became trapped「身動きができなくなった」　25 his collection of 〜「彼が集めた〜」
26 Apart from a small bed「小さなベッドを除いて」was completely filled … に続いていく
27 the publications「発行物」つまり本や雑誌のこと
28 which he had been hoarding for more than a decade「それを彼は過去10年以上にわたって集めていた」関係代名詞の連続用法　29 in such a way that 〜「〜のように」
30 he called for help「助けを呼んだ」　33 rescue operation「救出活動」
33 which took over three hours「そしてそれは3時間以上かかった」関係代名詞の連続用法
35 traits「(性格上の)特徴」　35 indecisive「優柔不断な」
36 make decisions about 〜「〜について決断する」
36 what to throw away and what to keep「何を捨て、何を取っておくか」
37 perfectionists「完璧主義者」　37 which is impossible「そしてだれもそんなことはできない」which は先行の do things perfectly をさす　38 procrastinate「(ぐずぐずと)引き延ばす」
39 In any case「いずれにせよ」　39 getting angry about them「彼らに腹をたてること」
39 making fun of them「彼らをあざ笑うこと」
40 professional as well as community help「専門家(心理学者や精神科医)の助力と地域の助力(理解)」

※http://www.ocd-net.jp/ 参照

43 Left-handedness

Long Passage ③

We all know that left-handed people are a minority. In fact, right-handers outnumber left-handers nine to one in all cultures. But perhaps most of us — we right-handers, that is — have never thought of left-handed people as victims of discrimination.

In fact, right-handers have looked askance at left-handers all through history. In ancient times, people believed that things that lay to their right represented luck and positive omens, while things on their left-hand side were unlucky. Thus, the Latin word for "on the left," *sinister*, has come to mean "ominous" or "evil" in modern English.

In more recent times, left-handers have been looked down on as inferior rather than evil. One prominent child psychologist in the 1930s said of lefties, "They are fumblers and bumblers at whatever they do." This perception of left-handers as clumsy and awkward no doubt stems from the fact that we live in a right-handers' world. Scissors, can openers, guitars, and golf clubs — you name it: all are designed for righties. Still, because left-handed kids were considered clumsy and inferior, many generations of parents and teachers sought to "cure" them of left-handedness by forcing them to favor their right hands. To this day, it is estimated that from 5 to 25 percent of the world's left-handers are unnaturally favoring their right hands.

We now know that left-handedness is a quite ordinary trait. The fact that it is often observed in the animal kingdom bears out the normality of this condition. Many cats favor the left paw over the right; many horses stomp more frequently with the left hoof than the right. Certain crabs motion mainly with the left claw, others with the right claw. The list is endless.

Why then, is it only among humans that we find an overwhelming dominance of the right hand? Some researchers have believed that human right-handedness was linked to another unique trait of humans, the use of language. However, experiments in recent years

耳練-43))) Left-handedness

have cast doubt on the connection between language and the dominance of right-handedness in humans. Simply put, we just don't know why most people are right-handed, but we do now know that there is nothing at all abnormal about being left-handed.

Thanks to these advances in our understanding, the practice of forcing left-handed children to use their right hands is gradually disappearing. We can now hope for a day when left-handers can live more comfortably in the predominantly right-handed world.

日本語訳 ―英文の内容を確認しよう!

左利き

　左利きの人は右利きの人よりも少ないことはみんな知っている。実際、すべての文化で右利きの人の数は左利きの人の数を9対1で上回っている。しかし、私たち、つまり右利き、の大半は左利きの人を差別の被害者と考えたことはないだろう。

　実際のところ、歴史を通じて右利きの人は左利きの人を白眼視してきた。古代では、人々は自分の右側にあるものは幸運と肯定的な前兆を表すのに対し、左側にあるものは不吉だとした。こうして、ラテン語で「左側に」を意味する sinister という言葉は現代英語では「不吉な」とか「邪悪な」を意味するようになった。

　もっと現代に近くなると、左利きの人たちは邪悪というよりもむしろ劣ったものとして見下されてきた。1930年代の著名な児童心理学者は左利きの人を「彼らは何をするにしても不器用でしくじる」と言っている。不器用でぎこちないという左利きに対するこの見方は、私たちが右利きの世界に住んでいるという事実からきていることは間違いない。はさみ、缶切り、ギター、ゴルフクラブなどありとあらゆるものが右利き用に作られている。それでも、左利きの子供は不器用で劣ると考えられていたので、親や教師は何世代にもわたって子供に右手を優先的に使うよう強制し、左利きを「治そう」としてきた。今日に至るまで、世界の左利きの5％から25％は矯正されて右利きになっていると推計されている。

　今や私たちは左利きはきわめて普通の習性だと知っている。動物の世界でもしばしば観察されるという事実は、左利きが正常であることを裏づけている。多くのネコは右前足よりも左前足をよく使う。馬の多くは右よりも左のひづめで足を踏み鳴らす。カニの中にはもっぱら右のはさみを動かす種類もいるが、左のはさみを動かす種類もいる。例は枚挙にいとまがない。

　それではなぜ人間だけに右利きが圧倒的に多いのだろうか。研究者の中には、人間の右利きはもう一つの人間だけに見られる特徴、すなわち、ことばの使用と関連があると考える人もいる。しかし、近年の実験は言語と人間に右利きが多いこととの間の関連に疑いを投げかけている。要するに、なぜ右利きが多いのかはわからないが、左利きであることは何も異常ではないことはわかっている。

　私たちの理解が進んだおかげで、左利きの子供に右手を使うよう強制する習慣は徐々に姿を消しつつある。これで、右利きが優勢な世界で、いつの日か左利きの人もより快適に暮らせる日が来ることが期待される。

耳練ポイント

Vocabulary & Key Expressions　－重要語句とフレーズを聴き取ろう！

01 left-handed「左利きの」　01 a minority「少数派」　01 right-handers「右利きの人」
02 outnumber left-handers nine to one
　「9対1の割で数において左利きの人を圧倒する」left-hander「左利きの人」
02 in all cultures「すべての文化において」どの文化的集団でもの意
03 most of us ── we right-handers, that is ──
　「私たちの大部分、つまり私たち右利きの人たち」と言い直している
03 have never thought of left-handed people as victims of discrimination
　「左利きの人たちを差別の被害者と考えたことがない」
05 look(ed) askance at ～「～を白眼視する、～を非難の目で見る、～に不信感を示す」
05 all through history「歴史を通じて、これまでずっと」　06 In ancient times「古代では」
06 things that lay to their right「自分の右側にあるもの」　07 positive omens「よい兆し」
09 ominous「不吉な」　10 look(ed) down on ～「～を軽蔑する、見下げる」反対は look up to ～
11 inferior「劣った」　11 rather than ～「～ではなく」
11 prominent child psychologist「著名な幼児心理学者」
12 lefties 米口語 = left-handers 反対は righty, righties
12 fumblers「不器用な人」Cf. fumble「不器用に扱う」
12 bumblers「へまをする人」Cf. bumble「よろめく、ぎこちなくやる」
12 at whatever they do「やることすべてに」
13 This perception of left-handers as ～「左利きの人を～のように見ること」
13 clumsy「不器用」　13 awkward「ぎこちない」　13 no doubt「おそらく」
14 stems from ～「～に端を発している」　15 can openers「缶切り」
15 you name it「そのほか何でも」「他に思いつくものの名前を挙げてごらんなさい」の意から
18 sought to ～「～しようとした」
18 cure ～ of …「～の…を治す」つまり「治療により～から…を取り除く」cure の引用符がふってあるのは、あたかも病気であるかのようにという意味
18 favor「優先する」　19 To this day「今日でも」　19 it is estimated that ～「～と推計されている」
20 are unnaturally favoring their right hands
　「不自然に右手を優先している」つまり「直されて右手を使っている」
23 animal kingdom「動物界」
23 bears out ～「（事実・結果などが人の言葉や仮説を）裏づける、実証する」
23 the normality of this condition「この状態（＝左利き）の正常さ」　24 left paw「左前足」
25 stomp
　「足を踏み鳴らす」馬は飼い主などが自分のところから去って行くのを呼び止めるときに、前足を踏みならす
25 hoof「ひづめ」　26 crabs「カニ」　26 motion with the left claw「左のはさみで呼ぶ仕草をする」
27 The list is endless.「このような例は枚挙にいとまがない」
28 overwhelming dominance of the right hand「右手を圧倒的に使うこと」
30 another unique trait of humans, the use of language
　「もう一つの人間独特の特徴、つまり言語の使用」同格
32 cast doubt on ～「～に疑問を投げかける」　33 Simply put「要するに」
36 Thanks to ～「～のおかげで」　36 practice「習慣、慣習」
39 the predominantly right-handed world「圧倒的に右利きの世界」

44 Why Not Go to the Movies?

Long Passage ❹

Most adult Americans have fond memories of going to movie theaters. Many can recall a nervous first date with a future spouse. Even more remember going to see a particularly thrilling film with a group of special friends. And in moments of boredom, practically everyone has gone to a theater alone, just to enjoy the companionship that comes with laughing or screaming or crying with a room full of strangers.

However, the custom of going out to the movies is rapidly dying out in the United States today. There are a variety of reasons for this trend.

The causes most commonly mentioned by people who have stopped going to movies concern the unpleasantness of the movie-going expe-rience. Obnoxious fellow patrons, including those who continuously talk to each other (or even to a faraway friend via cell phone) throughout the show, are the bane of serious film fans. Other critics blame theater owners for not keeping the theaters clean, or for not providing seats that allow patrons a clear view of the screen. Many older theaters still have gradually sloping floors, so that one's view of the screen may be blocked by a taller person.

Then, there are those who put the blame squarely on the filmmakers. Movies today are simply too long to sit through. In the 1930s and 1940s, the average film produced in Hollywood ran about ninety minutes. These days, the average is approaching the two-hour mark, and films that run over three hours are not uncommon. And that doesn't even count the twenty-odd minutes of previews and advertisements that moviegoers are subjected to before the main feature even begins.

Of course, the main villain in the slow death of the movie theater is technology. First, video cassette players spread to nearly all American households, and now DVD players have followed. With large-screen TVs and high-quality sound systems, many families are able to enjoy a first-rate movie-watching experience in their own homes.

耳練-44 ♪)) Why Not Go to the Movies?

　　It seems unlikely that movie theaters will ever die out completely. Indeed, many experts predict that they will make a comeback soon. But if this is to happen, theater owners have to take measures to ensure that theaters once again become places where people go to escape from the nuisances of daily life, not confront them. And filmmakers must do their bit by providing the kind of fast-paced, lively fare that was the rule in decades past.

日本語訳　－英文の内容を確認しよう！

映画に行こう

　アメリカ人成人のほとんどは映画館に行くという懐かしい思い出がある。将来の伴侶とのドキドキした初めてのデートを思い出す人も多い。特にスリル満点の映画を特別な友達の一団で見に行ったことを思い出す人はもっと多いだろう。また、退屈したときに、館内いっぱいの知らない人と一緒に笑ったり、叫んだり、泣いたりすることからくる連帯感を楽しむためだけに、一人で映画館に行ったことはほとんどだれにでもあるはずだ。

　しかし、今アメリカでは映画館に行く習慣が急速に衰退しつつある。この傾向にはさまざまな理由がある。

　映画を見に行かなくなった人たちが一番よく挙げる理由は映画に行って経験した不快さに関係している。映画の間中、絶え間なくおしゃべりをする人たち（携帯電話で遠く離れた友人と話す人さえいる）といった不快な観客は、まじめな映画ファン泣かせだ。ほかには、映画館の経営者が場内を清潔にしていないことや、スクリーンがよく見える座席を備えていないことなどを挙げる人もいる。古い映画館の多くは今も床の傾斜が緩く、背の高い人のために視界がブロックされる場合がある。

　また、責任は映画制作者にあると真っ向から言う人たちもいる。今の映画は最後まで見るには長すぎる。1930年代や40年代には、ハリウッドで作られる平均的な映画の上映時間はおよそ90分だった。現在、平均上映時間は2時間に近づきつつあり、3時間を越える作品も珍しくない。しかも、その中には、本編が始まる前に観客が見せられる20分あまりの予告編とコマーシャルの時間は入っていない。

　もちろん、映画館の衰退の元凶はテクノロジーだ。まず、ビデオデッキがほとんどすべてのアメリカの家庭に普及したこと、そして現在はDVDプレーヤーが普及している。大画面テレビと高品質サウンドシステムによって、多くの家庭では第一級の映画鑑賞体験を自宅で楽しむことができる。

　映画館が完全になくなってしまうことはなさそうだ。実際、多くの専門家はもうすぐ映画館が復活するだろうと予想している。しかし、そうなったら、映画館の経営者は人々が日常の生活のわずらわしさと向き合うのではなく、わずらわしさから「逃避する」ために行く場所に再び劇場がなるような対策をとらなければならない。また、映画制作者も、昔は鉄則だった速いペースの生き生きとした作品を提供して、少しでも協力しなければならない。

耳練ポイント

Vocabulary & Key Expressions　－重要語句とフレーズを聴き取ろう！

01 fond memories「懐かしい思い出」　02 a nervous first date「緊張した最初のデート」
02 a future spouse「未来の伴侶」
02 Even more（adult Americans）「さらに多くの人（＝大人のアメリカ人）」
04 in moments of boredom「退屈したときには」　05 companionship「交わり」
05 that comes with 〜「〜に伴う」
06 a room full of strangers「他人でいっぱいの部屋」映画館のこと
07 dying out「すたれる」　08 a variety of 〜「さまざまな〜」　08 trend「傾向」
09 The causes most commonly mentioned by people who have stopped going to movies
　「映画に行くのをやめてしまった人々が最も普通に挙げる理由」これが次の concern の主語
10 the unpleasantness of the movie-going experience「映画に行くという経験の不愉快さ」
11 Obnoxious「不快な、目／耳ざわりな」　11 fellow patrons「他の観客」patron は「常連」
11 including those（patrons）who continuously talk to each other
　「絶えず話をする人たちも含めて」
12 via cell phone「携帯電話で」　13 throughout the show「上映中ずっと」
13 bane「苦労の種」　13 Other critics「他の批判者」ほかに不平を持っている人たち
14 blame 〜 for … ing「…していることについて〜を責める」
15 allow patrons a clear view of the screen
　「観客にスクリーン全部を遮られることなく見えるようにする」
16 gradually sloping floors「緩やかな傾斜になっている床」
16 one's view of the screen「（一般的に）人のスクリーンの視界」
18 Then, there are those（critics）who 〜「〜する批判者もいる」
18 put the blame squarely on 〜「正面切って〜が悪いとする」
19 filmmakers「映画制作者、映画会社」
20 ran about ninety minutes「約90分の長さがあった」
21 These days「最近は」　21 the average「平均（上映時間）」
21 is approaching the two-hour mark「2時間の区切りに近づいている」
22 not uncommon「珍しくない」　23 twenty-odd minutes「20分あまり」
24 moviegoers are subjected to「映画愛好家がむりやり見せられる」
　subject 〜 to …「〜に…を受けさせる」
24 main feature「主要作品」その日上映の映画
26 main villain「一番の悪者」ここは比喩的に使っている
26 the slow death of the movie theater「映画館の緩慢な死」ゆっくりと映画館が衰退していくこと
30 first-rate movie-watching experience「一流の映画鑑賞経験」
32 It seems unlikely that 〜「〜ということはありそうもないように思われる」
33 they（= movie theaters）will make a comeback soon「映画館はじきにまた復活する」
34 if this is to happen「そうなるためには」
34 take measures to 〜「〜するよう対策を取る」
36 escape from the nuisances of daily life「日常生活での嫌なことから逃れる」
36 not confront them（= the nuisances of daily life）「それらに直面するのではなく」
37 do one's bit「分担を果たす」　37 fast-paced「早いテンポの」
38 lively fare「活発な作品」　38 the rule「きまり、通例」　38 in decades past「過去何十年かの間」

183

45 Is Curry Addictive?

Long Passage ⑤

When we describe someone as an "addict," we are making a serious accusation. The word implies that the person has an uncontrollable desire to consume some sort of drug, be it an illegal one such as cocaine or amphetamines, or a legal one such as alcohol or nicotine.

In recent years, a debate has raged in Britain on the question of the power of curry to cause addiction. It began when researchers at a British university concluded that the spices in curry are addictive. They found that eating a spicy curry causes the same kinds of reactions in the body, such as increases in the heart rate and blood pressure, that are caused by addictive drugs.

Even more interesting, the researchers found that curry-eaters build up a "tolerance" to spices remarkably similar to the tolerance for, say, alcohol that a budding alcoholic might experience. As a person develops a dependency on alcohol, he requires more and stronger drinks in order to reach a feeling of satisfaction. Likewise, curry addicts constantly seek hotter and spicier curries in order to feel satisfied.

Other scientists, however, are not convinced. The skeptics say that we must be careful to draw a distinction between a mere craving and a true addiction. One study revealed that the bodily reactions mentioned earlier — the increase in the heart rate and blood pressure — can be triggered simply by asking curry eaters to think about a spicy curry. This seems to indicate that the desire for spicy curry is purely in the mind: a craving, and not a physical addiction like addictions to nicotine or heroin. This is not to say that the craving is not terrifically strong. Researchers admit that the craving for curry falls into the category of seeking a "natural high." In this same category are the urges to shop, to gamble, or to play computer games constantly — all of which have become serious social problems.

But why curry, of all foods? Because curry contains a variety of tastes, it activates more areas of the tongue than most other foods —

耳練-45))) Is Curry Addictive?

especially in Britain, where staple foods are famously bland. Simply put, curry dazzles the tongue into a state of confusion, causing the diner to seek greater and greater thrills.

In the final analysis, British nutritional experts say that there is no need to fear curries. From a nutritional standpoint, experts warn consumers only to avoid curries with rich, creamy sauces. Stick with the less fattening sauces, they say, and it is perfectly all right to enjoy a good curry now and then.

日本語訳 ー英文の内容を確認しよう！

カレーは中毒性があるか？

　だれかについて「中毒だ」ということは、重大な非難をしていることだ。中毒という言葉は、コカインやアンフェタミン（覚せい剤）のような違法なものであれ、アルコールやニコチンのように合法的なものであれ、何らかの薬物を使いたいという抑えられない欲望があることを示唆している。

　近年、イギリスでカレーに中毒性があるかどうかという議論が盛んだ。この議論はイギリスのある大学の研究者たちが、カレーに入っているスパイスには中毒性があると結論づけたことから始まった。彼らはスパイスのきいたカレーを食べると、中毒性のある薬物によって引き起こされるのと同じような反応、たとえば心拍数や血圧の増加を身体に引き起こすことを突き止めた。

　もっと興味深いのは、カレーを食べる人たちは、たとえばアルコール中毒になりかかっている人が経験することもあるアルコールに対する「許容度」と驚くほど似た、スパイスに対する「許容度」を増していくことを、研究者たちは発見した。ある人がアルコールに依存するようになると、その人は満足感に到達するためにより多くのより強い酒が必要になる。同じように、カレー中毒の人は満足感を得るために常により辛くスパイスのきいたカレーを求める。

　しかし、これを疑う科学者もいる。そういう懐疑的な科学者たちは単なる渇望と本当の中毒を慎重に区別しなければならないと言う。ある研究は、前に言及した心拍数や血圧の上昇といった身体的な反応は、カレーを食べる人たちにスパイスのきいたカレーを想像するようにと言っただけで引き起こされることを明らかにしている。これは、スパイスのきいたカレーを食べたいという欲求は純粋に頭の中のことで、ニコチンやヘロインの場合のように肉体的な中毒ではないということを示唆しているようだ。ただしこのことは、渇望が非常に強いわけではないことは意味しない。研究者たちは、カレーを食べたいというのは「自然な高揚感」を求める部類に入ると認めている。この同じ部類には、買い物やギャンブルの衝動や、ずっとコンピュータゲームをしていたいという衝動など、すべて深刻な社会問題になっているものが含まれている。

　しかし、あらゆる食べ物の中でなぜカレーなのか？　なぜなら、カレーにはさまざまな味が含まれていて、特によく知られているように主な食べ物に味がないイギリスでは、ほかのほとんどの食べ物よりも舌の広い部分を活性化するからだ。要するにカレーは舌を驚かせて混乱状態に陥らせ、食べる人により大きなスリルを求めさせるのだ。

　最後に、イギリスの栄養学の専門家はカレーを恐れる必要はないと言っている。栄養の観点から、専門家はリッチでクリーミーなカレーを食べないようにと消費者に警告している。あまり太らないソースという点を守れば、おいしいカレーをときどき食べるのはまったく問題ないということだ。

耳練ポイント

Vocabulary & Key Expressions　－重要語句とフレーズを聴き取ろう！

- ■ Addictive「中毒性の、病みつきになる」
- 01 making a serious accusation「重大な告発、非難をする」　02 implies「意味する、ほのめかす」
- 03 some sort of「ある種の、何らかの」
- 03 be it an illegal one, or a legal one「それが違法なものであれ、合法なものであれ」one は drug をさす
- 03 drug「麻薬、薬物、ドラッグ」　04 cocaine「コカイン」
- 04 amphetamines「アンフェタミン（中枢神経興奮薬）」　04 nicotine「ニコチン」
- 05 In recent years「近年」　05 raged「盛んである、高調に達する」
- 05 on the question of ～「～の問題について」
- 07 concluded that「（that 以下）との結論をくだした」　08 spicy「香辛料のきいた、ピリッとした」
- 08 causes the same kinds of reactions in the body「身体に同じような反応を引き起こす」
- 09 heart rate「心拍数」　09 blood pressure「血圧」　12 build up「増やす、強める」
- 12 remarkably similar「驚くほど似通った」　12 tolerance「耐性、許容度」
- 13 budding alcoholic「アルコール中毒になりかかっている人」
- 13 As a person develops a dependency on alcohol「アルコールに依存するようになるにしたがって」
　as は「～するにしたがって」
- 15 Likewise「同様に、同じく」　18 are（not）convinced「納得する（していない）」
- 18 skeptics「懐疑的な人、懐疑的な科学者たち」
- 19 draw a distinction between（a mere craving and a true addiction）
　「（単なる食べたいと思う気持ちと本当の中毒）を区別しなければならない」
- 19 craving「渇望、欲しがること」　20 revealed「（新事実などを）明らかにした」
- 20 the bodily reactions mentioned earlier「先に述べられた身体的反応」
- 22 triggered「引き起こす、誘発する」
- 23 This seems to indicate that「（that 以下）ということを示唆しているようだ」
- 24 in the mind「頭の中」　25 This is not to say that「（that 以下）と言っているわけではない」
- 26 terrifically「（口語）ものすごく、猛烈に」
- 27 In this same category are ～「これと同じ部類に入るものは～です」
　この構文は ～ are in this same category というのが本来の語順で、in this same category の部分を
　先行文脈に引かれて are の前に出し、その代わりに主語を be の後ろに持ってきたもので、結果的に両者
　を be 動詞を中心にひっくり返したもの　28 urges「強い衝動、駆りたてられること」
- 28 urges to shop, to gamble, or to play computer games constantly
　「買い物癖、賭博癖、コンピュータゲーム癖」
- 30 why curry, of all foods「あらゆる食べ物の中でなぜカレーが（そのような性質があるのか）」
- 31 activates「活性化させる」　32 staple foods「主食」
- 32 bland「味（風味）のない」　32 Simply put「端的にいえば、簡単にいえば」
- 33 dazzles the tongue into a state of confusion「舌を驚かせて混乱に陥らせる」
- 34 thrills「興奮」　35 In the final analysis「全部を総合すると」という程度の意味
- 35 nutritional experts「栄養の専門家、栄養士」　35 there is no need to ～「～する必要はない」
- 36 From a nutritional standpoint「栄養の点からは」　36 warn consumers to avoid ～「～を避け
　るように消費者に警告する」つまりこの warn は強い意味の advise
- 37 Stick with ～, and...「～を守る／堅持するならば…」（命令文+andの構文）
- 38 fattening sauces「太るソース」　39 now and then「ときどき」

46 Ecotourism

Long Passage 6

For most people, the idea of "going on vacation" conjures up certain images: waking up in a spacious hotel room, ordering a huge breakfast in a restaurant, and hopping into a rented car for a long drive along the seacoast, to give some examples.

But for an increasing number of people, vacations involve more exotic activities. Some spend their time off hiking through the Amazon jungle of Ecuador with a trained naturalist, who explains the various plant and animal life and sometimes offers a tasty snack, like lemon-flavored ants that live on certain trees. Others board old Russian research ships for trips to frigid Antarctica and the chance to view colonies of penguins in their natural habitat.

The practice is known as "ecotourism," a movement that was born in the 1980s. Definitions of ecotourism vary, but ecotourists in general are more interested in viewing the natural beauty and experiencing the original cultures of their destinations than in their own personal comfort.

A guiding principle of ecotourism is that the visitors must be sensitive to the fragility of the earth's environment. One seeks to learn about the earth through ecotourism without in any way damaging the local environment or depleting its resources. Another key tenet of the movement is the preservation of local cultures. Ecotourists never impose themselves on the people who inhabit a region. Tours of such places as the Ecuadorian Amazon region should be planned with the consent and cooperation of local people, and these locals should be the main beneficiaries of the tourism business.

Since its birth, ecotourism has grown every year. The United Nations declared 2002 "the year of ecotourism," and, for countries such as Kenya, Ecuador, Nepal and Costa Rica, the income from ecotourism has become a major part of the gross domestic product, or GDP.

As with so many well-intended ideas, ecotourism has come to be abused. Some travel companies and developers attach the label of "ecotourism" to activities that do not attempt to adhere to the principles of the

耳練-46 ♪)) Ecotourism

movement. A common practice is for a developer to build a hotel in the midst of a natural paradise in an attempt to lure ecotourists, even though a great many animal habitats might be destroyed in the process of building the hotel, and the continued operation of the hotel might pollute the very same natural paradise that attracts its guests.

Despite such unfortunate cases, the ecotourism movement is widely seen as a great benefit to regions of natural wonder and cultures that had been in danger of being wiped out. And since ecotourism is only now beginning to attract attention in some developed countries, the number of adherents to the movement is expected to grow.

▌日本語訳 －英文の内容を確認しよう！

エコツーリズム

ほとんどの人にとって「休暇を取る」というと、あるイメージが頭に浮かぶ。たとえば、広いホテルの部屋で目を覚ますとか、レストランですごい量の朝食を注文するとか、レンタカーに飛び乗って海岸沿いをずっとドライブするなどだ。

しかし、休暇でもっと風変わりなことをする人が増えている。訓練された博物学者と一緒にエクアドル国内のアマゾンのジャングルをハイキングして時間を過ごす人もいる。博物学者はさまざまな植物や動物について解説し、時には特定の木に生息するレモン味のアリのようなおいしいおやつも与えてくれる。また、古いロシアの調査船に乗って極寒の南極に行き、自然の生息地でペンギンのコロニーを見る人たちもいる。

こういうことは「エコツーリズム」として知られており、1980年代に生まれた運動だ。エコツーリズムの定義はさまざまだが、一般的にエコツーリストは快適な旅行よりも、自然の美しさを見ることや旅先の独自の文化を体験することに関心を持っている。

エコツーリズムの原則は、ビジターは地球環境のもろさに対して敏感でなければならないということだ。絶対に現地の環境を傷つけたり資源を枯渇させることなく、エコツーリズムを通して地球について学ぼうとするのだ。この運動のもう一つの信条は現地の文化の保護だ。エコツーリストは決して地域に住む人々に負担になるようなことはしない。エクアドル国内のアマゾン地方のような場所のツアーは地元の人々の同意と協力のもとで計画されなければならないし、こういう地元の人たちこそが観光の恩恵をもっぱら被る人たちでなければならない。

エコツーリズムはその誕生以来、毎年伸びている。国際連合は2002年を「エコツーリズム年」と定めた。ケニア、エクアドル、ネパール、コスタリカなどの国では、エコツーリズムによる収入は国内総生産（GDP）の主要な部分になっている。

多くの善意のアイデアによくあるように、エコツーリズムも濫用されるに至っている。旅行会社や開発業者の中には、この運動の原則にそぐわない活動を「エコツーリズム」としているものもいる。よくあるのは、開発業者がエコツーリストを呼び込もうと自然の楽園の真ん中にホテルを建てる場合だ。ホテル建設の過程で非常に多くの動物の生息地が破壊されてしまう可能性があり、その後ホテルが稼動し続ければ、客を惹きつけるまさにその自然の楽園を汚染する可能性もある。

そのような残念なケースもあるが、エコツーリズム運動は消滅の危機に瀕していた自然の驚異や文化を持つ地域にとっては大きな恩恵になっていると広く考えられている。そして、一部の先進国ではエコツーリズムは最近注目を集め始めたばかりなので、この運動の支持者は増えると予想されている。

耳練ポイント

Vocabulary & Key Expressions　—重要語句とフレーズを聴き取ろう！

- Ecotourism「エコツーリズム、環境保護志向の観光（業）」
- 01 going on vacation「休暇を取る」休暇でどこかに行くこと
- 01 conjures up ～「～を呼び起こす」conjure ～ up としても用いる　　02 spacious「広い」
- 03 hopping into ～「～に（飛び）乗る」　cf. hop out「（～から）降りる」
- 04 to give some examples「いくつか例を挙げると」　06 exotic「エキゾチックな、風変わりな」
- 06 time off「休暇」　07 Ecuador「エクアドル」赤道（Equator）上にあるためこの名がついた
- 07 naturalist「博物学者、自然誌研究家」
- 08 plant and animal life「動植物」life は集合的に「生き物、生物」の意味
- 09 lemon-flavored「レモンの味がする」　10 frigid「極寒の」
- 10 Antarctica「南極大陸」the Antarctic とも言う
- 11 colonies「《生態学》コロニー」同じ種類の動植物が共生する集団　　11 habitat「生息地」
- 13 vary「異なる」　13 ecotourists「エコツーリズムに参加する人」　13 ～ in general「～一般」
- 15 destinations「（旅行などの）目的地、行き先」
- 15 personal comfort「個人的な快適さ」
- 16 guiding principle「指針、指導原理」　16 be sensitive to ～「～に敏感である、～に配慮する」
- 17 fragility「壊れやすさ」　17 One 一般的な人をさす　18 in any way「決して」
- 19 depleting「（資源などを）激減させる、枯渇させる」
- 19 its resources「その資源」「その」は local environment をさす
- 19 tenet「信条、主義」　20 preservation「保存、保護」
- 21 impose themselves on ～「～の負担になる」　21 inhabit ～「～に住む、居住する」
- 23 consent「同意」　23 locals「土地の人、地元民」　24 beneficiaries「受益者」
- 28 gross domestic product「国内総生産（略GDP）」
- 29 As with ～「～のように、～と同様に」
- 29 well-intended「善意の、（結果はともかく）よかれと思ってなされた」
- 29 abused「（地位、人の好意などを）濫用（悪用）する、誤用する」名詞は同じ綴りであるが [əbjúːs] と発音が変わることに注意　　31 adhere to ～「～を厳守する」
- 32 A common practice「よく行われていること」
- 32 for a developer to build a hotel ... この for は次の a developer が to build 以下の不定詞の主語であることを表している（「～にとっては」という意味ではない）
- 32 in the midst of ～「～の真ん中に」
- 33 in an attempt to ～「～しようとして、～しようと企てて」
- 33 lure「誘い出す、おびき寄せる」
- 35 the continued operation of the hotel「そのホテルを営業し続けること」
- 36 pollute「汚染する」　37 Despite ～「～にもかかわらず」
- 38 benefit「利益、恩恵」
- 38 regions of natural wonder and cultures「すばらしい自然と文化を持った地域」
- 39 in danger of ～「～の危険にある」
- 39 wiped out「絶滅させる、消す」他動詞 be wiped outは「絶滅する、姿を消す」wipe ～ out と wipe out ～ の両方の語順がある
- 41 adherents「支持者、信奉者（=followers）」
- 41 is expected to grow「増加が予想される」

47 Intrusive Marketers

Long Passage 7

In many developed countries in the world, the average consumer is besieged by salespeople offering unwanted products or services. A family sitting down to dinner may be interrupted more than once by telephone calls from total strangers offering stocks, credit cards, or telephone services. After dinner, one may decide to surf the Internet for relaxation, only to be overwhelmed by unsolicited emails, commonly known as "spam." And in the midst of typing this very paragraph, the author was forced to step away from his computer for a few minutes to deal with a particularly persistent door-to-door salesman offering units in a newly completed condominium building.

In the United States, angry consumers have begun to fight back. They have pressured their representatives in both state and national governments to take actions to protect average citizens from intrusive marketers.

The first major weapon in the battle against such marketers was the so-called "Do Not Call" list. In 2003, the Federal Trade Commission, a government agency, allowed consumers to register their phone numbers for inclusion on this list. The registration process is free and can easily be completed on line. Telephone marketers are obliged to obtain the list, for which they have to pay, and to avoid calling any of the numbers on it. If a marketer calls a single number on the Do Not Call list, it may be subjected to a very high fine.

So how well has the law worked? In the first two years, over 100 million numbers were registered for the list. In a survey taken half a year after the law went into effect, most citizens on the list expressed satisfaction. Ninety percent were getting significantly fewer calls than before, and a quarter said they had stopped receiving unwanted calls altogether. More recently, however, some of those same consumers report an increase in unwanted sales calls. Some say that the government has not penalized violators of the law strictly enough, and this has emboldened marketers to risk making more calls.

Still, the Do Not Call list is widely viewed as a step in the right direction, and it has inspired imitation. A small city in Ohio recently launched a "Do

耳練-47 Intrusive Marketers

Not Knock" list. Salespeople who knock on the door of any person registered on the list risk not only a fine, but possible jail time as well.

Of course, the hardest nut to crack is unsolicited email. Although the American government has also passed anti-spam legislation, which imposes severe penalties on persons who send unwanted email messages, the measure has had little effect. Most of the spam Americans receive comes from overseas sources which are beyond the reach of the law. The only hope for a real reduction in the pollution of our email is action at the United Nations, where the issue has been discussed without concrete results.

日本語訳 －英文の内容を確認しよう！

しつこい売込み

　世界中の先進国で、普通の消費者は欲しくもない商品やサービスを勧める販売員に悩まされている。家族で夕食を食べていると、株やクレジットカードや電話サービスはいかがですかと、まったく知らない人から電話がかかり、食事を邪魔されることが一度ならずということもある。食後に気晴らしにネットサーフィンをしようと思ったら、ものすごい数の、一般に「スパム」として知られている、勝手に送られてくる電子メールに圧倒されるばかりということもあるだろう。そして、今まさにこの文章を書いている最中にも、新築の完成したマンションの購入を勧めるとりわけしつこい訪問販売のセールスマンに対応するために、私はコンピュータの前を数分間離れるはめになった。

　アメリカでは、怒れる消費者たちが反撃を始めた。しつこい売込みから一般の消費者を守る措置を講じるよう州議会および連邦議会の議員たちに圧力をかけた。

　そういう売込みに対する闘いで最初に使われた主な武器はいわゆる「電話拒否」リストだ。2003年に政府機関である連邦取引委員会は、消費者が登録するとこのリストに自分の電話番号を載せられるようにした。登録は無料で、インターネットでも簡単にできる。テレマーケティングを行う業者はこのリストを入手することが義務付けられており、リストは有料で、掲載されている番号には電話をかけないようにしなければならない。もし彼らが1本でも電話をかけた場合、非常に高額の罰金を科される可能性がある。

　では、この法律はどれくらいうまく機能しているのだろうか。最初の2年間に1億以上の電話番号が登録された。この法律が発効して半年後に行われたある調査では、このリストに載っている市民の大半は満足感を表明していた。回答者の90％で以前よりも勧誘の電話が目に見えて減っており、25％は望まない電話がまったくなくなったと答えている。しかし、もっと最近になると調査時と同じ消費者の中に迷惑なセールスの電話が増えていると報告しているものもいる。政府が法律の違反者に対する罰則を十分厳しくしていなくて、そのためテレマーケティング業者が大胆になり、危険を冒してももっと電話をかけているのだと言う人もいる。

　それでも、電話拒否リストは正しい方向への一歩だと広くみなされており、これに刺激されて類似のものも生まれている。オハイオ州の小さな市では最近「戸別訪問拒否」リストを作り始めた。このリストに登録した人の住宅を訪問した販売員は罰金だけでなく、懲役刑を受ける危険を冒すことになる。

　もちろん、一番対策が難しいのは勝手に送られてくる電子メールだ。アメリカ政府は反スパム法も成立させており、それは迷惑な電子メールによるメッセージを送った人に厳罰を課すものだが、この対策はほとんど効果がない。アメリカ人が受け取るスパムの大半は、法律の適用外である海外から発信されたものだからだ。私たちの電子メールの汚染を本当に減らすための唯一の希望は国連における行動だが、そこでの議論は具体的な成果をあげていない。

耳練ポイント

Vocabulary & Key Expressions －重要語句とフレーズを聴き取ろう！

- Intrusive「うっとうしい、押しつけがましい」　01 developed countries「先進諸国」
- 01 average consumer「普通の消費者」　01 is besieged by ～「～に悩まされる、苦しめられる」
- 02 A family sitting down to dinner「食事をしようとしている一家」
- 03 may be interrupted「中断される、邪魔されることがあるかもしれない」
- 03 more than once「一度ならず」　04 total strangers「まったくの見ず知らずの人」
- 04 stocks「株、株式」
- 05 only to be overwhelmed by ～「～に圧倒される結果に終わる」この only to は結果を表す不定詞の用法
- 06 unsolicited emails「頼んでいないのに送りつけられた電子メール」
- 06 spam「スパム、メールによる大量広告」日本語では「迷惑メール」と訳されるが迷惑とは限らない
- 06 in the midst of ～「～の最中に(=during)」　08 deal with「対処する」
- 08 particularly persistent「ことのほかしつこい」
- 08 door-to-door salesman「訪問販売のセールスマン」
- 09 offering units in a newly completed condominium building「新築マンションの住戸を売り込む」
- 10 fight back「反撃する」　11 pressured ～ to …「…に～するよう圧力をかける」
- 12 take actions「行動をとる、措置を講じる」
- 13 The first major weapon「最初の主要な武器、対抗手段」
- 13 in the battle against ～「～との闘いでの」
- 14 the Federal Trade Commission「(米)連邦取引委員会(略FTC)」　15 register「登録する」
- 15 for inclusion on the list「リストに含める／載せるために」　16 registration process「登録手続き」
- 16 can easily be completed on line「簡単にインターネットで済ませられる」
- 17 Telephone marketers「テレマーケティングをする業者」
- 17 are obliged to ～「～しなければならない」ここでは to obtain …と to avoid …の両方にかかる
- 19 may be subjected to a very high fine「非常に高額の罰金を科される可能性がある」
- 22 half a year after the law went into effect「その法律が発効して半年後」
- 23 most citizens on the list「そのリストに載っている市民のほとんどは」
- 24 significantly fewer「(以前よりも)かなり少ない」　27 penalized「罰する、罰則を適用する」
- 27 violator「違反者」　28 strictly「厳しく、断固として」
- 28 emboldened marketers to risk ～「マーケティング業者に(危険覚悟で)～をやってみるよう勇気づけた」つまりその結果、危険を冒すことに大胆になったということ
- 30 is widely viewed as ～「広く～と見なされている」
- 30 a step in the right direction「正しい方向への一歩」
- 31 inspired imitation「模倣することを思いつかせた」
- 33 risk not only ～, but … as well「～ばかりか…の危険も冒す」
- 33 possible jail time「懲役刑を受ける可能性」
- 34 the hardest nut to crack「一番難しい問題」
- 35 imposes severe penalties on ～「～に厳しい刑罰を科す」
- 36 the measure「この措置、方法」
- 37 has had little effect「ほとんど効果がない」a little は「少し」、little は「ほとんどない」
- 38 beyond the reach of the law「その法律の効力が及ばない」
- 38 The only hope for ～「～の唯一の期待、希望は」
- 40 concrete results「具体的な成果、結果」

48 Fighting Plagiarism

Long Passage 8 オーストラリア

Plagiarism used to be an ugly word. For most young people these days, it is simply an unknown one.

A dictionary definition of the verb "to plagiarize" is "to use and pass off the ideas or writings of another as one's own," though a shorter and simpler version might be "to steal someone else's words." A college student copying a paragraph from a book into his research paper without identifying the source of that paragraph would be a simple example. A more extreme case might be a student purchasing an entire research paper written by someone else, and submitting it with his own name on it.

Plagiarism has been the bane of educators the world over for as long as schools have existed. In the 21st century, however, there is a sense that plagiarism has gotten out of control and reached epidemic proportions. According to one survey, 36 percent of American undergraduates admit to having plagiarized part of their written work at least once.

Why has plagiarism become so commonplace? Most reasons given by experts are related to advances in technology.

First, it is simply easier to plagiarize today than it ever was before. A century ago, plagiarism was hard work. A would-be plagiarizer first had to find some printed information suitable for stealing by visiting a library and searching through stacks of books. Since no photo-copiers existed, the copying itself had to be done by hand. In contrast, these days a student need only use an Internet search engine to find a wide variety of sites that contain long tracts of information suitable for stealing. With the copy and paste functions, the placing of the stolen words into the student's homework can be wrapped up in mere seconds.

Moreover, the fact that the information is in "electronic" form somehow makes the action seem less dishonest than if one were taking words from a "hard" copy of the source. A similar problem is

193

耳練-48 Fighting Plagiarism

seen in the music industry. While only a few young people would consider walking into a music store and stealing a CD, a great many have no qualms about downloading songs from the Internet without paying for them.

Finally, plagiarizers increasingly believe that they will never get caught. A magazine survey found that 90 percent of U.S. university students believe that cheaters are never punished. And to be sure, the challenge of catching a student in the act of plagiarizing is so daunting that many educators have simply given up. "Who wants to sit around looking for websites trying to find out if a paper is plagiarized or not? Pretty soon you're a private investigator," said one professor at a prominent university.

In response to the growing need to fight plagiarism, some entrepreneurs have begun to offer services. For a fee, these companies will act as "private investigators" to determine whether or not information in a student's paper has been plagiarized. It is sad to think that the problem has reached such a critical stage, and yet the demand for these on-line investigators is steadily growing.

耳練-48 Fighting Plagiarism

日本語訳 －英文の内容を確認しよう！

剽窃との闘い

　かつて剽窃（ひょうせつ）は忌まわしい言葉だった。しかし、現代の若者のほとんどにとってはこの言葉は単なる未知の言葉だ。

　辞書に出ている「剽窃する」という動詞の定義は「他人の考えや書いたものを使って、自分のものとして通用させる」ことだが、手短に簡潔にいえば「ほかの人の言葉を盗む」ということになるだろう。大学生が自分のレポートに出典を明記せずに本の一節を書き写すのは単純な例だ。もっと極端なものは学生が他人が書いたレポートをそっくり買い取り、それに自分の名前を書いて提出する場合だろう。

　剽窃は学校というものが存在する限り世界中の教育者にとってずっと悩みの種であった。しかし21世紀になって、ある意味で剽窃は手に負えないものになり、はびこっているといえる。ある調査によれば、アメリカ人大学生の36％が少なくとも一度は自分で書いたものの一部で剽窃をしたことがあると認めている。

　なぜ剽窃がこんなに広く行われるようになったのか？　専門家が指摘する理由はもっぱら技術の進歩と関係している。

　まず、現在は剽窃することがかつてないほど容易である。一世紀前には剽窃は大変な作業だった。剽窃をしようという人はまず図書館に行って、たくさんの本の中から盗むのに適した印刷された情報を見つけなければならなかった。コピー機がなかったので、写すのも手書きで行わなければならなかった。これとは対照的に、最近では学生はインターネットの検索エンジンを使うだけで、盗むのに適したさまざまな情報が入っている多様なサイトを見つけることができる。コピーと貼付け機能を使うことで、盗んだ文章を自分の宿題に入れるのはわずか数秒でできてしまう。

　さらに、情報が「電子的」であるという事実は、情報源の「印刷」物から文章を取る場合よりも剽窃の行為による不正の感覚を小さくするようだ。音楽業界でも同じような問題が見られる。ミュージックショップに行ってCDを盗むことを考える若者は少ないが、お金を払わずにインターネット上から音楽をダウンロードすることに良心の呵責を感じない若者はとても多い。

　最後に、剽窃を決して見つからないと思ってる人が増えていることがある。ある雑誌の調査によれば、アメリカの大学生の90％が剽窃をした人は絶対に罰せられないと信じている。そして、確かに、剽窃をしている学生を捕まえることはあまりに大変なので、多くの教育者があきらめている。ある有名大学の教授は「レポートが剽窃したものかを調べるためにウェブサイトを調べたいと思う人がどこにいますか？　そんなことをしていたら、すぐに私立探偵のようになってしまいます」と言った。

　剽窃対策の必要性が増していることに対応して、サービスを提供する企業家も出てきている。それらの会社は有料で学生のレポートに書いてある情報が剽窃されているかどうかを判断する「私立探偵」の役目を果たすことになる。この問題がそのような深刻な段階にまで達したことは残念なことだが、こういうオンライン探偵の需要は着実に伸びている。

耳練ポイント

Vocabulary & Key Expressions　−重要語句とフレーズを聴き取ろう!

01　plagiarism「剽窃(ひょうせつ)」(広辞苑:他人の文章などの文句または節を盗み取って、自分のものとして発表すること)
01　For most young people these days「今日の若者の大多数にとっては」these days は後ろから young people を修飾している
03　plagiarize「剽窃する」　04 pass off ～ as …「～を…として通す」
05　shorter and simpler version (of definition)「短い簡単な定義」
06　A college student copying ... that paragraph 全体で A college student を主語とする動名詞表現で、「大学生が…すること」で、would be a simple example の主語となっている
07　identifying the source「出典を明らかにする」
08　A more extreme case might be ～「もっと極端な場合は～であろう」～の部分がまた a student から文の最後までで、これも a student を主語とし、2つの動名詞を含む動名詞表現で、「学生が…すること」
09　submitting「提出する」　10 with his own name on it「自分の名前で」
11　bane「悩みの種」　11 the world over「世界中で」
11　for as long as schools have existed「学校というものができてずっと」
12　there is a sense that ～「ある意味で～である」in a sense ～を強めた言い方。there is a sense in which ～ともいう
13　gotten out of control「手に負えなくなる、押さえておくことができなくなる」
13　reached epidemic proportions「大流行する、多発する、まん延する」
14　under-graduates「学部学生」
15　admit to having plagiarized ～「～を剽窃したことを認める」admit to ～ing で「～することを認める」で、必ずしも完了形にしなくてもよいし、admit ～ing の形でも使える
17　commonplace「ありきたりの、広まっている」
20　A would-be plagiarizer「剽窃しようとする人」
21　suitable for stealing「盗むのにちょうどよい」
23　photo-copiers「コピー機」　23 In contrast「これに対して」
24　need only use an Internet search engine「インターネットのサーチエンジンを使うだけでよい」助動詞 need はこのように否定的に用いられることが多い
25　tracts「文書」書かれたもの
27　the placing of the stolen words into the student's homework「盗んだ言葉を学生の宿題の中に置くこと」　28 wrapped up「済ます、片付ける」
29　"electronic" form「電子的な形」つまり印刷物になっていないこと
30　the action「その行為」つまりコピーする行為　30 less dishonest than if ～「～の場合よりは不正直でない」　31 "hard" copy of the source「印刷された原典」
34　qualms「不安、気がとがめること、良心の呵責」通例複数形で使われる
38　to be sure「確かに、もちろん」　39 challenge of ～ing「～するという挑戦、課題」
39　catch ～ in the act of …ing「～が…しているところをつかまえる」
40　daunting「気が遠くなるような」　41 sit around ～ing「じっと～する」
43　prominent university「有名大学」　44 In response to ～「～に反応して、対して」
45　entrepreneurs「起業家」　45 For a fee「料金を取って」
47　information in a student's paper has been plagiarized「ある学生のレポートの情報が剽窃されている」ここでの plagiarize は他の文献から無断で取ってくるという意味
49　steadily growing「着実に増えつつある」

Abraham Lincoln

Long Passage 9

Abraham Lincoln's name is usually associated with two achievements: the abolition of slavery in the United States and the delivery of the Gettysburg Address.

It is often forgotten that as a candidate for president, Lincoln did not advocate an end to slavery. He merely sought to stop it from spreading to new areas as the country continued to grow larger by adding new states in the West. This position, however, did not satisfy the politicians in the slave-holding states of the South. As soon as Lincoln was elected president, these states began to secede from the United States in order to form a new and independent country where they could continue to practice slavery. Thus, the long and bloody Civil War broke out, during which the Northern states tried to force the rebellious states of the South to rejoin the United States.

It was not until the autumn of 1862, well into the second year of the war, that Lincoln issued the Emancipation Proclamation, which declared an end to slavery in all the rebellious states.

In the following year, the rebel army of the South, under the direction of General Robert E. Lee, made a daring attempt to force Lincoln to surrender by invading the North. Lee's troops penetrated deep into Pennsylvania and seemed likely to succeed until they met United States troops near the small village of Gettysburg. After three days of horrific fighting that left 7,500 soldiers dead, Lee retreated to the South in defeat.

Southern forces continued to fight to defend their "country" from "invaders," however, so the war dragged on. When his army failed to force the South to surrender, and the heavy costs of the war in terms of both lives and money mounted, Lincoln faced the possibility of losing his bid for reelection in 1864. Nonetheless, timely victories by his generals restored his popularity and allowed him to win a second term. He would live long enough to see General Lee surrender in April 1865, ending the war in a victory for the North. Less than a month later, Lincoln was shot to death as he watched a play in a Washington, D.C. theater. The assassin

耳練-49))) Abraham Lincoln

was an actor who had sympathized with the South.
   In the meantime, the citizens of Gettysburg devoted much of their time in the weeks following the battle there to burying the thousands of dead soldiers. It was not an easy task, since the dead of Gettysburg outnumbered the living three to one. A wealthy attorney purchased land for a new cemetery that would honor the fallen soldiers. A ceremony to dedicate the cemetery was held in November 1863. Edward Everett, America's most famous orator at the time, was invited to give the main address, while Lincoln was also invited to make brief "dedicatory remarks."
   While Everett's two-hour speech was well-received by the crowd, Lincoln's short "Gettysburg Address" lasted only two or three minutes, and received little applause. In the middle of his remarks, Lincoln stated that the world would little note, nor long remember what he said on this occasion. They are ironic words indeed for what remains the most famous speech ever made by any American president. He then concluded his speech with this memorable praise for the dead Northern soldiers:

It is for us the living, rather, to be dedicated here to the unfinished work which they who fought here have thus far so nobly advanced. It is rather for us to be here dedicated to the great task remaining before us — that from these honored dead we take increased devotion to that cause for which they gave the last full measure of devotion — that we here highly resolve that these dead shall not have died in vain — that this nation, under God, shall have a new birth of freedom — and that government of the people, by the people, for the people, shall not perish from the earth.

耳練-49 Abraham Lincoln

日本語訳　―英文の内容を確認しよう！

エイブラハム・リンカーン

　エイブラハム・リンカーンというと人は普通2つの業績を思い出す。アメリカにおける奴隷制度の廃止とゲティスバーグ演説を行ったことだ。

　しばしば忘れられていることだが、大統領候補のときにはリンカーンは奴隷制度の廃止を提唱しなかった。彼は、西部の新しい州を加えることでアメリカが大きくなり続ける中、新たな地域に奴隷制が広まることを止めようとしただけだった。しかし、この立場は奴隷を保有する南部の州の政治家たちを満足させなかった。リンカーンが大統領に選ばれるとすぐに、これらの州は奴隷制度を続けることができる新たな独立国家を作るためにアメリカ合衆国から離脱し始めた。こうして、長く、たくさんの血が流れた南北戦争が始まり、戦争中、北部の州は力ずくで反逆的な南部の州を再び合衆国に加わらせようとした。

　すべての南部の州で奴隷制の終結を宣言した奴隷解放宣言をリンカーンが発布したのは、戦争が始まって2年目もかなり経った1862年の秋になってからのことだった。

　その翌年、南部の反乱軍はロバート・E・リー将軍の指揮のもと、北部に侵入することでリンカーンを降伏させようという大胆な企てを試みた。リー将軍の軍はペンシルベニア州内深くに入り込み、ゲティスバーグという小さな村の近くで合衆国軍と対峙するまでは、この企ては成功するかに見えた。7,500人の戦死者をだした3日間にわたるすさまじい戦いの後、リー将軍は敗れて南部に撤退した。

　南部軍はその後も自分たちの「国」を「侵略者」から守るために戦いを続けたが、そのために戦争は延々と続いた。北軍が南部を降伏させることができず、人命と戦費の両面で戦争の大きな負担がかさんでくるにつれ、リンカーンは1864年の大統領選挙に再出馬しても負ける可能性に直面した。しかしながら、時宜を得た北軍の将軍たちの勝利によってリンカーンは人気を回復し、2期目の当選を果たした。彼は1865年4月にリー将軍が降伏し、北軍の勝利によって戦争が終わるのを自分の目で見ることになった。しかし、それから1か月も経たずに彼はワシントンDCの劇場で観劇中に銃で撃たれて亡くなった。暗殺者は南軍に共感していた俳優だった。

　一方、ゲティスバーグの住民たちは、戦闘の後、何週間にもわたって多くの時間を割いて何千人もの死んだ兵士を献身的に埋葬した。ゲティスバーグの戦いの死者数は3対1で生存者を上回ったので、それは容易なことではなかった。裕福な弁護士が、亡くなった兵士を埋葬する新しい墓地を造るために土地を購入した。この墓地を戦死者に捧げる式は1863年11月に行われ、当時アメリカで最も有名な演説家であったエドワード・エベレットが主演説をするために招かれていたが、リンカーンも短い「献辞」を述べるために招かれていた。

　エベレットの2時間の演説は聴衆に好評だったが、リンカーンの短い「ゲティスバーグの演説」はわずか2,3分の長さで、拍手もほとんどなかった。献辞の途中で、リンカーンはこの場で自分が言ったことに世界はほとんど注目しないであろうし、長く記憶することもないだろうと述べた。それは、アメリカの大統領が行った演説としては現在でも最も有名なものに対する皮肉な言葉であった。そして、彼は亡くなった北軍の兵士たちに対するこんな記憶に残る賞賛の言葉で演説を締めくくった。

　『ここで戦った者たちが、ここまでかくも気高く推し進めた未完の企てに、ここで身を捧げるべきはむしろ生きているわれわれである。われわれこそ、われわれの前に残されている偉大な任務に身を捧げるべきである。敬意をもって埋葬されたこれらの戦死者たちが命を捧げたあの大義に対する献身の心を、われわれは一層強くするのである。これらの戦死者の死が無駄にならないことを、この国は、神のもと、新たな自由を誕生させることを、そして、人民の、人民による、人民のための政府が地上から姿を消してはならないことを、われわれはここで固く決意するのである』

耳練ポイント

Vocabulary & Key Expressions　—重要語句とフレーズを聴き取ろう!

02 abolition「廃止、全廃」　02 delivery「演説をすること」Cf. deliver a speech「演説をする」
05 advocate（=support）「提唱する、擁護する」　05 merely ～（=just, simply）「単に（～にすぎない）」
05 stop ～ from … ing「～が…するのを妨げる、抑制する」
07 This position「この立場」すなわち他の州に奴隷制を広げない立場
09 secede「脱退する、分離する」　11 practice slavery「奴隷制度を実施／実行する」
11 the (American) Civil War「南北戦争」1861年4月～1865年4月　11 broke out「勃発した」
12 force ～ to do …「～に無理やり…させる」　12 the rebellious states「反乱州」独立しようとした州
14 It was not until ～ that …「～になって初めて…」　15 declared「宣言した」
17 under the direction of ～「～の指揮のもと」
18 General Robert E. Lee「リー将軍（1807～1870）」南軍の総指揮官
18 daring「大胆不敵な」　19 penetrated into ～「～に侵入した」
20 United States troops「合衆国部隊」形容詞的に使われているので the がない。troops は複数形で「軍隊、軍勢」
22 left 7,500 soldiers dead「7,500人の兵士の戦死者を出した」7,500 soldiers と dead は主語と述語の関係　22 retreated「退却した」
23 "country"「南部連合政府」"invaders" は南部から見た侵略者、つまり「北軍」
24 dragged on「だらだら長引いた」　25 in terms of ～「～の点での」
26 mounted「（自動詞）かさんだ」　27 bid for ～「（～を勝ち取ろうとする）努力、試み、企て」
27 timely victories by his generals「彼の将軍による時宜を得た勝利」この文の主語
28 He would live long enough to ～「～をするまで十分長生きをするであろう」大統領に再選された過去の時点におけるその後の見込みを述べている
29 ending the war in a victory for the North「（その結果）戦争を北部の勝利に終わらせた」この分詞構文の主語は、全文の主語の He=Lincoln ととるのが自然
32 sympathized with ～「～に共感した」had sympathized と過去完了になっているのは暗殺に至る前からなので　33 devoted ～ to …「～を…に捧げた、つぎ込んだ」
34 the dead, the living「死者、生者（the+形容詞=名詞）」　36 outnumbered ～「数で～に勝る」
37 honor「称える、敬意を払う」この場合は埋葬するの意　41 well-received by ～「～に好評を博す」
44 little note「ほとんど注目しないだろう」
44 what he said on this occasion「その際に言ったこと」時制の一致で said になっている
48 It is for us the living, rather, to be dedicated here to ... この前でリンカーンは「戦死者にこの土地を捧げる（dedicate）ためにここに集まった」と言っていて、それとの対比になっている
48 they who fought here = those who fought here「ここで戦った者たち」の古い言い方
49 so nobly「かくも気高く」とは「命によって」という意味
49 It is rather for us ... before us は前の文の言い換え。趣旨は「われわれが大義に身を捧げなければならない」ということの繰り返し
52 resolve「決意する、決心する」この後に続く3つの that 節はいずれもこの動詞の目的語なので、すべて shall を含んでいる
52 these dead shall not have died in vain「これらの死者は無駄に死んだのではないということ」未来において今日のことを振り返っているという想定なので完了形になっている
53 that this nation ... freedom　この that 節はその前の resolve の目的語
54 government of the people, by the people, for the people「人民の、人民による、人民のための政府」と訳されるが、the system of the people governing themselves（=the people） for themselves（=the people）という意味

Long Passage ⑩ — Martin Luther King, Jr.

　The "I Have a Dream" speech is the most celebrated moment in the career of Martin Luther King, Jr. and one of the most famous speeches ever given in the English language. King delivered the speech on the steps of the Lincoln Memorial in Washington, D.C., during the March on Washington for Jobs and Freedom in August 1963.

　The huge March on Washington was an amazing climax to a career as a civil rights leader that had begun only eight years earlier. In 1955 King, the son of a Baptist minister, earned his PhD in theology from Boston University while serving as pastor of Dexter Avenue Baptist Church in Montgomery, Alabama. Later that year, Rosa Parks, a black seamstress, refused to give up her seat on a Montgomery city bus to a white passenger. This refusal was a violation of an Alabama state law that gave preferential treatment to whites, so Parks was arrested.

　The arrest sparked calls for a response within Montgomery's black community, and King stepped forward to organize a boycott of the city bus system by black passengers. Since the majority of its bus passengers were black, the city soon felt an economic strain from the boycott, but tried to ignore it. Nearly a year later, the United States Supreme Court struck down the state law that segregated seating on public transportation according to race. King had won his first major victory and achieved fame in the process. He was 27 years old.

　This slow-working but effective use of nonviolent protest would serve as a model for similar activities throughout the rest of King's life. By calling worldwide attention to laws in southern states that restricted the freedoms and opportunities of African Americans, King generated pressure that gradually eliminated those laws.

　Thus, in the summer of 1963, King could look out upon an audience estimated at between 200,000 and 500,000 people to deliver his most famous address, saying, in part:

耳練-50 Martin Luther King, Jr.

And so even though we face the difficulties of today and tomorrow, I still have a dream. It is a dream deeply rooted in the American dream. I have a dream that one day this nation will rise up and live out the true meaning of its creed: "We hold these truths to be self-evident, that all men are created equal." I have a dream that one day on the red hills of Georgia, the sons of former slaves and the sons of former slave owners will be able to sit down together at the table of brotherhood.

By 1964, Lyndon Johnson, a powerful politician who was sympathetic to the Civil Rights movement, had become president. Owing to the constant pressure applied by King, the Civil Rights Act and the Voting Rights Act were passed in 1964 and 1965 respectively. These two laws ended most forms of legal discrimination based on race. In the midst of this progress, King was awarded the Nobel Prize for Peace in 1964.

King continued to work for racial equality through the years that followed while also becoming an outspoken opponent of the War in Vietnam. In April 1968 he traveled to Memphis, Tennessee to lead a march in support of the local union of sanitation workers, whose members were mostly African Americans. On the evening of April 4, a hidden assassin shot King as he stood on the balcony outside his motel room. He was pronounced dead one hour later.

耳練-50))) Martin Luther King, Jr.

▊日本語訳 －英文の内容を確認しよう！

キング牧師

　「私には夢がある」の演説はマーティン・ルーサー・キング・ジュニアの経歴の中で最高潮の瞬間である。また今までに英語でなされた演説の中で最も有名なものの一つだ。キング牧師は1963年8月の職と自由を求めるワシントン大行進の際に、リンカーン記念堂の階段でこの演説を行った。

　このワシントンでの巨大な行進は、わずか8年前に始まったばかりの公民権運動の指導者としての経歴にとっては驚くべき頂点だった。1955年、バプティスト派の牧師の息子であった彼は、アラバマ州モンゴメリーにあるデクスター・アヴェニュー・バプティスト教会の牧師を務めながら、ボストン大学で神学博士号を取得した。その後、同年中に黒人の針子だったローザ・パークスが、モンゴメリー市営バスで白人の乗客に座席を譲ることを拒否した。この拒否は白人を優遇するアラバマ州法違反だったため、パークスは逮捕された。

　この逮捕によってモンゴメリーの黒人社会の中から対応を求める声が沸き起こり、キング牧師は黒人乗客による市営バスのボイコットを組織する先頭に立った。市のバスの乗客の大半は黒人だったため、市はすぐにボイコットの経済的影響を感じたが、それを無視しようとした。1年近くたって、連邦最高裁判所が人種によって公共交通機関の座席を分離していた州法を違法とした。キング牧師は最初の大きな勝利を勝ち取り、その過程で有名になった。彼は27歳だった。

　この、時間はかかるが有効な非暴力抗議という手段を使うことは、キング牧師のその後の人生を通して同様の活動の模範となった。アフリカ系アメリカ人の自由と機会を制限する南部諸州の法律に世界の注目を集めることで、徐々にこれらの法律の撤廃につながる圧力を醸成していった。

　こうして、1963年の夏、キング牧師は推計で20万人から50万人の聴衆を前にして、以下のような内容を含む彼の最も有名な演説をすることができたのである。

　『今日の、そして明日の困難に直面してはいても、私にはなお夢がある。それはアメリカン・ドリームに深く根ざした夢なのだ。いつの日かこの国が立ち上がり、"すべての人間は平等につくられている"というこの国の信条の真の意味を現実のものとする日が来るという夢が私にはある。いつの日かジョージアの赤い丘の上で、かつての奴隷の子孫とかつての奴隷所有者の子孫が、兄弟が集う一つのテーブルに一緒につくことができるという夢が私にはある』

　1964年までに、公民権運動に理解を示していた有力政治家のリンドン・ジョンソンが大統領になっていた。キング牧師からの絶え間ない圧力のおかげで、公民権法および投票権法が1964年と65年にそれぞれ成立した。これら2つの法律は人種に基づく法的差別の大半に終止符を打った。この過程の途中で、1964年、キング牧師はノーベル平和賞を受賞した。

　キング牧師はその後も人種間の平等のために働き続けると同時に、ベトナム戦争に声高に反対するようになった。1968年4月、メンバーの大部分がアフリカ系アメリカ人である地元の清掃労働者の組合を支援する行進の先頭に立つために、彼はテネシー州メンフィスに行った。4月4日の夜、モーテルの部屋の外のバルコニーに立っていたところを、物陰から暗殺者が撃った。1時間後、キング牧師の死亡が宣告された。

耳練ポイント

Vocabulary & Key Expressions －重要語句とフレーズを聴き取ろう！

- 01 The "I Have a Dream" speech「"私には夢がある"の演説」全体で一つの名詞となっている
- 05 the March on Washington for Jobs and Freedom in August 1963 1963年8月28日に行われたワシントン大行進のこと
- 07 a career as a civil rights leader「公民権運動の指導者としての経歴」
- 08 that had begun only eight years earlier「その8年目に始まったばかりの」つまりキング牧師が公民権運動の指導者になったのは1955年
- 10 while serving as pastor of ～「～の牧師を務めながら」serve as ～「～として働く、務める」
- 11 Later that year「その後その年内に」ローザ・パークスの逮捕は1955年12月1日
- 12 refused to ～「～することを拒んだ」　12 give up ～ to …「～を…に明け渡す、譲る」
- 16 sparked ～「～の火付け役となる、煽りたてる」
- 16 calls for a response「対応することを求める要求」何か行動を起こすことを求める要求
- 17 stepped forward to ～「進んで～する役をかってでる」
- 18 the majority of its bus passengers「その＝モンゴメリー市のバスの乗客の大部分」
- 19 economic strain「経済的な負担」つまり収入が激減したこと
- 20 Nearly a year later「ほぼ1年後」実際には1956年11月13日。その前に特別連邦地方裁判所は6月5日に2対1で公的交通手段における人種差別が憲法違反であるという裁決を下していたが、市側がこれを連邦最高裁に控訴し、その判決が出たのが6月5日だった
- 20 the United States Supreme Court「合衆国連邦最高裁」　21 struck down「廃止した」
- 21 segregated「分離する」おもに人種により分離することをさす
- 22 according to race「人種によって」　24 slow-working「時間のかかる」
- 24 nonviolent protest「非暴力の抗議運動」
- 26 By calling worldwide attention to ～「～に世界の注意を引きつけることで」
- 28 generated「生み出す」　28 eliminated「除去する」　29 Thus「こうして」
- 31 saying, in part「部分的には次のようなことを言った」分詞構文の連続的用法
- 33 the American dream「アメリカン・ドリーム」『知恵蔵2000』には「独立宣言をよりどころとした」「だれもが機会を得て、天与の能力を可能な限り発揮し、より充実した豊かな生活を追求していけるという夢」とある
- 34 rise up and live out「立ち上がり、実践する」live out は「行う、経験する」
- 34 its creed「その＝この国の信条」以下の独立宣言に謳われていること
- 35 We hold these truths to be self-evident, that all men are created equal「われわれはこれらの真理が自明のものであると考える。即ちすべての人が平等に創造されたということ」原文ではこの後に、that they are endowed by their Creator with certain unalienable Rights, that among these are Life, Liberty and the Pursuit of Happinessと続く。these truths とはこの3つのこと
- 38 at the table of brotherhood「兄弟関係のテーブル」つまり比喩的に兄弟同士が集うテーブル
- 39 Lyndon Johnson 第37代合衆国大統領（1969-1974）
- 40 sympathetic to ～「～に理解のある」
- 40 had become president「大統領になっていた」president は役職の場合は無冠詞
- 42 respectively「それぞれ」
- 43 legal discrimination based on race「人種に基づく法的差別」
- 46 through the years that followed「その後何年も」
- 47 outspoken opponent of the War in Vietnam「ベトナムでの戦争に対する声高な反対者」
- 49 sanitation workers「衛生労働者」つまりゴミ回収に携わる労働者
- 51 assassin「暗殺者」

英語
徹底耳練

■さらに、本書を徹底活用するために！

Useful Expressions一覧
Listening Challenge 120

Useful Expressions 一覧

Useful Expressions ❶
1. You'd have to wait in line to register.
   (登録するなら、列に並ばなければなりません)
2. Your plan ought to work out all right.
   (君の計画はうまくいくはずだ)
3. I ran into an old friend of mine yesterday.
   (昨日ばったり古い友人に会った)

Useful Expressions ❷
1. He took a day off today.
   (彼は今日はお休みです)
2. Jack will never go for such an idea.
   (ジャックはそんな考えには賛成するはずがない)
3. That's exactly why I am here.
   (だからこそ私が来たのです)

Useful Expressions ❸
1. Did you get to rub elbows with your new colleagues?
   (新しい同僚と親しくなりましたか?)
2. Try to make a good impression on her.
   (彼女にいい印象を与えるようにしなさい)
3. It's a shame to waste all this food.
   (こんなに食べ物を無駄にするのはもったいない)

Useful Expressions ❹
1. Shall we go through all the details?
   (詳細をすべてチェックしましょうか?)
2. There's one problem with your proposal.
   (あなたの提案には一つ問題がある)
3. I will take the responsibility in that case.
   (その場合には私が責任をとります)

Useful Expressions ❺
1. What we need is a go-getter like you.
   (私たちが必要なのはあなたのような辣腕家です)
2. You should get a good look at this product.
   (この製品をよく見てみなさい)
3. Let's have a quick look at them now.
   (今はそれらをざっと見ておきましょう)

Short Conversation 編

Useful Expressions 6

1. Let's bring it up at our next meeting.
   (次の会議でそれを話題にしましょう)
2. They got bogged down in a series of lawsuits.
   (彼らは一連の訴訟合戦に落ち込んだ)
3. The last thing I want is to have to do it all over again.
   (それを最初からやり直すなんてごめんだ)
4. I give you my word that I'm serious.
   (誓って本気だよ)

Useful Expressions 7

1. (He can't help you.) He's got too much piled up on his desk.
   ([彼は助けてはくれない。]仕事がたまりすぎています)
2. You won't get much out of his book.
   (彼の本からはあまり得るものがない)
3. I doubt that he knows about this.
   (彼がこのことを知っているとは思わない)
4. Why don't you ask Bill?
   (ビルに聞いてみたらどうですか?)

Useful Expressions 8

1. I was wondering if you could help me.
   (助けていただけないかと思いまして)
2. Are you satisfied with the job you have?
   (あなたの今の仕事に満足していますか?)
3. We used to come here to dine.
   (ここに食事に来たものだ)

Useful Expressions 9

1. Did you see my cell phone around?
   (僕の携帯を見かけなかった?)
2. I haven't eaten beef in ages.
   (ずいぶん牛肉を食べていない)
3. Do you have any idea who he is?
   (彼がだれだかわかりますか?)
4. I guess you are right.
   ([考えてみれば]君の言うとおりだ)

Useful Expressions 10

1. Somebody will be available to assist you.
   (だれかお手伝いする者がいるでしょう)
2. I assure you that it will be delivered on time.
   (間違いなく期限内にお届けいたします)
3. His house will come up for sale next week.
   (彼の家は来週売りにでる)

Useful Expressions 一覧

Useful Expressions 11
CD 1-52

1. He usually flies United.
   （彼は普段はユナイテッド航空で飛びます）
2. I used to have to make this trip every week.
   （私は毎週この旅行をしなければなりませんでした）
3. You have to change planes at JFK airport.
   （JFK空港で飛行機を乗り換えなければなりません）

Useful Expressions 12
CD 1-53

1. I could certainly use a computer like this.
   （こんなコンピュータがあるといいな）
2. We've set up a meeting (on) next Monday.
   （次の月曜日に会議を設定しました）
3. Can I get back to you on this after the meeting?
   （この件は会議の後でいいですか？）

Useful Expressions 13
CD 1-54

1. Who seems to be the best player on your team?
   （君のチームで一番の選手は誰だい？）
2. I need to talk to your boss.
   （あなたの上司に話がある）
3. (Are) you sure you don't want to come?
   （本当に来たくないのですね？）
4. Make sure you have everything.
   （忘れ物がないように確認しなさい）

Useful Expressions 14
CD 1-55

1. Let's go over the list again.
   （リストをもう一度確認しよう）
2. He left the decision up to us.
   （彼は決断をわれわれに任せた）
3. His idea didn't turn out okay.
   （彼の考えはうまくいかなかった）

Useful Expressions 15
CD 1-56

1. They will name you chairman.
   （彼らはあなたを議長に指名するだろう）
2. I don't know if I would call him a genius.
   （彼を天才だと言っていいかどうかわからない）
3. I wonder what will happen next.
   （次に何が起こるのだろう）
4. What happened to your confidence?
   （君の自信はどうなったの？）

Short Conversation 編

Useful Expressions 16

1. Are you signing up for the job?
   (その仕事に申し込みますか?)
2. Could you tell me what time it is now?
   (今何時でしょうか?)
3. I'm not authorized to make that decision.
   (そのような決定をする権限を与えられていない)

Useful Expressions 17

1. I'm afraid it's too late.
   (残念ながら間に合いません)
2. I took the liberty of reserving a room for you.
   (勝手ながら部屋を予約しておきました)
3. You should have come earlier.
   (もっと早く来るべきだった)

Useful Expressions 18

1. I hear that you've just been promoted.
   (昇進したそうだね)
2. I'm sure this will work.
   (きっとこれでうまくいきますよ)
3. He didn't get my message.
   (彼は私の言っていることがよくわからなかった)

Useful Expressions 19

1. Will this work for you?
   (こちらだとうまくいきますか?)
2. The matter is out of my hands now.
   (その件はもう私の手を離れました)
3. How am I supposed to find him?
   (どうやって彼を見つければいいんだろう?)

Useful Expressions 20

1. All I have is just a few hundred dollars.
   (あるのは数百ドルだけだ)
2. I'd be willing to quit my job.
   (喜んで仕事を辞めますよ)
3. I don't blame you for quitting your job.
   (君が仕事を辞めるのも無理はない)

Useful Expressions 一覧

Useful Expressions 21
1. My boss wants you to get back to Mr. Smith on the new contract.
   （上司は、新しい契約についてあなたからスミスさんに連絡してほしいとのことです）
2. We're coming back about a week sooner than expected.
   （予定より約1週間早く帰ってきます）
3. So we wondered if you knew about it.
   （だからあなたがそのことを知っているかどうかと思ったのです）
4. It'd give you a chance to rub elbows with the board members.
   （役員と親しく話をする機会になりますよ）

Useful Expressions 22
1. Our car has a navigation system.
   （うちの車はカーナビが付いている）
2. Japanese cars get good mileage.
   （日本車は燃費がいい）
3. This contract needs rewording.
   （この契約書は語句の修正が必要である）
4. What is your asking price?
   （あなたの言い値はいくらですか?）

Useful Expressions 23
1. They named Bill their new candidate.
   （彼らはビルを彼らの新しい候補者に指名した）
2. Mary will become our new department head effective September first.
   （メアリーは9月1日付で私たちの新しい部長になる）
3. Mr. Black will begin serving as the section chief.
   （ブラック氏は新しい課長を務めます）
4. This move will play a key role in solving the financial problem.
   （この決断は財政問題を解決する上でカギとなる働きをするでしょう）

Useful Expressions 24
1. The next item on the agenda is the election of the new committee members.
   （次の議題は委員会の新委員の選挙です）
2. You have been asked to submit a proposal.
   （あなたは提案を提出することを求められています）
3. We have to make the final decision by the end of the day.
   （今日中に最終的な決定をしなければならない）
4. I will run through the candidates we have so far.
   （これまでに挙がっている候補［者］の名前を読みあげます）

Useful Expressions 25
1. This is Dr. Yamada calling from the City Hospital.
   （こちらは市民病院の山田医師です）
2. Two seats are available for the 11 o'clock flight.
   （11時の便は2席空いています）
3. Are you familiar with this library?
   （この図書館のことはよくご存知ですか?）

Short Talk 編

Useful Expressions 26

1. Everybody was tense from the moment the president entered the office.
  (社長がオフィスに現れたときから、みんなは緊張していた)
2. Our Company is behind in household electrical appliances.
  (わが社は家電で遅れをとっている)
3. I got the best deal on my computer.
  (コンピュータを安く手に入れた)
4. She is desperate to find another job.
  (彼女は別の仕事を探すのに必死だ)

Useful Expressions 27

1. I would like to begin by introducing our new board members.
  (新しい役員を紹介することから始めたいと思います)
2. We decided to ask you to reconsider.
  (あなたに考え直すことを求めることにしました)
3. Please look over the documents before we begin.
  (始める前に書類に目を通してください)

Useful Expressions 28

1. Please do not open the booklet until I tell you to do so.
  (指示をするまで冊子を開かないでください)
2. The committee consists of ten members.
  (委員会は10人の委員からなる)
3. Next you will fill out the questionnaire.
  (次にアンケート調査に答えていただきます)

Useful Expressions 29

1. This is my first time to visit your company.
  (御社を訪れるのは初めてです)
2. On behalf of President Morrison, it is my pleasure to welcome you all to our company.
  (モリソン社長に代わって当社への来訪を歓迎いたします)
3. The 1990s were difficult times for Japan economically.
  (1990年代は経済的に日本にとっては大変な時代でした)

Useful Expressions 30

1. I'll be showing you the important features of the museum in a minute.
  (すぐにこの博物館の重要な特色を案内します)
2. Let me first take you to the main entrance.
  (まず正面玄関にお連れします)
3. If you are all ready, let's get started.
  (準備がよければ始めましょう)

Useful Expressions 一覧

Useful Expressions 31
[CD 1-72]

1. It's a great pleasure to be able to make an opening speech for this conference.
   (会議の開会の挨拶をするのは大きな喜びです)
2. Then he worked part-time as a salesperson at a convenience store.
   (それから彼はコンビニの販売員としてパートタイムで働いた)
3. He attended graduate school while working part-time for an on-line broker.
   (彼はオンラインブローカーでアルバイトをしながら、大学院に行った)
4. Over the years he gradually became more and more short-tempered.
   (年を経るにしたがって彼はますます短気になった)

Useful Expressions 32
[CD 1-73]

1. I've been asked to make a proposal.
   (提案をするように頼まれました)
2. Will you lay out the project for this committee?
   (この委員会に企画を説明してくれますか?)
3. You should be able to get there by ten.
   (10時までにはそこに着くことができるはずだ)

Useful Expressions 33
[CD 1-74]

1. Before we begin our presentation I would like to provide a little background information on space science.
   (発表の前に宇宙科学についての背景知識を少し述べておきます)
2. Please go through registration procedures before going to your rooms.
   (各人の部屋へ行く前に登録の手続きをしてください)
3. We are planning to convert this into our second guest house.
   (これを2つ目のゲストハウスにする予定です)
4. The museum is well worth visiting.
   (その博物館は訪れる価値が大いにあります)

Useful Expressions 34
[CD 1-75]

1. New businesses are joining the field at the rate of three per month.
   (新規事業が月に3社の割合で参入しています)
2. I think it's safe to say that our company is the first to adopt this system.
   (わが社がこのシステムを導入した最初であると言っても差し支えない)
3. This area has a lot of attractive features to offer.
   (この地域には魅力的な点がたくさんある)

Useful Expressions 35
[CD 1-76]

1. I've been asked to remind you about the new law on copyrights.
   (著作権に関する新しい法律について皆さんに念を押すよう言われています)
2. Be sure not to inform any more people than necessary.
   (必要な人にだけ知らせてください)
3. Please pass this information on to your direct subordinates.
   (この情報を直属の部下に伝えてください)

Short Talk 編

Useful Expressions 36

1. I had no idea what he was talking about.
   (彼が何のことを話しているのかわかりませんでした)
2. Our section deals with customer complaints and product improvement.
   (この課は顧客の苦情処理と製品改良を行います)
3. I will drop by your office late this afternoon.
   (午後遅くに御社に立ち寄ります)

Useful Expressions 37

1. The Red Sox lead the Yankees 5 to 3.
   (レッドソックスがヤンキーズを5対3でリードしています)
2. Our new flat screen TV is expected to do well in the next quarter.
   (わが社の新しい薄型テレビは次の四半期に健闘するものと期待されています)
3. It's a bit surprising that exports increased despite the rise in yen.
   (円高にもかかわらず輸出が増えたのはやや意外です)

Useful Expressions 38

1. In order to apply for the job, you have to be an experienced system engineer.
   (その仕事に応募するためには、経験のあるシステムエンジニアである必要があります)
2. My boss didn't tell me exactly what he meant by "major shake-up."
   (「大人事異動」が一体何であるのか上司ははっきり教えてくれなかった)
3. We make every effort to keep our customers satisfied.
   (当社はお客様に満足いただくためにあらゆる努力を行います)

Useful Expressions 39

1. It's an honor to be invited to Sunburst Coffee to talk about tea production around the world.
   (サンバースト・コーヒーに招かれて、世界のお茶の生産についてお話するのは名誉なことです)
2. In the field of flat screen TVs it is difficult for any company just to survive.
   (薄型テレビの分野では、どの会社も生き残るだけでも難しい)
3. We should not waste our energy on such trivial things.
   (われわれはそのような些末なことにエネルギーを浪費すべきではない)

Useful Expressions 40

1. Thanks for inviting us to your managers' conference.
   (管理職会議に私どもを招待いただきありがとうございます)
2. The only thing that changes is the way you make your payment.
   (唯一変わるのは支払いの方法です)
3. We can save money on office paper.
   (会社で使う紙のお金を節約できる)
4. I'm going to turn things over to our next speaker.
   (では次の講演者にバトンタッチします)

Listening Challenge 120

🔊 **CDの音声を聴き取り、以下の質問にチャレンジしてください。**
（質問および選択肢の音声は収録されていません）

🔊 CD 1-02　耳練1　A Man in a Hurry

Q1. What is the man's problem?
- A. He has to go a long distance quickly.
- B. He doesn't know where he should go.
- C. He doesn't have enough money for his trip.
- D. He has been transferred too many times.

Q2. Why doesn't the woman recommend the subway?
- A. It is very expensive.
- B. It takes too much time.
- C. It is hard to find at this time of day.
- D. It is currently out of order.

Q3. How does the man feel at the end of the conversation?
- A. Relieved.
- B. Anxious.
- C. Irritated.
- D. Confused.

🔊 CD 1-03　耳練2　Absenteeism

Q4. What are the speakers mainly discussing?
- A. Their children.
- B. The food in the cafeteria.
- C. A problem in their company.
- D. Plans for a holiday.

Q5. What criticism does the man make about management?
- A. It provides poor services to customers.
- B. It wastes money on day care.
- C. It doesn't care about the cafeteria.
- D. Its priorities are wrong.

Q6. What does the man propose doing about the problem?
- A. Reporting all absentees' names.
- B. Holding a meeting in the cafeteria.
- C. Preparing a report for management.
- D. Hiring employees who don't have kids.

耳練3 Ankle Injury

Q7. Why can't the man attend the reception?
- A. He has no car.
- B. He injured himself.
- C. He has an important game.
- D. He has a doctor's appointment.

Q8. Who will be at the reception?
- A. The woman's family.
- B. Famous movie directors.
- C. Important people in their company.
- D. The president of a country.

Q9. What does the man want the woman to do later?
- A. Apologize to the Board of Directors.
- B. Bring him some medicine.
- C. Pick up some work for him at the office.
- D. Tell him about the reception.

耳練4 Contract

Q10. Where do the man and woman work?
- A. In a small business that they own.
- B. In different companies.
- C. In the same department of a large company.
- D. In different departments of a large company.

Q11. What does the woman want the man to do?
- A. Make a change in a contract.
- B. Move up the project deadline.
- C. Demonstrate the new software.
- D. Apologize for an engineering mistake.

Q12. What will the man send the woman?
- A. Some money.
- B. New software.
- C. A proposal for a project.
- D. A revised contract.

Listening Challenge 120

CDの音声を聴き取り、以下の質問にチャレンジしてください。
（質問および選択肢の音声は収録されていません）

耳練5　A Commercial Property

Q13. What kind of business does the man want to open?
- A. A clothing store.
- B. A glassware shop.
- C. A moving company.
- D. A car dealership.

Q14. What is the woman's occupation?
- A. The man's assistant.
- B. A limousine driver.
- C. A banker.
- D. A real estate agent.

Q15. Why is the man eager to make a deal quickly?
- A. He thinks interest rates will rise.
- B. He knows there aren't many good locations.
- C. He is losing money.
- D. He is concerned about moving costs.

耳練6　Agenda

Q16. What are the speakers doing now?
- A. Taking a break.
- B. Cleaning something.
- C. Reading a memo.
- D. Preparing for a meeting.

Q17. What is probably the problem with the break room?
- A. Employees spend too much time there.
- B. Only section leaders can use it.
- C. It is often dirty.
- D. Not enough people use it.

Q18. What does the man promise to do?
- A. Conduct the meeting smoothly.
- B. Send a memo to the president.
- C. Explain the problem in detail to the staff.
- D. Change the agenda.

Q13-24

★正解は234ページで確認できます。

耳練7　Managers' Conference

Q19. Why won't the woman attend the conference?
- A. She never attends such events.
- B. She plans to move her office this weekend.
- C. She did not make an airline reservation.
- D. She has to deal with personnel changes.

Q20. What does the woman say about last year's conference?
- A. She was unable to attend.
- B. It was in a more convenient location.
- C. It was not very useful.
- D. The guest speaker was interesting.

Q21. What does the woman say about this year's guest speaker?
- A. She met the speaker many years ago.
- B. The speaker's advice may be out of date.
- C. The speaker did not deserve to win a prize.
- D. It is the same speaker as last year.

耳練8　A Telephone Sale Call

Q22. What is the purpose of the woman's call?
- A. To get advice from the man.
- B. To sell the man a service.
- C. To test the man's telephone.
- D. To offer the man a job.

Q23. What aspect of her company's service does the woman emphasize?
- A. Fast service.
- B. Customer care.
- C. Low cost.
- D. Security.

Q24. Why does the man try to be polite to the woman?
- A. He understands how hard her job is.
- B. He is interested in her company's service.
- C. He remembers meeting her once.
- D. He has some time to relax now.

Listening Challenge 120

CDの音声を聴き取り、以下の質問にチャレンジしてください。
（質問および選択肢の音声は収録されていません）

CD 1-10　耳練9　An Ambitious Young Man

Q25. How does the man feel about the news about Jeffrey?
- A. Pleased.
- B. Shocked.
- C. Disappointed.
- D. Envious.

Q26. What is Jeffrey's long-term goal?
- A. To found a company.
- B. To become a professor.
- C. To return to his former company.
- D. To live on the East Coast.

Q27. What field is Jeffrey especially interested in?
- A. Automobile parts.
- B. Architecture.
- C. Computers.
- D. Police work.

CD 1-11　耳練10　Faulty Product

Q28. Why is the woman unhappy about the email filter?
- A. The installation is behind schedule.
- B. It blocks messages that she sends out.
- C. It doesn't work very well.
- D. It caused damage to her computer.

Q29. What does the woman plan to do if the problem is not fixed?
- A. File a lawsuit.
- B. Hire a different company.
- C. Buy a new computer.
- D. Renew the current contract.

Q30. How soon does the man promise to fix the problem?
- A. The very same day.
- B. The next day.
- C. The end of this month.
- D. The beginning of next month.

Q25-36

★正解は234ページで確認できます。

耳練11 Crowded Airplane

Q31. What is the relationship of the speakers?
- A. Co-workers.
- B. Old friends.
- C. Strangers.
- D. Flight attendant and passenger.

Q32. What did the woman dislike about her previous job?
- A. The travel.
- B. The supervisors.
- C. The standard of living.
- D. The salary.

Q33. What is the purpose of the woman's trip?
- A. To celebrate an event with her husband.
- B. To take part in a sports competition.
- C. To do volunteer work for her church.
- D. To help her husband find a job.

耳練12 Headhunting

Q34. What does Bob want Jennifer to do?
- A. Join his company.
- B. Buy his company's products.
- C. Give another presentation.
- D. Meet with one of his clients.

Q35. How does Jennifer feel about Bob's request?
- A. Confused.
- B. Interested.
- C. Indifferent.
- D. Offended.

Q36. How will Jennifer contact Bob?
- A. By email.
- B. By phone message.
- C. By calling him directly.
- D. By postcard.

Listening Challenge 120

CDの音声を聴き取り、以下の質問にチャレンジしてください。
（質問および選択肢の音声は収録されていません）

耳練13　A Million Messages

Q37. What is probably the woman's job?
- A. Head of maintenance.
- B. Budget planner.
- C. Postal worker.
- D. Secretary.

Q38. Who will the man talk to first?
- A. The school principal.
- B. His wife.
- C. The vice president.
- D. His son.

Q39. What is the matter with the man's son?
- A. He does nothing seriously.
- B. He is having a difficult time.
- C. He cannot concentrate on his work.
- D. He is having a good time.

耳練14　Weekend Plans

Q40. What had the speakers been discussing earlier?
- A. The woman's supervisor.
- B. Plans for the weekend.
- C. A meeting with the legal department.
- D. A mistake in a contract.

Q41. What happened to interrupt the conversation?
- A. The woman's boss spoke to her.
- B. The legal department called.
- C. The woman had a headache.
- D. Jeff called.

Q42. What will the woman do this afternoon?
- A. Depart for the beach.
- B. Attend a meeting.
- C. Revise a contract.
- D. Visit another company.

Q 37-48

★正解は234ページで確認できます。

耳練15　Shake-up

Q43. What happened to Marcia Waterston?
- A. She was shaken up in an accident.
- B. She had an unpleasant surprise.
- C. She was named Director of Human Resources.
- D. She got a promotion.

Q44. Who is Miles Butterman?
- A. A former executive.
- B. President of the company.
- C. Director of company housing.
- D. The company lawyer.

Q45. How does the woman feel about what happened to Miles?
- A. Delighted.
- B. Shocked.
- C. Angry.
- D. Unimpressed.

耳練16　Franchise Seminar

Q46. What is probably the man's long-term career goal?
- A. Seminar instructor.
- B. Owner of a hamburger shop.
- C. French-speaking tour guide.
- D. Bank employee.

Q47. What information does the woman refuse to tell the man?
- A. The number of new franchises.
- B. The deadline for applications.
- C. How to submit an application.
- D. How difficult it is to be accepted for training.

Q48. What will happen to all applicants after the seminar?
- A. They will be given tests.
- B. They will begin a training course.
- C. They will be taken to Chicago.
- D. They will compete for quarters.

Listening Challenge 120

CDの音声を聴き取り、以下の質問にチャレンジしてください。
（質問および選択肢の音声は収録されていません）

耳練17　Baseball Tickets

Q49. Why does the woman want tickets to a baseball game?
- A. To impress some clients.
- B. To cheer for her favorite team.
- C. To support a charity.
- D. To entertain her family.

Q50. How does the woman feel about the man's first news?
- A. Satisfied.
- B. Elated.
- C. Upset.
- D. Unmoved.

Q51. What does the man say about the tickets that he got?
- A. They were difficult to get.
- B. They were very cheap.
- C. They are for seats in a good location.
- D. They are for a rescheduled game.

耳練18　Employee Orientation

Q52. What new assignment will the man begin next month?
- A. Training new employees.
- B. Meeting new customers.
- C. Writing new company policies.
- D. Conducting a sales conference.

Q53. What does the woman want the man to tell the new employees about?
- A. How to dress properly.
- B. How to send email messages.
- C. How to talk to customers.
- D. How to introduce themselves.

Q54. What will the man do about the woman's suggestion?
- A. Forget about it.
- B. Write it down.
- C. Think about it.
- D. Give it little attention.

Q49-60

★正解は234ページで確認できます。

耳練19　Office Renovation

Q55. How did the woman find out about the renovation of the offices?
- A. She saw a notice on a bulletin board.
- B. The man informed her by mail.
- C. An announcement was made at a meeting.
- D. The president of the company told her.

Q56. What does the man say about the woman's complaint?
- A. He thinks it is unreasonable.
- B. He has heard the same thing from others.
- C. He will tell the president about it.
- D. It is based on a misunderstanding.

Q57. What does the man apologize for?
- A. The damage done to her office.
- B. The loss of her files.
- C. His rude attitude toward her.
- D. His inability to satisfy her request.

耳練20　Looking for a Job

Q58. What does the woman say about the jobs that she finds?
- A. They don't pay enough money.
- B. They don't fit her schedule.
- C. They don't suit her qualifications.
- D. She isn't tough enough to do them.

Q59. What kind of job does the woman most hope to find?
- A. Sales manager.
- B. Nurse.
- C. Cashier.
- D. Typist.

Q60. What does the man advise the woman to do?
- A. Lower her expectations.
- B. Try not to be discouraged.
- C. Try to be more realistic.
- D. Work in a supermarket.

Listening Challenge 120

CDの音声を聴き取り、以下の質問にチャレンジしてください。
（質問および選択肢の音声は収録されていません）

耳練21　A Mountain Bike Prototype　[CD 1-22]

Q61. In what part of the company does Larry probably work?
- A. Research and Development.
- B. Human Services.
- C. Accounting.
- D. Marketing.

Q62. What will Mr. Hendricks and his team do on the 7th?
- A. Test a new product.
- B. Go for a long run.
- C. Appear in a courtroom.
- D. Visit Larry's office.

Q63. What would Larry be able to do if he accepted the invitation?
- A. Make suggestions.
- B. Test-ride a bike.
- C. Help paint a product.
- D. Get advice on his work.

耳練22　Radio Flea Market　[CD 1-23]

Q64. Who is Lisa?
- A. A radio announcer.
- B. A customer looking for a car.
- C. A person trying to sell a car.
- D. A spokesperson for Honda Motors.

Q65. According to the announcement, what part of the car is not in top condition?
- A. The sound system.
- B. The exterior.
- C. The transmission.
- D. The air conditioner.

Q66. If someone wants to buy the car, what should he or she do?
- A. Telephone the owner directly.
- B. Get proof of having 4,000 dollars.
- C. Visit the car dealership.
- D. Drop by the owner's home in the evening.

Q61-72

★正解は234ページで確認できます。

耳練23　Business News

Q67. What is Edward Klepp's current position?
   A. Vice president.
   B. Chief accounting officer.
   C. CEO.
   D. Public relations officer.

Q68. Who is George Hipple?
   A. A former employee of Avanti.
   B. The CEO of Avanti.
   C. Avanti's spokesperson.
   D. Avanti's new chief accountant.

Q69. According to the CEO, what is Avanti's goal?
   A. Reduction of staff.
   B. Cutting costs.
   C. Further growth.
   D. Moving to a new stage.

耳練24　New Annex

Q70. At what sort of event is this talk being given?
   A. A dinner party.
   B. An executive committee meeting.
   C. A sales presentation.
   D. A departmental meeting.

Q71. When will the name of the new annex be decided?
   A. Within the next few minutes.
   B. By this evening.
   C. By the end of the week.
   D. By next month.

Q72. Why has "West Annex" been suggested as a name for the annex?
   A. It is the name of the president's relative.
   B. It describes the building's location.
   C. It is the name of an important person.
   D. It parallels the names of other annexes.

Listening Challenge 120

CDの音声を聴き取り、以下の質問にチャレンジしてください。
（質問および選択肢の音声は収録されていません）

耳練25　Banquet Hall Reservation

Q73. Who is the speaker?
- A. A restaurant manager.
- B. A colleague of Mr. Jacobs.
- C. A customer of Mr. Jacobs.
- D. An employee of Mr. Jacobs.

Q74. What does the speaker imply about the banquet hall?
- A. It is already reserved.
- B. It is too big for the party.
- C. It is suitable for making speeches.
- D. Its tables will be replaced.

Q75. What does the speaker want Mr. Jacobs to do?
- A. Come to see a room in person.
- B. Make an apology.
- C. Contact her soon.
- D. Confirm his plans by December.

耳練26　Book Commercial

Q76. What is the commercial for?
- A. A car dealership.
- B. Sporting goods.
- C. A book.
- D. A trade school.

Q77. According to the commercial, what can we get if we buy this product?
- A. A free car.
- B. Useful knowledge.
- C. A good job in sales.
- D. Tickets to a sporting event.

Q78. What must we do in order to get the product?
- A. Make a telephone call.
- B. Write an email message.
- C. Visit a dealership.
- D. Guess the lucky number.

Q73-84

★正解は234ページで確認できます。

🔊 CD 1-28 耳練27 Condominium Association Meeting

Q79. Who is being addressed?
- A. Stockholders.
- B. Security guards.
- C. Victims of crimes.
- D. Condominium residents.

Q80. What is Quintomex?
- A. A video rental store.
- B. A telephone service provider.
- C. A maker of security systems.
- D. A condominium management agency.

Q81. Why does the speaker mention a video camera?
- A. This meeting is being filmed.
- B. It may make the building safer.
- C. He will soon show a film he made.
- D. A company is providing it as a gift.

🔊 CD 1-29 耳練28 Spanish Test

Q82. What is the main topic of the talk?
- A. Ways to improve Spanish ability.
- B. Instructions for the test center's staff.
- C. Rules for taking a test.
- D. Strategies for doing a translation exercise.

Q83. How is the writing section different from other sections of the test?
- A. Dictionaries may be used.
- B. Questions are not multiple choice.
- C. It is all right to use pencils.
- D. Answer sheets are not used.

Q84. What will happen next?
- A. The writing section will begin.
- B. Test booklets will be handed out.
- C. Dictionaries will be provided.
- D. Answer sheets will be collected.

Listening Challenge 120

CDの音声を聴き取り、以下の質問にチャレンジしてください。
（質問および選択肢の音声は収録されていません）

耳練29　Association of Small Publishers

Q85. What is the speaker's goal?
- A. To sell books.
- B. To attract new members.
- C. To publish a book.
- D. To get a new job.

Q86. According to the speaker, what can his group do for the audience?
- A. Save money.
- B. Buy more books.
- C. Design a website.
- D. Reduce membership fees.

Q87. What will the speaker do next?
- A. Show a website.
- B. Collect membership fees.
- C. Make a presentation.
- D. Introduce a new speaker.

耳練30　Factory Tour

Q88. Who is the speaker?
- A. A tour guide.
- B. A bus driver.
- C. An aircraft engineer.
- D. A food server.

Q89. What will the tour group be able to watch?
- A. The construction of a large building.
- B. Test flights of new aircraft.
- C. A meeting of top executives.
- D. Airplanes being built.

Q90. Why will the tour be conducted by bus?
- A. The facility is very large.
- B. It is not safe to walk.
- C. It is raining.
- D. The main building is far away.

Q85-96

★正解は234ページで確認できます。

🔊 CD 1-32 耳練31 Pet Lovers Incorporated

Q91. What is the purpose of the talk?
   A. To introduce the main speaker.
   B. To explain how the company got started.
   C. To promote gentle treatment of animals.
   D. To attract new customers.

Q92. What does Pet Lovers Incorporated do?
   A. It runs a chain of pet shops.
   B. It rescues pets from bad homes.
   C. It trains pets to help people.
   D. It supports pet owners' rights.

Q93. What aspect of the treatment of animals does Ms. Huffington emphasize?
   A. Kindness.
   B. A healthy diet.
   C. Strictness.
   D. Good grooming.

🔊 CD 1-33 耳練32 Outsourcing

Q94. What is the purpose of the talk?
   A. To explain why outsourcing is a bad idea.
   B. To sell a software development service.
   C. To compare the prices of two companies.
   D. To help a committee reach a decision.

Q95. What does the speaker say about the software engineering industry?
   A. It is very competitive.
   B. It has many drawbacks.
   C. Its services are too expensive.
   D. Its leaders are wealthy.

Q96. What does the speaker recommend doing, if the company outsources projects?
   A. Asking a lot of questions.
   B. Maintaining high standards.
   C. Using foreign firms.
   D. Laying off staff.

Listening Challenge 120

CDの音声を聴き取り、以下の質問にチャレンジしてください。
（質問および選択肢の音声は収録されていません）

耳練33　Ellis Island　[CD 1-34]

Q97. Where does this talk take place?
- A. On a boat moving toward Ellis Island.
- B. In front of the Main Building.
- C. On the second floor of the Main Building.
- D. Inside a museum.

Q98. What purpose does the Main Building serve today?
- A. It houses a museum.
- B. It is an immigration office.
- C. It exhibits immigrants' works of art.
- D. It protects the country from immigrants.

Q99. What does the speaker recommend doing at the end of the tour?
- A. Shopping in the museum store.
- B. Asking questions.
- C. Repeating the tour.
- D. Watching a movie.

耳練34　Sunburst Coffee　[CD 1-35]

Q100. Why is Charles Finkleman well known?
- A. He founded a famous company.
- B. He led a small business to great success.
- C. He discovered a new way to make coffee.
- D. He has appeared in television commercials.

Q101. How many Sunburst Coffee shops are there in the world?
- A. Three hundred.
- B. Seven hundred.
- C. Over a thousand.
- D. Over twelve hundred.

Q102. According to the speaker, what is Mr. Finkleman's outstanding talent?
- A. Finding good coffee farms.
- B. Hiring excellent staff.
- C. Breaking into various markets.
- D. Eliminating competitors.

Q 97-108

★正解は234ページで確認できます。

🔊 CD 1-36 耳練35 Paper Reduction

Q103. To whom is the talk addressed?
- A. Vice presidents.
- B. Secretaries and part-time workers.
- C. The heads of departments.
- D. Maintenance personnel.

Q104. What is the main purpose of the talk?
- A. To explain how the printers work.
- B. To reduce paper costs.
- C. To protect company secrets.
- D. To improve the working environment.

Q105. What does the speaker say about documents containing sensitive information?
- A. They should be shredded.
- B. They should not be stapled.
- C. They should be put in recycle boxes.
- D. They should be printed on both sides.

🔊 CD 1-37 耳練36 Job Fair

Q106. What is the purpose of the talk?
- A. To sell services to the audience.
- B. To list the speaker's achievements.
- C. To introduce the speaker's company.
- D. To invite people to a party.

Q107. To whom is the talk addressed?
- A. Senior citizens.
- B. University students.
- C. Unmarried men.
- D. Potential clients.

Q108. Why does the speaker mention politicians?
- A. They are among his company's customers.
- B. There are several in the audience.
- C. Some of them used to work for his company.
- D. It is a career that he recommends.

Listening Challenge 120

CDの音声を聴き取り、以下の質問にチャレンジしてください。
（質問および選択肢の音声は収録されていません）

耳練37　Election Report

Q109. Who are Harkin and Klosterman?
- A. Political candidates.
- B. Campaign managers.
- C. Vote counters.
- D. News reporters.

Q110. What does the reporter say about the vote counting?
- A. It has just begun.
- B. It is more than half finished.
- C. It will be completed in an hour.
- D. It will take several days.

Q111. What does the reporter say about the outcome of the election?
- A. Klosterman is sure to win.
- B. Harkin is likely to win.
- C. A minor party's candidate might win.
- D. It is not at all clear who will win.

耳練38　Enterprise Zone Program

Q112. What is the purpose of the talk?
- A. To attract customers to a new business.
- B. To get voters to vote for a new program.
- C. To inform businesses of a government policy.
- D. To persuade the government to lower taxes.

Q113. What does the speaker promise to do soon?
- A. Explain an unclear term.
- B. Hand out application forms.
- C. Lead a tour of depressed areas.
- D. Introduce the state governor.

Q114. Who is the audience for this talk?
- A. Business owners.
- B. Government officials.
- C. Unemployed workers.
- D. Tax accountants.

Q 109-120

★正解は234ページで確認できます。

耳練39　Conflict Resolution

Q115. Who is the speaker?
- A. A sports coach.
- B. A successful author.
- C. A corporate executive.
- D. A university administrator.

Q116. Who is the audience for this speech?
- A. Owners of various businesses.
- B. Student athletes.
- C. Recently hired employees.
- D. Executives of a company.

Q117. What does the speaker hope to teach the audience?
- A. How to avoid internal conflicts.
- B. How to start their own businesses.
- C. How to attract more investors.
- D. How to get rid of rivals.

耳練40　Clean Electricity

Q118. What does the speaker's company provide?
- A. Garbage treatment.
- B. Clean electricity.
- C. Business consulting.
- D. Electronic goods.

Q119. What do some of the customers of the speaker's company worry about?
- A. Interruption of service.
- B. Inability to pay their power bill.
- C. How to keep their offices clean.
- D. Where their energy comes from.

Q120. What will the speaker do next?
- A. Let his colleague speak.
- B. Demonstrate his product.
- C. Show some charts and graphs.
- D. Give the audience a present.

Listening Challenge 120

正解記号一覧

Q	A	Q	A	Q	A	Q	A	Q	A	Q	A
1	A	21	B	41	A	61	D	81	B	101	C
2	B	22	B	42	B	62	A	82	C	102	C
3	A	23	C	43	D	63	A	83	B	103	C
4	C	24	A	44	A	64	C	84	B	104	B
5	D	25	A	45	B	65	A	85	B	105	A
6	C	26	A	46	B	66	A	86	A	106	C
7	B	27	C	47	A	67	A	87	C	107	B
8	C	28	C	48	A	68	A	88	A	108	A
9	D	29	B	49	A	69	D	89	D	109	A
10	B	30	B	50	C	70	B	90	A	110	A
11	A	31	C	51	C	71	D	91	B	111	D
12	D	32	A	52	A	72	B	92	C	112	C
13	A	33	A	53	A	73	A	93	A	113	A
14	D	34	A	54	B	74	C	94	D	114	A
15	A	35	B	55	B	75	C	95	A	115	B
16	D	36	A	56	B	76	C	96	B	116	D
17	C	37	D	57	D	77	B	97	B	117	A
18	A	38	B	58	C	78	A	98	A	118	B
19	D	39	B	59	A	79	D	99	D	119	A
20	C	40	B	60	B	80	C	100	B	120	A

index

A

a career as a civil rights leader	204
A common practice	189
a complete product line	128
a cottage at the beach	64
a couple of hours	28
a day off	16
A family sitting down to dinner	192
a few dozen	164
a future spouse	183
a good part of our own staff	136
a great many ~	140
a household word	144
a million messages	60
a minority	180
A more extreme case might be ~	196
a nervous first date	183
a number of ~	177
a raised dais	108
a room full of strangers	183
a series of	72
a step in the right direction	192
a trial run	92
a type of	177
a variety of ~	140, 183
A would-be plagiarizer ~	196
abolition	200
about a week sooner than expected	92
absenteeism	16
abused	189
accept	72
acceptable	48
access	84, 108
accommodate	108
according to race	204
act as ~	80
activates	186
Actually	28
acute	174
Addictive	186
address	136
adhere to ~	189
adherents	189
admit to having plagiarized ~	196
ado	144
adopted	174
advantage	136
advertise	124
advertising	152
advocate	200
affect	16
after all	76
agenda	32
agree to ~	68
air conditioner	96
all ~ is/are …	88
All of this	128
All right	24
all through history	180
allow patrons a clear view of the screen	183
amphetamines	186
an executive committee	104
an hour at least	12
and there ~	156
animal behavior	132
animal kingdom	180
annex	104
announce	100, 116
annual membership fee	124
answer sheet	120
Antarctica	189
Any ideas come to mind?	104
anything relevant	36
Anyway	56, 72
Apart from a small bed	177
apology	108
applicants	72
application form	72
application process	160
apply to ~	160
appreciate	48, 174
are (not) convinced	186
are accepted for the training course	72
are obliged to ~	192
are referred to as ~	177
are unnaturally favoring their right hands	180
argument	32
art	164
As a person develops a dependency on alcohol	186
As a result	174
as a whole	164
as if	174
As part of the tour	128
As soon as possible	28

235

index

as well as…	164
As with ~	189
as you know	124
asking price	96
assassin	204
associates	148
assure	48
astonishing	80
at a reasonable price	136
at any time	120
at least an hour	12
at present	160
at the end	24, 128
at the rate of ~	144
at the table of brotherhood	204
at this point	88
at whatever they do	180
attend	36, 152
attendee	72
attention	80
attract ~ to …	160
automatic transmission	96
available	40, 48, 108
available for ~	40, 108
available to ~	48
average consumer	192
awkward	180

B

background information	140
bandaged up	20
bane	183, 196
banquet hall reservations	108
banter	174
bargain	40
be concerned about ~	64
be desperate to	112
be driven by ~	177
be impressed with ~	56
be in favor of ~	84
be it an illegal one, or a legal one	186
be satisfied with ~	40
be sensitive to ~	189
be supposed to ~	84
be sure that ~	148
Be sure to ~	148
be wiped out	189
bears out ~	180
beat	112
became trapped	177

become friends with ~	20
before ~	128, 148
behavior	177
behind	36, 112
beneficiaries	189
benefit	160, 189
benefits and drawbacks	136
Besides	36
Best of luck to you	72
best-selling book	164
beyond the reach of the law	192
bid for ~	200
bill	168
blame ~ for …	32
blame ~ for …ing	183
bland	186
block	48
blood pressure	186
board	128
bonus minutes	40
book ~	64
book ~ for two nights	64
break room	32
bright	44
bring up ~	32
brochure	116
broke out	200
budding alcoholic	186
budget	16
budget proposal	60
build up	186
building materials	160
bumble	180
bumblers	180
burden for ~ing	174
burnout	174
business	44
by (3 o'clock)	12
By calling worldwide attention to ~	204
by hand-writing ~	120
by offering a wealth of services	124

C

cafeteria	16
call	116
Call now at our toll-free number	112
calls for a response	204
can easily be completed on line	192
can openers	180
candidate	156

cannot help ~ing	177
can't see the forest for the trees	174
career	100
cares about ~	174
case	68
cast doubt on ~	180
catch ~ in the act of ⋯ing	196
catch a taxi	12
ceiling	60
celebrate	52
challenge of ~ing	196
challenger	156
changing planes	52
channel	164
chronic problem	174
classic case of ~	174
clause	24
cleaner sources	168
client	48
closure	140
clumsy	180
cocaine	186
colleague	168
colonies	189
come along	92
come by	48
come to ~	84, 104
come up	168
commercial aircraft	128
commercial property	28
committee	136
common	112
commonplace	196
companionship	183
company dress code	80
competitive	72, 136
complain	177
comply with ~	64
Compulsive hoarders	177
concealed video camera	116
concluded that	186
concrete results	192
conduct	80, 128
conducting your tour of ~	128
confirm	108
conflict resolution	164
conjure ~ up	189
conjures up ~	189
consent	189
consequence	24

consist of ~	120
constantly	174
consumers and businesses	168
contain	148
contract	24, 64
controller	100
convert	140
convert ~ into ⋯	140
could you tell me ~	72
crabs	180
craving	186
crowded	52
crucial	136
cruelty	132
crutches	20
cubicle	84
cure ~ of ⋯	180
current	168
cut you some slack	40

D

damage	60
Damn it!	88
daring	200
dark blue	96
Darn it!	88
data processing	88
daunting	196
day by day	124
day care center	16
dazzles the tongue into a state of confusion	186
deadline	72
deal with	32, 48, 152, 174, 192
decided to ask ~ to do ⋯	116
declared	200
degree	132
deliver a speech	200
delivery	200
dent	96
Department of Commerce	160
depending on ~	168
depleting	189
describe	104
desperate	112
Despite ~	189
destinations	189
detail(s)	64
developed countries	192
devoted ~ to ⋯	200
diner	108

237

index

dinner reservation 76
discussion 32
dishonest 196
display window 28
distribute 120
do one's bit 183
do without ～ 84
documents 148
don't even think about it 12
don't keep her in the loop for important decisions 174
door-to-door salesman 192
double-sided copy 148
down side 136
draft 16
dragged on 200
draw a distinction between (a mere craving and a true addiction) 186
draw up ～ 24
drive you to ～ 28
drop by 64, 152
drug 186
during 140, 192
dying out 183

E

Each department has been asked to submit ～ 104
earlier 64
earn 40
eccentrics 177
economic activity 160
economic strain 204
economically depressed area 160
economically disadvantaged 160
Ecotourism 189
ecotourists 189
Ecuador 189
editorial 124
effective 48, 100
election return 156
electronic device 120
electronic form 196
eliminated 204
elsewhere 136
emboldened marketers to risk ～ 192
emergency room 174
emphasis 132
emphasize 80
ending the war in a victory for the North 200
energy provider 168
engineer 48

enjoy a sense of superiority 177
enterprise zone 160
entrepreneurs 196
envy 164
Equator 189
eraser 120
escape from the nuisances of daily life 183
establish 132
even as we speak 84
Even if ～ 164
Even more 183
Evidently 80
exception 148
executive 164
exemption 160
exhibit 140
exotic 189
expenditures 148
extension 92
exterior 96

F

facility 140
fall upon ～ 174
familiar with ～ 108, 152
family business 144
fast-paced 183
fattening sauces 186
favor 180
fax 24, 72
featuring 177
federal law 64
feel overwhelmed 174
fellow patrons 183
field 116
fight back 192
figure out 174
filmmakers 183
find out 112
finger-pointing 32
finishing touches 92
firm 136
first of all 108
first-rate movie-watching experience 183
flea market 96
flight 52
fly this route 52
follow 68
followers 189
fond memories 183

For a fee	196
for as long as schools have existed	196
for inclusion on the list	192
For instance	177
For most young people these days	196
for some reason	24
for the better	152
for the good of ~	164
for the last (five) years	100
for the meeting	64
For those of you ~	152
force ~ to do …	200
founder	132
fragility	189
franchise owners	72
free up	136
frigid	189
From a nutritional standpoint	186
From the moment you enter a car dealership	112
front door	116
front row	76
fumble	180
fumblers	180
functioning	96

G

gained control of ~	144
gas mileage	96
gateway	140
gave him the choice	68
generate	168, 204
get ~ down	88
Get ~ on the line	60
get ~ to …	76
get a chance	20
get a feel for ~	140
get a good look at ~	28
get accepted	44
get across town	12
get along (well)	174
get back to ~	56
get back to ~ on …	108
get bogged down ~	32
get into the details	168
get more involved with ~	174
get much out of it	36
get old	52
get right on it	48
get started	128
get through ~	124

gets good gas mileage	96
getting angry about them	177
getting fired	68
give advice on ~	124
give me a call	92
give up ~ to …	204
go for	16
go over ~	64
go through ~	24, 140
go-getter	56
going on vacation	189
good for ~	44
gotten out of control	196
grab a taxi	12
gradually	174
gradually sloping floors	183
graduate	152
graduate courses	132
grand scheme	44
ground floor	28
guide dogs for the blind	132
guiding principle	189

H

habitat	189
had become president	204
half a year after the law went into effect	192
hand-write	120
has a lot to offer	144
has had little effect	192
have a problem with ~	16
have a quick look at ~	28
Have a seat	48
have access to ~	84, 108
have time	28
having a bad day	174
He wondered if ~	92
He would live long enough to ~	200
headhunt	56
health care industry	88
hear from ~	60
heart rate	186
help herself	174
help you to ~	164
helping workers cope with workplace burnout	174
higher-ups in the organization	174
his collection of ~	177
his whole life	44
honey	64
honor	144, 200

239

index

hoof	180
hook up	84
hop out	189
hopping into ~	189
hour by hour	124
how am I supposed to ~?	84
How soon	28
how to ~	80
Human Resources	68
humane treatment	132

I

I appreciate your coming by	48
I assure you that ~	48
I can hold the room for you	108
I can now confirm that ~	108
I can speak for ~ when I say …	56
I don't blame you for ~ing	88
I don't know if I'd call it ~	68
I don't think ~	20, 144
I doubt that ~	36, 144
I give you my word that ~	32
I guess ~	20, 44
I hear that ~	80
I hear what you're saying	84
I know what that's like	52
I see what you mean	36
I tell you what	36
I think it's safe to say that ~	144
I used to ~	40, 52
I wanted to talk to you about ~	76
I was hoping ~	64
I was wondering if I could ~	40
I wonder who ~	68
I won't let ~	32
I'm at extension 5712	92
I'd be willing to ~	88
I'd like to begin tonight by ~ing	116
I'd like to provide a little background information	140
Ideally	28
identified	174
identified ~ as …	174
identifying the source	196
If interested	96
if one goes by	12
if there are no questions	120
if this is to happen	183
if you agree …, that is	56
if you choose	128
I'll be ~ing	128

I'll be conducting ~	80
I'll pause now for any questions	136
I'll talk to you later	20
I'm afraid ~	76, 84
I'm at the end of my rope!	88
I'm calling for~	40
I'm not too excited about ~	104
I'm not too wild about ~	104
I'm sure ~	28, 80
immigrants	140
immigration procedure	140
implies	186
imply	104
important decisions regarding ~	174
impose themselves on ~	189
imposes severe penalties on ~	192
impression	20
improper clothing	80
improvement	48
in a good location	28
in addition	136
in advance	116
in ages	44
in all cultures	180
in an attempt to ~	189
In ancient times	180
In any case	177
in any way	189
in case ~	24
in common	40
In contrast	196
in danger of ~	189
in decades past	183
In fact	40
in general	189
in honor of ~	104
In just a moment	120
in moments of boredom	183
In order to ~	160
In recent years	186
in relation to ~	104
In response to ~	196
in such a way that ~	177
in terms of ~	128, 200
in the battle against ~	192
In the final analysis	186
in the midst of ~	189, 192
in the mind	186
in the order that people called	60
In this same category are ~	186

240

in town	36
inconvenience	108
incumbent senator	156
indecisive	177
inevitable	136
inferior	180
informal meeting	56
inhabit ~	189
inspired imitation	192
install	48, 116
instead	12
instruct	120
interest rates	28
interest you in ~	40
internal struggle	164
interruption	168
intrigued	56
introduction	164
Intrusive	192
is approaching the two-hour mark	183
is besieged by ~	192
is expected to grow	189
is not consulted on ~	174
Is that right?	80
is widely viewed as ~	192
it is a bit surprising that ~	156
it is difficult for ~ to…	164
it is estimated that ~	180
It seems unlikely that ~	183
It was not until ~ that…	200
It was only a few years ago that ~	152
it was that hard to get in	72
It's a great honor for me to be able to introduce ~	144
it's nice to do ~	152
It'd give you a chance to ~	92
item	32, 96
It's a great pleasure to be able to ~	132
It's an honor to be invited to talk to ~ about…	164
It's because ~	16
It's just a suggestion, but	80
It's just that ~	32
It's kind of fun at first	52
It's kind of you to say so	56
It's my first time	80
it's nothing serious	60
it's out of my hands	84
I've been asked to ~	136
I've been asked to remind you about ~	148
I've got to ~	28

J

jealousy	164
job fair	152
job satisfaction	174
job-seeker	88
jokingly	177
junk mail	177
just	200
just like when ~	174

K

keep ~ing	88
kids	16
know of ~	28

L

Later that year	204
lay out	136
lay out for …~	136
lead ~ X to Y	156
left ~ out of …	174
left ~ up to …	64
left paw	180
left-handed	180
left-hander	180
leftover	148
legal department	64
legal discrimination based on race	204
lemon-flavored	189
less dishonest than if ~	196
Let Bob show you ~	112
let me begin ~	124
Let me just ~	128
let me think	76
level	112
liberty	76
Likewise	186
lip service	16
listen to ~	177
listings	28
live out	204
live out of one's suitcase	52
lively fare	183
locals	189
locations	144
Look	40, 84
look for ~	28, 88
look it over	116
look over this whole list	60
look (ed) askance at ~	180

241

index

look (ed) down on ~	180
low-grade paper	148
lure	189

M

main feature	183
main production facility	128
main villain	183
maintenance	60
make a sale	112
make an application to ~	160
make an offer on ~	112
make decisions about ~	177
make every effort to ~	160
make good mileage	96
make improvements to his house	68
make it	20
make sure ~	60
make the final decision	104
make the playing field level	112
make this trip	52
making a serious accusation	186
making fun of them	177
manage	177
management	16
market	88
Marketing	92
master's degree program	44
match	56, 88
maximize	164
may be interrupted	192
may be subjected to a very high fine	192
may have ~	174
medication	20
meet the deadline	24
memo	32
merely	200
message	80
minor parties	156
More specifically	136
more than once	192
moreover	168
most citizens on the list	192
most of	24, 156, 180
motion with the left claw	180
mounted	200
move	36, 100
move ~ back and forth	84
moviegoers are subjected to	183
moving in	28

multinational corporation	152
multiple choice	120
multiple choice items	120
my apologies for ~	108

N

name	68, 100
naming	104
naturalist	189
naturally	160
Nearly a year later	204
need ~ing	96
need only use an Internet search engine	196
need to ~	60
nervous about ~	80
nicotine	186
no doubt	180
no longer~	174
non-profit group	124
nonviolent protest	204
not confront them	183
not just physically tired, but tired of her job itself	174
not merely ~	174
not uncommon	183
notice	48, 84
now and then	186
now that ~	44
nutritional experts	186

O

Obnoxious	183
obtain	132
Obviously	128
off hand	28
(Oh,) didn't you hear?	44
old	52
ominous	180
on behalf of ~	124
on business	52
on display	28
on edge	12
on exports	64
on schedule	24
on the East Coast	44
on the Internet	88
on the question of ~	186
on their own	174
on time	24
Once ~	174
one way or the other	108

242

one's view of the screen	183
on-line bookstore	124
only to be overwhelmed by ～	192
opening	88
opening day	76
organization	164
Other critics	183
out of town	76
outnumber left-handers nine to one	180
outnumbered ～	200
outsource	136
outspoken opponent of the War in Vietnam	204
Over the years	132
overall	124
overwhelming dominance of the right hand	180
owner	96

P

pack rats	177
parking garage	60
particularly persistent	192
pass ～ on (to…)	148
pass off ～ as …	196
pass out	116
patron	183
pause	136
peer into ～	88
penalized	192
penetrated into ～	200
perfectionists	177
personal comfort	189
personnel change	36
persuade ～ to …	76
pets to serve ～	132
petty	164
photo-copiers	196
photocopying machine	148
physical challenge	132
physically disadvantaged	160
piled up	36
pin ～ on…	174
plagiarism	196
plagiarize	196
plan to ～	72
planning	152
plant and animal life	189
play a key role in ～ing	100
Please do not ～ until …	120
please join me in welcoming ～	144
plus side	136

podium	108
poll	156
pollute	189
polluting	168
posing	177
positive omens	180
possibilities	28
possible jail time	192
postpone	76
potential client	80
power bill	168
power locks	96
power windows	96
practically	124
practice	112, 180
practice slavery	200
prepare	32
presentation	56
preservation	189
press release	100
pressured ～ to …	192
pretty well known	116
prevention	132
preview	128
previous job	52
priorities	160
private citizen	152
private phone line	84
privately	174
problem with ～	32
procrastinate	177
productivity	16
proficiency	120
prominent	152, 180, 196
proof	96
pros and cons	136
prototype	92
provide	16, 48
provide ～ with…	64
provide services for ～	152
provided	120
provider	168
psychologists	177
public health problems and fire hazards	177
public relations	152
pull it off	76
punch in	116
put in ～	84
put the blame squarely on ～	183

243

index

Q
qualifications	88
qualify for ~	160
qualms	196
quarter	72, 100
quit	44, 68

R
raged	186
raised by ~	177
ran about ninety minutes	183
rate	144
rates	40
rather than ~	180
reached epidemic proportions	196
ready	24, 92
realistic	88
rearrange	76
reasonable price	136
receipt	96
reception	20
recruiter	152
reduce	124, 148
refer ~ as ...	177
reference	116
refused to ~	204
regarding	144
regions of natural wonder and cultures	189
register	192
registration process	192
remaining	156
remarkably similar	186
remind	148
remind ~ about/of ...	148
renewal	48
renovate	84
repair	60
replace ~	100
reports	156
reputation	132
rescue missions	132
rescue operation	177
Research and Development	92
resign	68, 100
resolve	200
resources	164
respectively	204
responsibility	24
retail	168
retail provider	168
retail sales	88
retreated	200
revealed	186
revised	64
right in front of ~	12
right now	28
right-handers	180
rip-off	112
rise up and live out	204
risk not only ~, but ...as well	192
route	52
rub elbows with ~	20
run into	12
run through ~	104
rural areas	156

S
sales know-how	112
sales staff	52
salesperson	112
sanitation workers	204
save money on ~	168
saying, in part	204
scam	112
scratch	96
search engine	44
secede	200
section leader	32
see ~ around	44
seem to be ~	60
segregated	204
selection	72
seminar	72
seniors	152
sense of isolation	174
sensitive	148
serious	60
serve as~	204
serving as ~	100
set up	84
set up ~ at/on ...	56
shake hands with ~	20
shake-up	68
shipping	124
shorter and simpler version	196
should be able to ~	136
should have ~	76
should take about 45 minutes	140
show them a good time	76
showing on the second floor	140

Term	Page
shred	148
sign up	72
significantly fewer	192
simplify	160
simply	200
Simply put	180, 186
Since ~	64
sit around ~ing	196
six-cylinder engine	96
skeptics	186
slack	40
slow down	12
slow-working	204
so much energy is wasted on ~	164
so nobly	200
so that ~	28, 116
so-called	168
sold out	76
some sort of	186
sought to ~	180
sound system	96
sounded anxious to ~	60
spacious	189
spam	48, 192
sparked ~	204
speak for ~	56
special occasion	52
specify	24
spicy	186
sprain one's ankle	20
staff	120
staff meeting	32
stages of manufacture	128
staple	148
staple foods	186
start out as ~	88
start up a business	44
start-up firm	152
Stay tuned for ~	156
stay with it	88
steadily growing	196
stems from ~	180
stepped forward to ~	204
Stick with ~, and…	186
Still	48
stocks	192
stomp	180
stop ~ from …ing	200
stressed out	174
strict	68

Term	Page
strictly	192
strive to ~	136
struck down	204
struggle	164
subject ~ to …	183
submit	104
submitting	196
subordinates	148
subway	12
suffer from doubt or anxiety	174
suggestion	80, 92
suitable	104
suitable for stealing	196
supervise	52
supervisor	64
supply	168
supply ~ with…	64
support	156, 200
surprise	68
surprising	44, 156
survival	164
survive	164
suspect	56
suspect(ed) ~ of …ing	68
switch	168
switch from ~ to…	168
sympathetic to ~	204
sympathized with~	200

T

Term	Page
take a day off	16
take a vote	116
take actions	192
Take care	20
take measures to ~	183
take place	128
take your call	108
taking days off	16
tax credit	160
tax incentives	160
telephone access system	116
Telephone marketers	192
tend to ~	174
tenet	189
tentatively	116
terrifically	186
test booklets	120
Thanks for inviting us here	168
Thanks to ~	180
that comes with ~	183

index

That makes me wonder if ~	36	tip(s)	148
that sort of thing	80	tired	174
That'd be fine	56	to be sure	196
That'd be great	24	to give some examples	189
that's a shame	20	To make matters worse	48
That's all very good	24	to some extent	136
That's all well and good	24	to take another position	100
that's fine for the computer	84	To this day	180
that's not going to happen	32	tolerance	186
that's precisely why ~	144	toll-free	112
That's right	52	took the liberty of ~ing	76
That's why	16, 40	top management	68
That's wonderful	52	top-flight	56
The first major weapon	192	total strangers	192
the first person to ~	84	totally	84
the individual's need to ~	177	tough	40
The last thing I want is ~	32	tour	128
The list is endless	180	tracts	196
The next item on the agenda is ~	104	training course	72
the normality of this condition	180	traits	177
The only exception to this rule	148	transfer	12, 164
The only hope for ~	192	translate	120
The only thing that changes is ~	168	transmission	96
the publications	177	trash	177
The purpose of …is to ~	160	trend	183
the rule	183	triggered	186
the sense of anxiety	177	Trust me	32
the slow death of the movie theater	183	turn out all right	76
the vote	156	turn out okay	64
the way that your electricity is generated	168	turn things over to~	168
the world over	196	turn up	88
Then, there are those (critics) who ~	183	turned her attention to ~	132
there is a sense that ~	196	twist one's ankle	20
there is no need to ~	186	type up	88
There's no clause to specify ~	24	typical	168
These are difficult times	124		
These days	183	**U**	
things that lay to their right	180	Ultimately	174
This is ~ calling from …	108	Um	72
This is my ~ time to…	124	unbelievable	68
This is Shirley	92	under the direction of	200
This perception of left-handers as ~	180	under-graduates	196
This seems to indicate that	186	uneasy	174
This way, please	28	unit	80, 116
though	72	unsolicited emails	192
thrills	186	up to ~	108
through the years that followed	204	update	116
throughout the country	168	upgrades	48
throughout the show	183	up-to-date	48
time off	189	urban areas	156

urges	186
use	56
used car dealership	112

V

valuable	174
vary	189
vehicle	96
via cell phone	183
vice president	60
violator	192
volume	128
vote count	156

W

walk	128, 140
walk this tour	128
warn consumers to avoid ~	186
was reopened to the public	140
We are going to begin ~	120
We could certainly use ~	56
we see that ~	164
well-intended	189
well-received by ~	200
What are you talking about?	68
What do you say?	56
What do you think?	24
what happened	20
What happened to ~ ?	68
what have I got to lose?	72
what he said on this occasion	200
what to expect	128
what to throw away and what to keep	177
what we mean by ~	160
what with ~ and …	36
whenever possible	148
where ~	156
which is impossible	177
which is where	156
while serving as pastor of ~	204
wholesale	168
Why don't you ~?	36
wiped out	189
with his own name on it	196
Without further ado	144
without interruption	168
won her several awards	132
work for ~	84
work on ~	92
work out all right	12
work out solutions	174
work things out	174
working ~	132
worth ~ing	140
Would you mind ~ing?	40
wrapped up	196

Y

year by year	124
you are welcome to	128
you name it	180
You should have told me sooner	76
You sure ~?	60
you will ~	120
You'd have to ~	12
you'll do fine	80
You'll have to excuse me now	40
Your desk should be cleared of ~	120

● **執筆者紹介**

外池滋生（とのいけしげお）
1947年滋賀県生まれ。東京都立大学人文科学科大学院修士課程修了、ハワイ大学大学院言語学科博士課程修了（Ph.D.）。現在、青山学院大学教授として生成文法理論を中心に言語の背後にある規則性の不思議を教えている。専門は理論言語学、日英語比較統語論。本書では語彙、表現、文法、発音解説等を担当。主な著書に『新英語学辞典』（共著、研究社）、『チョムスキー小事典』（共著、大修館書店）、『一歩すすんだ英文法』（共著、大修館書店）、『英語徹底口練！』（共著、実務教育出版）などがある。

Joseph T.McKim（ジョセフ・マキーム）
1955年イリノイ州生まれ。テンプル大学教育学修士課程修了（MEd）。明治学院大学教養教育センター講師を経て現在関東学院大学准教授。本書では英文執筆を担当。著書に『英語徹底口練！』（共著、実務教育出版）がある。

外池一子（とのいけかずこ）
1954年大阪府生まれ。津田塾大学大学院修士課程修了。CNNニュース等の通訳、翻訳活動のかたわら、明治学院大学講師としてリスニング等を指導。本書では日本語訳、発音解説を担当。

● **CD英語音声**

　女性：Kimberly Forsythe（アメリカ）
　　　　Jojo Newsom（イギリス）
　　　　Carolyn Miller（カナダ）
　　　　Donna Burke（オーストラリア）
　男性：Chris Wells（アメリカ）
　　　　Steven Ashton（イギリス）

　　　　　　　　　　　カバーデザイン／イラスト　◆　齋藤信也
　　　　　　　　　　　本文レイアウト／DTP　　　◆　レミントン社
　　　　　　　　　　　録音／CD編集　　　　　　　◆　巧芸創作

英語 徹底耳練！

2006年 8月20日　初版第 1 刷発行
2020年10月10日　初版第12刷発行

編著者　外池滋生
発行者　小山隆之
発行所　株式会社 実務教育出版
　　　　163-8671 東京都新宿区新宿 1-1-12
　　　　電話　販売 03-3355-1951
　　　　振替　00160-0-78270

印刷／奥村印刷　製本／ブックアート

©Shigeo Tonoike　ISBN978-4-7889-1433-9 C0082
本書の無断転載、無断複写（コピー）を禁じます。
本書の内容についてのお問合せは、書面かFAX（03-5369-2237）にてお願いします。
乱丁・落丁本は本社にておとりかえいたします。